UNSHAKEABLE

UNSHAKEABLE

MY MOTORCYCLE RACING STORY

SHANE BYRNE

WITH MATTHEW ROBERTS

MACMILLAN

First published 2020 by Macmillan
an imprint of Pan Macmillan
The Smithson, 6 Briset Street, London EC1M 5NR
Associated companies throughout the world
www.panmacmillan.com

ISBN 978-1-5290-3432-5

3 5 7 9 8 6 4

A CIP catalogue record for this book is available from the British Library.

Typeset in Fairfield LT Std by Palimpsest Book Production Ltd, Falkirk, Stirlingshire
Printed and bound by CPI Group (UK) Ltd, Croydon, CR0 4YY

Visit **www.panmacmillan.com** to read more about all our books
and to buy them. You will also find features, author interviews and
news of any author events, and you can sign up for e-newsletters
so that you're always first to hear about our new releases.

Contents

Foreword by Jonathan Rea   IX

Prologue   1

1. The Maze   7

2. BMX Bandit   16

3. A 'Secondary' Education   25

4. Going Underground   42

5. Captain Clueless   55

6. Life on Track   66

7. Cover Stories   74

8. From Now On, You're Twenty-Two!   81

9. What Happens When You Crash   91

10. From the Backmarker to the Birdman   101

11. Chicken and Ducs   113

12. Mastering the Cube   124

13. A Dog Ran Out, Man!   139

14. Visual Flight Rules   152

15. Getting the Hump   166

16. What Will Be   178

17. Strong to the Finish   195

18. The Wright Stuff   202

19. Losing My Milk Money   213

20. Better the Devils You Know   227

21. What Doesn't Kill Us   240

22. Friend or Foe?   247

23. Seeing Red   255

24. May Day Mayday   274

25. Braced for the Worst   288

26. The Devil Wears a Halo   295

Epilogue   311

Acknowledgements   323

For Petra
It will always be you

For Zack and Lilly
Everything I do is for you
Everything I am is because of you

To a select few
I will be forever grateful

To the rest of you
Enjoy the ride!

Foreword

BY JONATHAN REA

I started my road-racing career in 2003 and launched my-self from a dirty motocross paddock into the glitz and glamour of the British Superbike Championship where a young Shane Byrne was quickly making his mark on the competition. I first came across Shakey when a girl I was friends with had some kind of family personal sponsorship deal with him, so I got the whole rundown about what a great guy he was. To be honest she seemed more into Shakey than me, but I let that go because he was a pretty big deal.

Something you remember about your rookie year is the guys you look up to at the track and, while I didn't have too much success in my first year on the tarmac, I really enjoyed seeing this smiley guy on top of the podium on his MonsterMob Ducati. I wanted to be just like him. He seemed like he had it all, and I particularly liked the big-ass motorhome that came with it. I can still vividly remember his whole get-up – leather suit, sponsor badges on leathers and green and red lightning-style helmet.

I sat around the TV that year and watched Shakey deal out the justice as a wild card at the Brands Hatch World Superbike round. Back in the late 1990s and early 2000s, wild cards were the big rage, but to go out and dominate with a double win as a wild card, on a year-old bike, was the stuff of fairy tales. From that moment on I became a huge fan, and Shakey was no longer just the talented BSB rider, he was headed to the big stage of MotoGP, fast-tracked from *Fast Bikes* magazine tester, hooning around the roads of the UK.

After a few years riding Aprilia and KTM MotoGP bikes, our paths crossed again in 2006, where we lined up along-side each other on the BSB grid again. Now I had to race against the guy I looked up to. One of my fondest memories was winning my first BSB race at Mondello Park in 2007. Shakey was second, and when he congratulated me on the podium he seemed genuinely chuffed for me. He said, 'Soak it up, this will be the first of many, mate.' That meant the world to me. When you are in that racing bubble you don't get the chance to take in all the good moments, but I'll remember that one for ever. We raced in World Super-bike together a few years later, but this time I was on the official bike and Shakey – like in MotoGP – had a second-string bike.

Unfortunately for us riders, we never get to pick our career route, we have to go with the opportunities that present themselves. Shakey's route made him the most successful British Superbike rider ever. Over the years, watching from the sidelines, I was impressed with his technique, effortless riding style and work ethic. Together with the right package around him, I'm sure he would have had World Championships to add to his *palmarès*.

Riding qualities aside, it's been Shakey's off-track personality that I really admire. Now, having a family, I can appreciate that even more. Watching from afar, it's endearing the love he has for his family: Petra, Zack and Lilly. Before I became a father, I worried about the potential negative effect that having kids would have on my racing career, but I only had to look at Shakey to see that it was possible to do it all together. I'm sure he would sit back and wonder what the hell all his younger rivals would do with their time, while he was knee-deep in being dad, husband and athlete. That motivation would be enough to rock up to the next race and kick their arses.

When I heard the news of Shakey's neck injury, I was gutted for him. Immediately I thought, I hope he can recover, but then I thought, surely he's had enough of racing now? But that's the thing, you want to leave this sport on your own terms. Throwing himself into TV as a pundit has been great to watch, and must be a great distraction from not being able to race a bike around a track. Not many can offer up experienced opinion like Shakey, and it comes so naturally. Whether he has his trademark Shoei in his hand, or a TV mic or whatever else he decides, I'm sure he will be giving it his all to be the best!

Good luck in the future, buddy!

JR

Prologue

Petra Byrne, June 2018
Isle of Sheppey, Kent, UK

Whenever Shane is riding and I'm not there, I try to find a quiet spot to watch the live timing app on my phone. With the kids at school and Shane at Snetterton for a one-day test, the house was silent. Just after ten o'clock, the peace was interrupted by my phone.

Ping!

A text from Shane.

> I'm just changing in the back of the van.
> I love you, speak to you later.

The session was due to start at ten minutes past, so I put some washing in the machine, made myself a coffee and I was just sitting down at the kitchen table when my phone beeped again. Another text. This time from a friend who works in the British Superbike paddock.

Is he OK?

What is she on about?

Is who okay?

Shakey. I've just seen he crashed.

How can he have crashed? The session has literally only just started . . . I refreshed the live timing page and saw the red flag icon in the top corner of the screen. My heart sank through my chest.

I flicked the app closed with my thumb and rang Shane's crew chief. Giovanni would know exactly what was going on. It rang and rang and eventually went to his voicemail. I tried Stuart Higgs, the race director . . . no answer. I rang everybody in the team, anybody I knew that might be there at Snetterton, but not one single person picked up. Nobody.

Normally if Shane has crashed and there's a red flag somebody would answer straight away. They would know I was watching and would probably be panicking. 'Don't worry, he's OK.' I'd heard those words so many times. But not this time. Not for forty-five minutes.

I sat at my kitchen table going absolutely crazy. I don't know how many times I must have tried Stuart but he ignored every call. I was shivering, feeling sick. It was the longest forty-five minutes of my life. Eventually, I ran to the kitchen sink and threw up. I had a really bad feeling.

Then, finally, my phone rang.

'He's fine,' said Stuart dismissively.

'Really? So why did it take so long?'

'Sorry, it was a bit busy here but he's fine. He's talking to the medics, he looks OK but he has suspected broken ribs.'

I can never forget how cold his words sounded, but still I breathed a big sigh of relief.

'So . . . I guess they're going to take him to hospital for the broken ribs then?'

'Yes, I think they're going to take him to the medical centre first.'

He sounded vague. The medical centre? This was forty-five minutes after the crash. Forty-five minutes, nobody has answered my calls, and he's only just going to the circuit medical centre? The last time Shane had a crash and was taken to hospital he called me from the helicopter on the way there. The guy is superglued to his phone. Something wasn't right. I packed a bag of Shane's clothes and called the kids' school to tell them I would be picking them up early.

I must have been in a panic, because all I could think was, 'I need to take his socks and shoes.' I remember tucking his socks inside his shoes and making a conscious effort to pack some pants, because that's the one thing I normally forget. I was talking to myself, trying to think of anything but what might have happened to my husband.

The kids came running out of the school gates and jumped in the car.

'What's happened, Mum?'

'Nothing,' I replied, trying to sound relaxed. 'We're just going to have a road trip.'

'A road trip to where?'

'To Snetterton.'

'Yay! We're going to see Daddy! But why are we going in our school uniforms?'

'I don't know, I thought we'd just go as a surprise.'

I didn't want to tell them. I didn't know what to tell them. So I just drove.

I was halfway up the A11 when Giovanni finally called me back. All he would tell me was that he had been with Shane the whole time and they were at Norfolk and Norwich University Hospital.

'Are you coming quickly?' he asked. I could sense something urgent in his voice.

'I'm coming as quickly as I can. If he's just got broken ribs, I'm sure he can wait, can't he?'

'Just try to get here quickly.'

I tried to imagine Shane at Giovanni's side, impatient for me to get there, wanting only to go home. Was that too much to wish for?

An hour later Giovanni met me at the door of the accident and emergency department. He was alone. 'Where is he?' I asked, looking over his shoulder.

My eyes met with Giovanni's and from the look of them, it was like he knew Shane's career – or worse, Shane's mobility – could be over. I quickly rushed through things in my head. Surely they wouldn't have sent Giovanni to give me this news, would they? Where was the doctor? Stuart had been so calm on the phone. Maybe he was just trying to make sure I didn't panic?

'He's having a CT scan,' Giovanni said. 'That's all I know.'

'OK. Sit down, kids, we'll have to wait for Daddy.'

A little while later some nurses came out to Giovanni and me, but said nothing other than that they just needed more time with Shane, to do some more tests. Then they turned to the children and offered them a picnic. The kids had been as good as gold, but the waiting was torture. Was it a broken leg? A femur maybe? An open fracture? Shane had told me before how bad an injury like that could be. I just didn't know and nobody seemed to want to tell me.

We had been sitting there for an hour when, finally, a smiling face came over and introduced himself as Dr Andrew Cook. I guess I was expecting somebody older – he was around Shane's age – but he came across looking really happy and confident. I took this as a positive sign and I felt much calmer as he instructed some nurses to clear another area and took me away from Giovanni and the kids to deliver his prognosis. Dr Cook slotted a memory stick into the computer and loads of images popped up. I had no idea what I was looking at. 'Right, let's start with the easy bits,' he said, turning to face me. 'As it stands at the minute, Shane has broken a lot of ribs.' It was just over a week until the next race at Snetterton, and my immediate thought was that there was no way he was going to make it with broken ribs.

Dr Cook continued. 'He's also fractured his left collar-bone and his sternum.' I didn't know what a sternum was in English, so I had to interrupt him to ask. It seemed that with each injury, the severity was getting worse. I hoped he was getting towards the end of his list when he took a deep breath and swung back to his computer. 'And I'm afraid those are the least of your husband's problems.'

On the screen there was an image of Shane's spine and, with a pen in his hand, Dr Cook started tapping the screen from the bottom and working his way up, all the way into his neck. 'This vertebra is fractured, this one is broken, that one is completely crushed. His broken ribs have punctured

5

his lung and the swelling in his neck is making it very difficult for him to breathe.' He turned back to face me. 'In the next twenty-four hours we need to prioritize, so let's concentrate more on his injuries after we've settled him down a bit. The first thing we need to do today is to save your husband's life.'

1

The Maze

You know when you're a kid and you do one of those mazes in your puzzle book? You have to take a pen and trace the correct line from point A to point B? Well, I believe that's how life is. Imagine if every human being, on the day of their birth, gets given a piece of paper with one of those puzzles on it. Point A is where you're born and point B is your ultimate destiny. At first glance the maze seems like pure chaos but, ultimately, there is always a way to the other side. All you have to do is stay on the right path and keep moving forward, even if you do take the odd wrong turn along the way.

I have always been convinced that my ultimate destiny was to be a champion motorcycle racer. I don't know why, I had no reason to believe it, but I never dreamed of anything else. Maybe it was fate, maybe it was good fortune. Maybe it was all down to genetics, although I will never know that for sure. Because the route to that destiny from point A on my life's maze was more complicated than most.

I was born in London, on the south bank of the River Thames, in Lambeth Hospital. It was two weeks before Christmas, but I was an unwanted early gift for my biological parents. All I know about them is that they were both Irish; my father was apparently a folk singer in his forties who seemingly had his wicked way with an underage checkout girl from the local supermarket. It must have been a bit of a scandal.

Actually, I do know one more thing about one of my birth parents: their surname. And I know it because for the first six weeks of my life, my name was Steven Price.

Baby Steven spent his first Christmas being passed around between foster homes until, one day early in the February of 1976, a lady in Sittingbourne, Kent, received a letter she'd been desperately hoping for. It had been two years since Janet Byrne and her husband Peter had suffered a terrible tragedy, when their only son Stuart fell into a cesspit at Janet's brother's farm and suffered a heart attack. Stuey was just four years old when he died, and the days and months that had passed since then had been horrendous for them both. They had even tried for another baby, but it just wasn't happening.

They were so traumatized, the doctor told them, that they'd probably never be able to have any more children. They applied to adopt, through Dr Barnardo's and a few other centres in and around London, and even though the police and the other authorities had been to visit them to complete all the necessary background checks and assessments, they hadn't heard back. The weeks and the months

8

passed until, finally, a letter came through from an adoption centre in Lambeth to tell them they had a six-week-old child who matched their profile.

Janet and Peter Byrne jumped on the next train to London, and later that very same day they were making the return trip, bringing their new son home to their little two-bedroomed house on the Snipeshill estate, a short walk from Sittingbourne station. The following morning, they dropped me round at my new nan's house while they went out to shop for new baby clothes, a cot and a pram. 'He's a gift from God,' my nan whispered to my mum when she saw me for the first time.

Mum had to agree. She always said that from the first moment she saw me, she felt like she was looking back at her Stuey as a baby. In fact, I looked so much like him that in years to come, Mum and Dad would look at old photos of me and Stuey at the same age and argue which one was which. Nan was convinced it was God's way of saying, 'Don't worry, everything's going to be all right.'

My new parents gave me a new start and a new name. They would have to allow an appeal period of six months before they could make it official, but from that first train journey home to Kent from London, I became known as Shane Daniel Byrne.

Just like my biological father, Dad was from an Irish family – it was one of the reasons they matched us – with thirteen brothers and sisters, all of whom had plenty of kids of their own. Mum says she picked the name Shane because it was pretty much the first one she could think of that hadn't already been taken by one of my cousins, and Daniel just because she liked it. Six months later, with no appeal lodged by my biological parents, I was formally renamed at the Swale Borough Council offices.

Mum and Dad told me everything; I knew from the word go that I was adopted. They always said that if I ever wanted to find my biological parents, it was no problem for them, but I never wanted to. I loved Mum and Dad to bits and they did so much for me growing up that I always felt it would be hurtful to them to go and look for somebody else, just because of a genetic bond. To me it was never an issue and, honestly, I never gave it much thought.

More recently there has been the odd occasion when I have wondered if my biological parents might know who I am and who I became. It doesn't happen often, but once or twice I have looked up into the thousands of people in the crowd on the banking at Brands Hatch before a Superbike race and thought, 'For all I know, the woman who gave birth to me could be sitting up there.' She could even be sitting up there and not have a clue who she was looking at.

As anybody would be, my mum had been in a real dark place – almost suicidal – when she lost Stuey. I honestly don't know whether it was because my introduction to my parents' lives had helped ease their grief but, despite what the doctors had told them, two years later they did conceive again and they had a little girl, my younger sister Kelly.

Kelly was definitely the brighter of the two of us, and she studied hard. Like a lot of brothers and sisters, we had different interests and plenty of fallouts along the way. I think I can say for both of us that we loved each other and irritated each other in equal measures. There were times when we pleaded with our mum and dad to leave the two of us together in a room for just one minute so that we could sort out our differences in the old-fashioned way. Needless to say, they never let us do it, but sometimes we both had so much anger and frustration with each other bottled up inside that it seemed like the only option.

I don't think that's any different to any other family but I can look back now and see that there were times when perhaps I felt a little jealous that Kelly biologically belonged to my mum and dad. I might hear them all giggling together in another room and wish it was me in there, purely because I loved them all so much and wanted to be involved. On the flip side, Kelly would argue that I got more attention because I was adopted, and if I'm honest she was probably right – I think I did get spoiled a bit more at Christmas and on birthdays.

Whenever one of us caused trouble, if neither of us owned up to something then we both got a clump. Mum had a fierce temper, and the smallest thing could spark off a massive eruption. She used to wear these furry, flip-flop type slippers with the hard, plastic soles, and if I ever did something a bit naughty, no matter how trivial it was, she would pin me down and belt me with it – once for each word of the bollocking, with some extra ones thrown in. 'You won't, won't, won't . . . break, break, break . . . anything, anything, anything . . . in this room, room, room . . . ever . . . *again!*' – finishing with a big whack at the end. I swear I've still got 'Made in Taiwan' imprinted on my legs from some of those hidings!

There was one day when Kelly had done something and I got clumped for it, so I was not happy at all. I would only have been ten or eleven years old. I turned to my mum and said, 'Do you know what? If you keep treating me like this, I'm going to go and find my real mum.' I'm still gutted I ever said it, but I was just so angry that I'd got the slipper for nothing, I came out with the most awful thing I could think of.

Mum was really upset, as you would be, although unusually for her on this occasion, she didn't really react. Then when my dad came home he pulled me to one side. I knew what it was going to be about and I thought I was really in for it. I have to say there weren't many times that my dad gave me a hiding; he was always really fair. If I ever stepped out of line, my mum was happy to give me the slipper or a smack, but if that didn't solve it and Dad had to get involved, I knew it was serious.

Dad was short and powerful, a former boxer in the army, where they'd given him the nickname 'Popeye', which I used to love calling him. When he came home I was bracing myself for the mother of all hidings but it never came. Instead, he stayed completely cool and calm.

'I'm not going to tell you off,' he said. 'I just need to explain something to you. One day you will understand that words are powerful, and that what you said to your mum, you could have punched her, kicked her, stabbed her or shot her in the chest, but nothing you could ever do to her will hurt her as much as that one comment.' His words really hit home, so much so that they still come back to me every now and again. And whenever they do, I always think to myself, 'You horrible little so-and-so, why did you ever even say that?'

The truth is, I love my mum to bits and I was always

made to feel special, so the occasional encounter with the sole of her slipper did nothing to change that. I don't think it's unfair to say that she was carrying a lot of anger around with her. My dad used to excuse it sometimes, if it was around the anniversary of when Stuey died, or coming up to his birthday. She would go a bit quiet then, but generally, I think she had a short fuse and nine times out of ten she was just on the warpath anyway.

Sittingbourne is a small, ordinary industrial town in Kent, about forty-five miles east of London and twenty-five miles down the road from the famous Brands Hatch circuit where, one day, my dream of becoming a professional motorcycle racer would come true. It might only have been twenty-five miles in distance but, back then, as far as I was concerned, it might as well have been a million. Until I was sixteen years old, the estate was pretty much all I knew.

The first house we lived at was number 61 Prince Charles Avenue, an unremarkable two-bedroomed house on an unremarkable council estate that is split in half by the busy A2 that runs from Rochester to Dover. On one side is Snipeshill, where we lived, and on the other is Murston. Snipeshill was much like any other council estate in the Eighties: lots of kids out playing on the street while their mums hung the washing out and chatted over the garden fence, older boys roaring around in flash cars trying to impress the groups of girls that huddled around in groups on the benches and walls. For me it was a happy place, and it was home.

When Kelly came along we needed an extra room and we swapped houses with my nan and grandad, who lived directly across the road. Number 104 was a three-bedroomed semi, meaning me and Kelly got a bedroom each. Of course, poor Kelly got the box room and, me being the golden boy in the eyes of my parents, I got the biggest bedroom in the house – even bigger than Mum and Dad's. The best thing about that house, though, was that it was right next door to the Goldsmiths.

There were three Goldsmith brothers: Steven, who was the eldest, Terry who was a year older than me, and Gary, the youngest. I got on well with the three of them, mainly because they raced BMXs and they always had the trickest bikes for miles around. Their dad Glenn kept them in tiptop shape and it was him who first taught me to ride one.

Glenn was brilliant, a proper wide boy, a real-life Del Trotter. You couldn't help but like him, and I'd have done whatever he told me to do. My dad had been trying to teach me to ride for a bit on my own little first pushbike – we'd taken the stabilizers off but I kept crashing and getting the hump, so Glenn offered to have a go with me instead.

At the bottom of Prince Charles Avenue there was a long path that ran alongside the green, all the way down to the A2, so Glenn took me down there one day with the other lads. 'Right, Shane,' he said in his broad Kent accent. 'I'm gonna teach ya how to ride this bike. What I'm gonna do is run along with ya, you just keep pedalling and I'll be right behind ya!'

I put my head down and started pedalling with all my might, not looking back. Pretty soon the end of the path was approaching, so I panicked and put my feet down. I turned around, expecting to see Glenn, but he was miles away. My first thought was, 'How did he run back there so quick?' Then I realized I'd done it all myself, and I pedalled all the way back feeling absolutely made up with life. Learning to ride a bike is a big moment in any kid's life, but to me it was absolutely everything.

I've been on two wheels ever since.

2

BMX Bandit

My dad was a track engineer for British Rail and my mum worked in a factory. This was in the early Eighties, when mortgage rates were at an all-time high and families like ours were struggling to make the payments. But Mum and Dad had promised me I could have a BMX of my own and they were always true to their word. In the October of 1982 they took me down to the local bike shop, Dean's Bicycles, to choose one, so that they could start the weekly payments and have the thing in time for Christmas. There was no point pretending Santa Claus existed.

There was one particular bike that I wanted from Dean's: a Raleigh Ultra Burner. It had a black frame but everything else on the thing was gold: the wheels, the handlebars and the Dia-Compe brake set. This thing was 'full factory', but there was no way my mum and dad could afford it, so I got the cheaper version – the Night Burner – instead. The

Night Burner had dark graphite-grey paint, with magenta-red wheels and brake sets, but Glenn Goldsmith stripped the frame back to the chrome for me and it looked the nuts.

That BMX became my life, and every evening after school, or all day during the holidays, I would be out and about, either playing on the street with the Goldsmith boys and the rest of the kids from the estate, or pedalling off on my own. I used to cruise about making motorbike noises, going: *'Braap! Braap! Braap! Braap!'* My bike must have had an 18,000-speed gearbox with the amount of gear changes I used to make!

If I was on my own I'd ride around the estate or venture out into the wheat fields and fruit farms that surrounded it. I used to love to find a big haystack, lean my bike up against it and climb to the top and chill out with a bag of sweets until the farmer came out and chased me off. Finding an orchard was the best – I'd be a bit tired and hungry from riding my bike and I'd climb up a tree and pull an apple straight off the branch. Funnily enough, the farmers didn't like that one either too much, but it definitely got me pedalling harder.

My other favourite spot to ride was an indoor shopping precinct in Sittingbourne town centre called The Forum. It had tiled floors, and right in the middle there was a big feature garden display – maybe ten metres long by four metres wide – with seats all around it. On a Sunday morning when the precinct was closed, I used to get up nice and early, pedal over there and sneak in through the multi-storey car park.

As sure as eggs is eggs, the Saturday night winos would have left a load of empty bottles lying around, so I'd fill one up with water from the bathrooms and go and make a puddle in each of the four corners of the tiled floor around this garden feature. Then I'd do lap after lap on my bike, pedalling as fast as I could down the straight bits and sliding it around the corners through the wet patches, skidding about for as long as it took for the security guards to clock on and chase me out of there.

Most days, on the estate, there'd be a group of about five to ten of us. We'd get up in the morning and be out on our BMXs until teatime. In the summer we'd be back out again after tea until we were called in for bed, pulling wheelies and finding good places to build a jump out of whatever old junk we found lying around.

One trick to master was the 'American bunny hop', where you lift the front wheel up in the air at the top of a ramp and have to land on the back wheel. Dead opposite the entrance to my house was a little alleyway between some garages, which the big boys would come flying down, hit a little ramp and attempt to bunny hop the whole width of the street and land on the other side. They used to do this until one day one of them hit the kerb and went straight over the bars into the neighbour's garden. I was desperate to show the older boys that I could do anything they could do, and the day I mastered the bunny hop I felt like I could conquer the world.

Gary Goldsmith was a couple of years younger than me, but he soon became my best friend. GG, as I call him, is the kind of mate you might not see for four years and then the moment you get back together it's like you've never been apart. That's me and GG – there is never an awkward moment between us.

The Night Burner was a great little bike but it used to rattle like hell, until I washed it with a hose and suddenly it stopped rattling. I thought I'd fixed it, but actually I'd just put a load of water in the bearings, and as soon as it dried out it started rattling again. Eventually, when I was around eleven or twelve, Mum and Dad bought me a better bike, a Rickman Racer, from Gary's elder brother Steven. This thing was built purely for racing, and to me it was the coolest bike in the world. Glenn used to really look after his sons' bikes, so it was in absolutely perfect condition.

Gary had a GT Pro Performer, a proper freestyler imported from California that we had only seen cool American kids riding in magazines, and Terry had one too. The Performer had a wider frame around the seat clamp, so you could get your foot in and stand up on it. The trick was called a 'frame stand' and Terry was the first to master it, although we used to pray for him to hit a stone and fall off! My Rickman had a round tube so it was much harder on that, but I sussed it out in the end and I loved nothing better than to do frame stands, rolling down the road with my arms out, thinking I was the best thing since sliced bread.

My speciality, though, was my wheelies, and I used to practise them all the time until I was the best on the estate. The pavement on Prince Charles Avenue was made from these huge concrete slabs, and I will never forget the first time I wheelied across three whole slabs. That was a landmark moment because I'd set it as a target in my head. I got better and better and eventually I could wheelie all the way from one end of the avenue to the other, which was just about one of the coolest things you could lay claim to on our estate.

Just past the Murston side of the estate was the Eurolink Industrial Park, which became one of our favourite places to ride. Sometimes there would be flatbed lorry trailers lying around, so we'd ride from one end to the other, flat out on our BMXs, and jump off the end. If we were really lucky we'd find the ramps they used to load stuff on to the back of the trailers and dare each other to ride up them and jump off.

We would sit together on our bikes, looking at a ramp that was quite big, arguing about who was going to go first. In the end it would always be me who said, 'Ah fuck it, I'll have a go!' The consequences didn't seem to matter. Whether you landed it or not, fell off and broke your wrist or smashed your face in, you had the kudos because you'd gone for it.

At one end of Prince Charles Avenue was Rectory Road Park, another favourite hangout for the kids on the estate. That was a great place to ride, especially the day we discovered that somebody had left a big pile of dirt there. I don't know why it was there, or what it was for, but there was a nice little lip off the top of it and some of the older boys – Gary's brothers and his mates – were there pussyfooting around on their BMXs, trying to jump it.

Some of them were half jumping it, some were just rolling over the top. I didn't need much encouragement before I found myself pedalling down one of the park's bankings, flat out towards this big pile of dirt. I hit the lip and flew so high through the air that I almost needed to check in with air-traffic control, and came down in a massive heap. I'd cut my arms and legs and smashed my face up, but I dusted myself down and I was absolutely made up with myself. All the other kids were laughing but I turned and shouted, 'At least I did it, you pussies!' as I limped off, pushing my buckled Night Burner all the way home, beaming with pride.

Me and my little group of mates would stray from one end of town to the other without a care in the world, having so much fun that I never even thought about how far away from home I was. All I knew was that if I couldn't hear my mum shouting me in from the front door, I was likely to be in deep shit. The distance that her voice carried across the estate – which was pretty far, to be fair – was effectively the radius I was allowed to operate in.

She'd have had a heart attack if she'd known where I'd been half the time. Like when me and a couple of mates from my secondary school decided we were going to cycle to Gillingham. It was only seven miles away, but to us it was the other end of the Earth. We'd done plenty of shorter runs before, to the Isle of Sheppey Bridge and back, and I probably covered way more than seven miles on any normal day riding around the estate, but this felt like undertaking the Tour de France. My mum had a big mouth, but even she couldn't shout all the way to Gillingham.

The only time I wasn't outside was if the weather was really – like, *really* – bad. Only torrential rain would keep me indoors, in which case I'd spend the hours in my bedroom, creating little imaginary tracks for my Matchbox cars and making screeching sounds as they drifted around the corners. Every now and then my mum's unmistakable shriek would come through the floorboards from down-stairs. 'Shat aaaap! Stop making those bleedin' noises!'

The boot is on the other foot now, and it's funny because

I often find myself saying something similar to my son Zack, although it's more along the lines of, 'Come on, Zack, can't you play with something quieter? Get your iPad out or something!'

Mum was hardcore, but our home was a happy place, especially when we were all together – me and my sister lying on the rug in front of the gas fire, my parents sitting in their chairs, watching the television. A special treat for us was to watch *M*A*S*H*, an American comedy set in an army field hospital during the Korean War. I absolutely loved that show, especially the opening sequence with the Bell 47 helicopters coming in to land. It was always on quite late, so for me and Kelly to be allowed to stay up with Mum and Dad to watch it was a pretty big deal to us.

Unfortunately, spending time as a family didn't happen a lot because Dad worked so bloody hard as a track engineer on the railways. Most weekends he worked twelve-hour shifts just to make ends meet, so often on a Saturday or Sunday, when the other kids were off doing things with their parents, I was left to entertain myself. At the time I didn't understand it, I just wished Dad could be around more. On Monday mornings at school the other kids might be talking about their weekend, 'Me and Dad did such-and-such,' or 'Mum and Dad took us there . . .' It bothered me a little that my family couldn't have that life together.

Our best times were on holiday. Even though my mum and dad never had a driving licence between them, we could go anywhere in the country for free on the train – it was one of the few perks of Dad's job with British Rail. So our big annual summer holiday was to take the train from

Sittingbourne to London Victoria and then on to Bognor Regis on the south coast, and the Butlin's Holiday Park, where we'd meet up with other family members – usually Auntie Pam and Uncle Jeff, who would drive down from Gillingham with my cousin, Tim.

Tim was like the big brother I never had. He was a few years older than me and a lot cooler, so I used to follow him around like a shadow, swimming and playing, hanging out with the other kids in a little group of mates that we always seemed to make at Butlin's. Usually the highlight of our day came in the evening, when we were given a pound to go and spend in the video game arcades.

There was this one game called *Hard Drivin'*, where you drove what looked like a red cardboard box on all these stunt tracks. You had to really drive the thing, do the gear changes and everything, and I absolutely loved that game. I was good at it too. I would always be that annoying kid who takes up all the highest scores on the leader board with my initials *SDB*. I knew that if I played a football game, or *Space Invaders* or whatever, my ten-pence credit would be gone in ten seconds. But on driving games like *Hard Drivin'* or *Outrun*, I could make every checkpoint and easily be on the thing for ten minutes at a time.

By far the best thing they had at Butlin's, though, was a little tarmac oval where they hired out 50cc scramblers called Puch Magnums. Our parents didn't allow us to ride them, but I used to beg Tim to take me up there just to watch the other kids. I was supposed to be on holiday having a good time, but I spent hours and hours of it just sitting on the banking around the oval, watching these other kids go round and round.

Tim got to know the lads who were in charge of the scramblers and must have worded them up that his annoying little cousin wouldn't shut up until he'd had a turn on a bike. Technically I wasn't old enough, but these guys were really cool about it and they let me have a ride, showing me how to twist the throttle to make it go and running alongside me in case I fell.

Mum and Dad would have gone nuts if they'd known what we were up to, but I was in heaven – every part of my body was tingling with excitement. The only feeling I can compare it to is the cool-down lap of a championship-winning race. You want to look at every single face that's looking back at you, acknowledge every single clap and soak up the moment as this feeling of pure elation rushes through your veins. The very first time I rode a motorbike had been everything I had expected and more.

Whatever happened from now on, I decided, I was going to become a motorcycle racer. And nobody was going to tell me otherwise.

3

A 'Secondary' Education

One of the worst things anybody can ever do is try and tell me what to do. If I ask you for advice, I'll take it on board and use it to achieve what I need to achieve. But if you come in and start telling me I'm doing this wrong or I need to do it more like that, I won't listen to a single word. On many occasions in the past, I've had team managers try and tell me to take second or third place in a race, because we need the points and can't afford to risk crashing, but that just makes me go out and try harder to win it.

It's a trait I can trace back as far as one very specific moment in my life, in 1983. The year stands out in my head because I vividly remember spending most of it outside my headmaster's office at Canterbury Road Primary School, watching from the corridor window during every break and lunchtime while my mates chased each other around in the playground outside.

It had only been a few years earlier that I'd been all excited about starting school. My aunties and uncles were always asking me about it and they got me so excited, I couldn't wait to begin. They got me thinking it was going to be something amazing, but unfortunately – I guess like for a lot of kids – school didn't turn out to be the big party I'd expected.

Having a routine and being told what to do and when was my worst nightmare, it still is; but once I'd realized there was no choice but to accept it for the next twelve years, I settled in at Canterbury Road and mixed well with the other kids. I wasn't a bad lad, and as time went on there were teachers who tried to nurture the good in me. But there was one teacher who I could never get on with and, in his eyes, I could do no right. Mr Webb had been one of my infant class teachers and he stayed on my case even as I moved up through the school. Eventually, on this one particular day in 1983, I decided I'd had enough.

The school was built up around a central sports hall, where they had assemblies and school plays and everything else. I was in there conducting one of those science experiments where you attach two paper cups with a long piece of string and make a telephone. The classroom wasn't big enough for the length of string we had to use, so me and another boy were sent down to do the experiment in the sports hall and report back. Next thing, this Mr Webb comes barging in and, without even asking what I was doing in there, he started shouting at me and carrying on. I knew I wasn't doing anything wrong, so I stood my ground and told him to get stuffed.

Mr Webb grabbed me by the arm, dragged me back to

my classroom and swung me around in front of my whole class. I'd already been kicking and struggling all the way, shouting that I was going to get my mum, but when he embarrassed me like that in front of my mates it was the last straw. I wriggled free, turned around and booted him straight in the bollocks.

I left the bastard doubled up on the floor, sprinted for the main school doors and kept on running, all the way to my mum's work at Barrow's bakery in Sittingbourne, a place I still go to now with my kids for a cup of tea and a bit of cake. As you can imagine, my actions went down like a concrete kite at school, and my mum and dad were summoned to see the headmaster and straighten the whole thing out.

I had to apologize to Mr Webb and it grated on me so badly, because I knew there was no justice. From that day onwards, something just clicked in me that I wasn't going to take it any more and I would have to look after myself. Dealing with other people's bullshit would become a big part of my life when I became a professional motorcycle racer, but I always felt equipped to handle it. Kicking Mr Webb in the bollocks was the moment that put me on that road.

It sounds like a cliché now but whenever the teacher or careers officer used to ask what I wanted to be, all I ever said was 'motorbike racer'. I'm sure there were kids who put 'astronaut' or 'fireman' or 'footballer' and didn't really mean it, but I was deadly serious, and Mum still has the end-of-year report cards to prove it. Neither of my parents held a driving licence, yet here was their son, Billy Big Spuds, who had sat on a motorcycle for five minutes at a

Butlin's Holiday Park in Bognor Regis, telling anybody who'd listen that he was going to race them one day for a living. There was simply no doubt in my mind that that's what I was going to do.

When I say my dad never had a driving licence, that's actually not strictly true, because when he was in the army he must have had some kind of forces permit. For a period before he met my mum he was stationed in Germany, and while he was out there he was driving a lorry during a storm when he came past a woman riding a bicycle while holding an umbrella. The wind picked up and blew her straight into his path, and even though Dad managed to swerve and avoid her, the whole thing popped his head. From that day on he never drove a car again, and he certainly never went near a motorcycle.

My dad never had a problem with me riding bikes, though, and he certainly never discouraged me from racing them. Even so, I knew that if I was going to fulfil my dreams then I wasn't going to get much help from my parents – it was going to be all down to me. I knew what had to happen, I just didn't know how to make it happen. Safe to say, I didn't think school held the answers to my problem.

By the time I got to secondary school, I wasn't overly bothered about my education at all. I wasn't particularly academic and it wasn't like there were any girls to chase either, because St John's High was an all-boys school. I would far rather be out in the real world, and from being fourteen or fifteen years old I would bunk off most Fridays and head down to the local car auction at Paddock Wood instead.

The car auction was heaven for me. I would spend ages walking around, poring over the motors before they went through to the auction hall, which would be buzzing with excited chat from all these dodgy-looking geezers. The auctioneer would introduce each car: 'Aaaaaand, here we 'ave a Sierra Sapphire. It's a 1.8 GLX, one laydee owner – where we gonna start? A fahsand pahnd?' And all these hands would go up, giving the auctioneer a nod here and a wink there. And then he'd start: 'Fiftypoundfiftypoundwho's gonnagivemefiftypound?' I just loved the atmosphere and the whole spectacle of it.

Usually I would have a good idea of roughly what each car was worth, and I loved setting myself the little challenge of guessing how much it was going to go for and to who. Then I'd sit in the cafe with a cup of tea and listen to all these supposedly 'reputable car dealers' talking about what they'd bought, working out how much money they'd spent and what they might be able to make on their day's work. I'd figure that they might have spent twenty-five grand on four or five cars in one afternoon, but I knew they could give them a clean and polish and put them through their showroom the following week for thirty-five grand. I loved the fact that these people were trying to make a few quid and crack on a bit with life, using nothing but their own enterprise.

Of course, I didn't have any money of my own to spend at the auction, but I would love to spend time picking out the bargains, working out what I reckoned I could get each one for if I had the money and how much I might be able to make on them. Going down the auction was like a lesson in maths, economics, business studies and life all in one, but sadly my school didn't see it that way.

Eventually one of the teachers pulled me to one side and said, 'Shane, I need to talk to you about your attendance.'

'What's up?'

'Well, you never seem to be here on a Friday.'

'All right,' I said. 'So what do you want me to do? Change it to Thursday?'

I had been on the borderline of being sent to grammar school, so I know I could have done much better than I did in secondary school. But the truth was that the longer it went on, the less interest I had in it. In my head I was going to be a motorcycle racer and that was the only thing that mattered. The closer I got to being sixteen years old, the closer I was to being able to race, and everything else was irrelevant. I couldn't see the point in knowing what $\frac{x}{y}$ meant when all I needed to get on in life was a motorbike and a racing licence.

While I was sure that school wasn't for me, I would soon start to discover that I wasn't much cut out for a working life either – especially when I went and did my work experience with my cousin Tim, who by now had his own painting and decorating business. I went with him to work on a big job in London, which – other than maybe on the odd school trip as a kid – was probably the first time I'd been back there since I was born.

We were working at these big offices on Great Marlborough Street and I was blown away by the grandeur of it all. I looked around and thought, 'This is the bollocks, I'm right amongst it here!' One of the lads on the site asked me to go and buy him some cigarettes from the shop. I was only fifteen and I had never bought cigarettes before in my life, but I wandered down there in my decorator's gear and got served straight away. I thought, 'This is the nuts!'

I loved the whole thing, especially being with Tim, but the actual painting and decorating bit was a bloody nightmare. I hated that part and – probably like most fifteen-year-olds – I was bloody useless at it too. It didn't help that I was having to stay the night before at Tim's house on the other side of Sittingbourne so that we could get up at four in the morning to be in London for five, work all day and come home. After a week of that I was put off painting and decorating for good.

What I needed was a job that was going to help me become a motorcycle racer, and I had just the plan for that. In Sittingbourne there was a shop called Colwin Motorcycles, which was the local Kawasaki, Suzuki and Yamaha franchise, and from the age of eleven I used to trail over there to gawp at the bikes. I loved going in and picking up the brochures of any new models that were out, so that I could take them home and pore over every word, and then cut the pictures out and stick them on my bedroom wall.

Colwin's was right at the far end of town, so really I wasn't supposed to be that far away from home, but I was given the perfect excuse when my nan was put into a big old people's home, called Mockett Court, that they had just built directly opposite the shop. I didn't really need an extra excuse to go and visit Nan because I loved her just as much as she loved me, but the fact that she now lived opposite Colwin's was the icing on the cake.

I could do no wrong in the eyes of my nan. She was so proud of me, if I did a poo she thought it was a gold bar. I'm pretty sure it was because of what I did for her daughter, my mum, in coming into their lives when I did. When Nan told my mum that I was a gift from God she must have meant it, because that's definitely the way she treated me. When she and my grandad, who died when I was about six, lived across the road from us on Prince Charles Avenue, I used to go over there all the time – especially if I was in any trouble.

If I crashed my BMX and tore my clothes I would be straight round to Nan's and she would clean me up and fix my pants before I went home and got the 'Made in Taiwan' treatment from my mum's slipper. She knew just what Mum was like, so she'd soften her up by phoning ahead and saying, 'Shane's here and the poor boy is all upset because he crashed his bike and he's hurt his arm.' It didn't usually make much difference and I got the slipper when I got home anyway, but it was nice of her to try.

The residents at Mockett Court all had their own accommodation, with their own cooking facilities, but they also had a social room so they could spend time together, and it was a great little place for my nan to be with people her own age. But she loved nothing better than when I went around to see her, which of course I did regularly.

At the same time, Colwin's became a hub for me – a real home from home. I used to hang around the place so much that eventually I persuaded them to give me something to do and they agreed to pay me ten pounds a week to wash the bikes. Every Saturday morning I'd go straight over there for about nine o'clock, wheel all the bikes out onto the forecourt, wash them all off and then go around to Nan's for my favourite lunch of fish fingers, chips and peas. I'd spend an hour or two sitting with her, then go back over to the shop and hang about for the rest of the afternoon, talking bikes with the lads who worked there and the customers who came in. I heard just about every story going – 'Oh yeah, I drifted my GSX-R1100 onto the slip road of the motorway at a hundred and sixty miles an hour, leaving thick black darkies on the road' – and all the rest of it. I knew for a fact that most of it was bullshit, but I lapped it up anyway.

Some of the boys occasionally put their money where their mouths were, and I distinctly remember in 1989 there being a lot of excitement when the Yamaha OWO1 came out. It was Yamaha's first proper Superbike – their answer to the Honda RC30, which was dominating what was essentially the World Superbike Championship (WSB) at the time, before it was named as such. This thing was more expensive than anything else around, and I was in the shop the day a guy came in and bought one for just shy of thirteen grand. I couldn't believe what I was seeing!

All those hours in the shop paid off the day I was at Colwin's when a guy came in looking to sell a black DT50MX, Yamaha's entry-level 50cc scrambler-style road bike. They gave him peanuts for it, like they always did, and agreed to sell it on for the same price to my parents, allowing them to pay for it in instalments so that it was ready for my sixteenth birthday. Mum and Dad had never been massively keen on the idea of me riding, but I hadn't stopped banging on about motorbikes since that fateful holiday to Butlin's, and they knew there was nothing else in my life that meant more to me.

We kept the bike up at a local farm, where they held junior club trials and a load of other kids used to ride on the weekends and during school holidays. Trials is a slow-paced sport, all about throttle control and patience, so riding with the other kids and entering the odd event was a good grounding for me, but really all I wanted to do was ride motocross. Nine times out of ten, rather than perfecting a trials section without putting my feet down, which is the idea, I was just trying to go over it as fast as I could. Still, the techniques I picked up stood me in good stead and, even when I made it through to Superbikes, people would often comment on how smooth I looked on the bike, and how easy I appeared to find it. In some ways I used to find that frustrating, because in reality I always have my balls to the wall just like everybody else out there.

Mum and Dad were happy for me to keep the bike up at the farm, their idea being that I could ride it up around the country lanes for hours and hours, feeling total freedom while keeping myself out of trouble, although it didn't quite work out that way. I'd gone from playing around on the estate, being at Mum's beck and call, to wandering a bit further afield on my BMX, and now I had an engine in my bike – the world was my oyster! I rode the DT50 whenever I could, even in the winter, when it was dark and freezing cold, even as far as Hastings once. I didn't realize England went on that far but I set off south down the A229 out of Maidstone and just kept going until I got to the sea.

I used to take the bike to local gravel car parks, sneak under the barriers and do exactly the same things I'd been doing on my BMX at the Forum – drifting it round and round in circles until I was chased off by security guards, or the police, who had no chance of ever catching me. Then I'd take it down to the Eurolink or this little dirt track over on the Murston side of the estate and do lap after lap, getting faster and faster without even realizing it.

Just down the road from the track at Murston was a permanent site for travellers called Three Lakes Park, named after the three fishing lakes down there. My favourite movie is *Snatch*, and one of my favourite scenes in it is when Turkish and Tommy go down to the gypsy camp. Turkish says something like, 'Now, there was a problem with pikeys or gypsies – you can't really understand much of what's being said. It's not Irish, it's not English, it's just . . . well, you know, it's just pikey.'

Well, this one particularly freezing night I went down and I was riding around on my own in the dark. I'd done a load of laps and had stopped for a rest when in the glow of my headlight I thought I could see some movement in the shadows. I revved the engine to make the light shine brighter and I could just make out the silhouette of a bunch of figures pushing their way through a gap in the fence. Suffice to say, they weren't speaking English, and they weren't speaking Irish . . .

Whatever it was they were shouting at me, I was pretty sure they weren't offering me a warm blanket and a cup of tea, so I dumped the DT50 in gear and shot as fast as I could towards the nearest gap in the fence. Somehow, these guys were multiplying around me, and blocking off every way out of the place, but I knew that the wall into the church grounds had been partly knocked down, so I turned and went flying down there, bounding through the grass and over the loose rocks and potholes.

Finally, the wall came into view in the dim light of my headlamp. At its lowest point the wall still stood about two feet high, but I knew that if I hit the pile of loose bricks that were scattered on the ground in front of it, I could get enough air to clear it. I ripped open the throttle and took off, landing on the flat paving stones on the other side, and blasted my way between the gravestones and back up towards the safety of Snipeshill.

I started work as a part-time mechanic at Colwin's as soon as I'd finished my exams, earning £40 a week, but the switch from washing motorbikes to servicing them proved trickier than I'd hoped. The first job I was given was to perform a first service on a Yamaha FJ1200. The bike was virtually brand new, so all I had to do was drop the oil out of the bottom of it, change the filter, check the thing over, make sure everything worked and give it a wipe down. The mechanic who was supposed to be training me up handed me this big bar with a socket on the end. 'Make sure you tighten that sump up properly so it don't leak,' he said. I followed his instructions to the letter and tightened the sump plug up so hard that I stripped the threads out of it which, needless to say, didn't go down too well. 'What you doing, you bloody idiot?' he shouted. 'I gave you the big bar so that you didn't have to make so much effort tightening the bolt!'

Thankfully, I hung on to my job at Colwin's, and in 1993 the parts manager Dave Moore even arranged for the shop to sponsor me to have a first go at motocross racing in the East Kent Schoolboys Scramble Club, on a Yamaha YZ125. The step up to motocross racing felt totally natural to me, and within four or five months I was winning at club level on the 125, so Dave was keen to get me on a 250 as soon as possible. One of the events we were entered in on the 125 was supposed to be a non-championship round, so we decided to skip it and went off to a different meeting on a 250 instead. I won every race there but, unfortunately, the 125 event that we skipped was made into a championship round without us knowing, so I ended up losing a load of points and finishing fourth overall. Otherwise my first season in the East Kent Schoolboys Scramble Club could easily have seen me finish in the top three in the championship, which for somebody who had literally never raced a motocross bike before would have been a pretty decent effort.

Colwin's always seemed to end up with the odd stolen-recovered bike being delivered by the police to be kept in storage until the insurance claim was sorted, and it was around this time that we had a rather cool delivery – a 1991 Honda CR500. Anyone who knows anything about motocross bikes of old will know that they were a proper handful, but we decided to do a few practice sessions on the big 500, just to build up my strength for the 125. I was sixteen years old and ten stone dripping wet, so when I took off on this bloody thing I was waving around like a flag in a strong wind. The CR500 was an absolute bloody animal, but the exercise did the trick because the 125 felt like a step-through moped when I got back on it.

I went to Canada Heights – a really tough track in Swanley, where they hold a round of the British Motocross Championship – for an event where all of the local club championships were running together. The top ten riders there would be selected to go to the British Schoolboy Motocross Association finals to race against the best in the country. With a lap or two to go, I was running around in tenth place, just high enough to qualify, when my chain came off. It turned out the same mechanic who had bollocked me for misusing the big bar on the FJ1200 hadn't put the wheel in properly, and the spindle had ended up all crooked. I guess we all make mistakes.

For me, the long-term goal was always to go road racing, but the opportunity to race in motocross filled a massive void at the time. Over the years there have been some fast motocross guys who made the switch, and while I never had a particularly high level of success on the dirt, I only did it for a short period of time. I guess I just saw it as a way to get fit, pull some skids and wheelies and develop some skills that would eventually help me when I became a road racer. But I wanted to win and I worked hard at it.

One thing I was sure about was that I wasn't going to make it as a mechanic. Being on the spanners were not a bit of me and, clearly, I wasn't very good at it either, but I still loved working at Colwin's. The job got a whole lot more interesting when I turned seventeen and they allowed me to take out any 125s we had in on my lunch break. I would ride back home to my mum's as fast as I could, gulp a sandwich down, shove my helmet back on and then spend the rest of the hour roaring around town, full gas and in my element.

My boss was a hard but fair character who could be pretty forgiving at times, which was an important trait with me around – especially when a local lad called Gloaky brought in his beloved Honda NS125 for a service. Gloaky was a bit older than me, but I knew him from being around town and we'd always have a chat about bikes whenever he came into the shop. He was super excited about his little Honda, to which he'd fitted some trick new tyres and a fancy exhaust. After it had been serviced, I convinced my boss it would be a good idea for me to give it a runaround, check everything was OK. So I went flying around Sittingbourne on this thing, absolutely flat out everywhere, and somehow must have caught the attention of the police.

They gave chase, but I had absolutely no idea they were behind me, I was having too much fun, and eventually I must have lost them. As usual I got back just in time for the end of my lunch break, put the bike back in the workshop and casually strolled back into the shop as if I'd just been out for a steady ride home for a sandwich.

Nobody batted an eyelid until two days later, when the police came barging in, demanding to know who had been riding like a lunatic all over town on an NS125. They'd checked the plates and had already been round Gloaky's house trying to arrest him, but he was able to show them the paperwork that proved the bike had been in for a service on the day in question, so it was clear it must have been one of the boys from the shop. Everybody just acted dumb and we all denied being anywhere near the thing. All my boss could do was apologize, and eventually the police gave up and swept the whole thing under the carpet.

Another regular at Colwin's was a local guy called Eric who'd done a bit of racing himself in his day, but he'd had a big crash and taken a bang on the head. Poor old Eric had never been quite the same since the accident, and he couldn't ride his motorbike any more, but he still used to come into the shop to hang out, and we all liked having him around because he was such a cool guy. I used to tell

Eric all about how I was going to be a motorbike racer and, as a former racer himself, he loved listening to my ambitious plans.

My boss and Dave would sometimes go for lunch at the same time and leave me in charge of the shop, but if Eric was there I used to say, 'Right, Eric, here's the plan. You're going to man the phone for a minute, because I am *going to the toilet*. And if I'm *in the toilet* and the phone rings, you need to answer it and say that I am *in the toilet*. OK?'

'Yeah . . . okay, Shane,' he'd slur back.

'Look, just tell whoever it is to call back in twenty minutes.'

With Eric in charge of the shop, I'd grab the keys for one of the 1000s or 750s that were on display, stick my crash helmet on and go roaring off out of the shop and down the road. After half an hour blasting around town, I'd come back in and stick the price tag back on the bike, take my helmet off and pop it back under the desk. According to Eric, nobody ever called or came into the shop while I was gone, and as soon as Dave and my boss came back from their lunch, they would let me go for mine on one of the 125s. So all in all, I was getting about two hours of road-racing practice in every day.

One of the customers at Colwin's was a local policeman, who owned one of the first Yamaha FZR400s to come out as a non-import model. The bike was trick, and he was so happy with himself because he had the fancy RR version, so he used to come into the shop, banging on about how fast his bike was. Obviously, as soon as the thing came in for a service, I was straight on to Eric to man the telephones.

'What you taking out today then?' he drawled.

'I'm taking out the FZR400, Eric,' I replied, rubbing my hands.

'You can't do that!' he protested. 'He's a policeman!'

Eric's protests were drowned out by the roar of the FZR400 as I blasted out of the front doors and ripped the absolute shit out of the thing all over Sittingbourne. It was a small victory for me, because if there was one thing I loved to do as much as riding motorbikes, it was winding up the local constabulary.

They were fun times working at Colwin's, but I knew that if I was ever going to be able to afford a bike of my own and race it, then I needed to earn some proper money. I really didn't like the idea, but the big wide world of full-time employment was calling.

4

Going Underground

It wasn't just my racing career that needed an injection of cash. After years of battling to keep us afloat, my dad was finally made redundant from his job at British Rail after they were privatized, and we lost the house that my sister and I grew up in. For a period, we ended up moving in with my mum's cousin. Aunt Margaret and her husband Uncle Richard lived in a similar-sized three-bed semi to ours, but they had two kids too, so we had to squeeze in where we could and Kelly and I ended up sleeping on the bedroom floors. Mum and Dad were struggling to even get a council house, so they were looking around for somewhere cheap to rent. Even then, they needed to make quite a hefty payment upfront, and with Dad out of work, spare cash was non-existent.

I was always good at saving the little bit of money I did earn, plus whatever I was given on birthdays and at

Christmas, so without my parents knowing, I went down to the bank, drew all my savings out of my junior account and gave it to them. There was about three or four hundred pounds there, enough for the first month's rent on a new house. No matter how tight money had been, my parents had never charged me board or anything like that, so I felt it was the least I could do. 'If this gets us out of this house,' I said, 'let's just do it.'

They found a place on the other end of town, which was a bit of a drama for me because the 'other end' of town was also the 'wrong end' of town. I would be moving in right next to the gang of kids who were rivals with the mates I grew up with. It was just the usual kids' stuff – arranging fights with each other just because we were from different ends of town, things like that – so I was a bit worried at first, but in the end it proved pretty handy because I made friends on both sides and usually ended up mediating whenever there was some trouble kicking off.

I took a few run-of-the-mill Youth Training Scheme jobs – roofing, building, mechanics – but there was no immediate money to be made on a YTS and, besides, I didn't feel like I needed a trade. I was going to be a motorbike racer, remember? So off I went into town to the Job Centre and had a look at all the little cards lined up on the walls advertising the various full-time positions that were going in and around town.

The first one I took was at a place down on the Eurolink Industrial Park where I used to ride my BMX, working for a company that refurbished alternators. I'd start the day with a big basket of knackered old starter motors and alternators that needed taking apart before they were sandblasted, cleaned out and rebuilt with new brushes. I hated the job with a passion and I dreaded going into work every single morning for as long as that job lasted, which wasn't too long as it turned out.

Part of the job involved working with air tools with changeable ends, like flat-head or Phillips screwdrivers. Now, I don't know what I was doing to them, but I managed to break at least one every couple of days. I would have to go in to my supervisor each time to tell him I needed a new bit, and eventually he got so sick of me that he sent me in to see the boss, who gave me a bit more of a serious talking-to and another new part. Two days later, I was back in his office with another broken bit in my hand. He looked at me and sighed. 'This ain't working out for you, is it, son?' he said.

I couldn't agree more with his assessment of the situation, so we decided that it was better for us both to go our separate ways. I vividly remember walking out of that place, heading back towards the fence that separated Eurolink from the estate, thinking to myself: 'Do you know what? You're really not cut out for this work malarkey. We're going to have to try and think of something else.'

It dawned on me that working in a factory like that was only really making money for somebody else, and that concept didn't sit right with me. My parents couldn't understand what my problem was. To them you went to work, you took your wage and you came home – that was just what you did. But that life wasn't for me and I knew that one day, sooner or later, I would have to be my own boss. I just had to get to the point where I could stand on my own two feet.

By this time Dad had managed to find employment as a railway engineer again, subcontracting and working permanent nights on the London Underground. Eventually, with nothing better on the horizon, it seemed logical for me to join him. I knew it was going to be a tough job, but I wasn't planning on doing it for long; the money would be good, plus it was a chance to be around my dad. If I couldn't see him so much at home because he was always working, then maybe the next best thing was to go along with him and earn a few quid while I was at it.

You know when you're on a train and it makes that sound: *Der-dun-der-dun . . . der-dun-der-dun . . . der-dun-der-dun . . . ?* Well, that sound is because the sleepers have become dislodged or worn, and replacing them on the London Underground is a constant task. I would get assigned to a team of around twenty or thirty other blokes, and we'd get to work at 11.30 p.m., after the lines had all closed. We'd have about an hour before they turned the power off to lift all these generators onto little trolleys that fitted on the rails, and then push them down to whichever section of track we'd be working for the rest of that night. Each night there might be an area of about thirty sleepers that needed replacing.

We'd set all the lights up and then we fired up the gennies and got to work. We'd bar all the stones and loosen it all up, get the shovel, shift the stone back, unkey the sleeper, drag the sleeper out and put it on the trolley. Then we'd slot the new sleeper in, pack all the stone back around it and move on to the next one.

It was hard labour but the idea was that once you had completed your quota of sleepers for the night, you could pretty much leave. I used to partner up with a big, strong Jamaican guy called Tony, and between the pair of us we got so good at it that we always used to finish our lot first. Our enthusiasm didn't last long because, with me being the foreman's son, my dad didn't want to be seen letting me leave early. Plus, he had to wait until the end anyway to sign the track back over to put the power back on, so me and Tony would end up getting sent off to help the slower workers get finished. After a while we got cute at making sure we just tickled along, got our quota of sleepers done in the slowest possible time and had a bit of a giggle together along the way.

Working on the railways with my dad didn't turn out to be the father–son bonding experience I had hoped, because there were always so many other people around and he was the boss. The only time I really got to spend with him was on the journey to and from London, either side of a night shift. The drive up from Sittingbourne would take an hour, maybe an hour and a half, depending on which station we were working at and which route we took – either through the Blackwall Tunnel, over Blackheath, or right the way around the M25. Most nights we'd get a lift and there'd be four or five of us in the car, but once I had a decent set of wheels, I made sure I took the opportunity to drive up there a couple of times, just me and him.

For a very short period I had a Peugeot 309 GTi that I'd bought off a friend. He'd had it parked outside for a long time so the paintwork was all faded, but I spent ages T-cutting and polishing it up until it looked brand new – I was so proud of it. I went into the living room where my dad was getting his things ready for work and said, 'Come on, Dad, I'll drive us tonight.' We ended up getting done early that night so on the way back the roads were empty and I was driving this GTi absolutely flat out. Dad was just staring out of the window into the darkness so he didn't have a clue how fast we were going, but after a while he must have seen a road sign and he looked down at his watch.

'Shane, it's three thirty in the morning,' he said.

'Yeah . . . so what?'

'We left London at three o'clock.'

'Yeah . . .'

'We're only ten minutes from home! How bloody fast are you going?'

He craned over to look at the speedo and the poor sod nearly had a heart attack!

I'd not had that Peugeot more than a couple of weeks when one of my colleagues on the Underground, another big Jamaican guy called Gary, offered to buy it off me. Gary had taken one look at the thing and said he just had to have it, so I added a grand on to whatever I'd paid for it – partly because I didn't want to sell it and partly because I practically wore my fingers out polishing the thing – and made the best part of a month's take-home money in the space of a few days.

Ever since my days visiting the car auctions a few years earlier, I'd always known that if ever I had a bit of money in my pocket I'd always be able to do something with it, and wheeling and dealing came naturally to me. I had a knack for knowing how much I could get away with paying for something and how much I could sell it on for, and on our estate there was always somebody looking to shift something quickly – whether it was car stereos, radio-control cars, pushbikes, motorbikes or cars. I always looked after my cash, so if ever a mate needed some up front, I would be ready to take something off his hands at a knockdown price.

Working on the Underground brought me in a good, solid wage, and because my mum and dad never charged me board, I could easily get away with spending no more than thirty quid out of my wages in a month. If I set my heart on something and worked out it was going to take me, say, four months to save for it, I would work for two months, buy a car with the money I'd earned and sell it – and with the profit I'd reach four months' worth of income while I was still working the third. Whatever my target was, I always hit it early and I got a proper buzz out of doing that.

When GG was about sixteen or seventeen, I did him a favour and shifted on a cut-and-shut Peugeot 205 GTi for him that he'd stupidly bought. I reckoned it must have been three different cars welded together, but I let him trade it in for this bright red Renault 5 GT Turbo that I'd only had myself for a week or two. I was made up with that Renault, it looked the nuts, and the best thing about it was that it had a dump valve that let out a huge *TSSS!* sound every time you changed gear. Gary had the thing about three weeks when it overheated and turned into a fucking cappuccino maker. He still gives me grief about that but, to be fair, he sold it on to another mate of ours and made a profit, so he can't complain!

Before I knew it, I was turning around cars all the time – XR3is, RS Turbos, Astra GTEs, SR Novas and the other 'hot hatches' that were all the rage round our way in the Nineties. Funny thing is, if you'd have asked any of us what our dream motor was, we'd have said a Ford Escort RS Turbo. That might sound stupid to anybody who dreams of owning a Ferrari or a Lamborghini, but to us those cars were from another planet. Even a Sierra Cosworth was next level.

As far as I was concerned, an RS Turbo with a big stereo in it was about as good as life could get. If you had one of them on our estate, you were Captain Cool, believe me. I had a Series 1 RS Turbo with the big 'whale tail' spoiler on the back that I bought from a guy a few years older than me. It had a monumental sound system and it was chipped to put out 215 bhp. At the time, anything with that much horsepower might as well have been a fucking jet. One of my mates has a fully restored one now, and I'm always trying to buy the thing off him. Not long ago he phoned and offered to take me out for a coffee. He said, 'I'll pick you up in the RS Turbo and you can see how shit they really were!'

They say old habits die hard and in my case it's true. Even now I'll buy an old car, something like a 1967 Mustang that I've been looking at on eBay recently, get my mate to give it a respray, keep it for a few months and then move it on and make a few quid. Or I'll buy a 4x4 in the middle of summer when the value is not that high, stick it in the garage until November, when Britain is expecting a snowflake, and then suddenly everybody wants a 4x4 and the price goes through the roof. I'm always figuring out what I need, when I can give the best price for it and when I need to sell. Over the years I've had Porsches,

Lamborghinis, Mercedes, and they've hardly cost me a penny because I've timed it all right and they hardly depreciate. Owning a Ferrari is the next itch I need to scratch, but I just have to make sure my head rules my heart on that one.

In the Nineties I always went for nice-looking cars that I could cruise around in for a bit, use to meet some girls, then work into somebody else for a profit. I must have looked a right Billy Big Spuds in my RS Turbo, driving around with a wad of cash in my pocket, buying the drinks and throwing twenties on the bar. To be honest, I was never one for drinking myself, or going to pubs or nightclubs too much, but what I did enjoy was hanging out with my mates and trying to impress the girls with my latest flash motor.

One of my favourite pastimes was winding up the local coppers, and we'd often drive past the police station, pull a handbrake turn and make them come after us, just for the thrill of the chase. Whenever it snowed I'd get my motocross bike out and ride flat out on the roads because I knew there was nothing they could do to catch me.

After I sold that white RS Turbo, I bought a black one that was an absolute deathtrap. The easiest way to chip these things was to cut through the pipe that carried the air into the turbo and put a boost valve in so that you could adjust it. On this one it had been done really cheaply, and somebody had shoved in a copper tube with a load of holes drilled into it. The car ran like a bag of shit and you could never guess what it was going to do next. One minute it had no power, the next it would over-boost, just when you didn't expect it to.

GG was with me one afternoon when I'd been meddling

about with the thing and we decided to head out from my mum's house for a cruise about. I came around the corner at the end of Mum's street, up to this little mini-roundabout at the entrance to the estate, hit the gas and the car just took off.

There was a brief moment of euphoria when I thought, 'Yes! I've done it!', but rather than turning left when I yanked the steering wheel, the car just lunged straight forwards, bounced over the top of the roundabout and cleared the kerb on the opposite side, smashing straight into a brick wall just a couple of feet to the right of a massive shop window. Sure enough, the police turned up and, standing next to the wrecked car, I had to explain to them that some bastard had just stolen it, crashed into this wall and must have run away. God knows why, but they bought the story and I managed to get away with it.

Buying and selling cars was my life in those days, and probably still would be if it wasn't for motorcycle racing. I would pick them up from the local free ads, or even the local salvage yard. I didn't care that much what had happened to them, as long as it hadn't been recorded as an insurance job. I never touched anything that was a write-off, even though plenty of my mates were up to all kinds of stuff like that.

Some of the lads I knocked about with were proper naughty boys. Even though I generally tried to steer clear of any trouble, I did like being one of them. Where I came from, if you wanted to be somebody that others looked up to and respected, you did what you had to do.

At heart I just wanted to be respected, and my ambition to be a professional motorcycle racer was definitely a part of that. In lots of ways it has lived up to my expectations because nowadays, if a kid comes up to me for a photograph, or a fan says that meeting me has made their day, I love all that. It feels good to me to know that I can have a positive effect on people and make them happy.

Some of the other guys I knocked around with had their own ways to gain respect, and knives and guns were pretty commonplace on the estate. People like that weren't the sort of friends whose house I would go around to for a cup of tea, but it was definitely better to have them think of you as a mate rather than an enemy.

By now, it might not come as a surprise to hear that some of my mates did end up doing a bit of time inside, and probably the worst trouble I ever got in was when one of them had just come out of prison. He was a good lad who had gone the wrong way, but he convinced me he was going straight, he was going to try and get a job and do everything right this time. I agreed to pick him up and hang out for a bit, cruise around and see who we could find. One day we were driving about in an XR3i when the police came past and straight away they clocked him. 'Fuck . . . I'm so sorry, Shane, I'm so sorry!' he stuttered as the blue lights came on.

'What's wrong?' I said.

'You've got to get me out of here!'

'What have you done?'

'Just go, go, GO! Get me the fuck out of here!'

Before the police had even turned around, I took off. I gassed it all around Sittingbourne, absolutely flat out. Nobody knew those roads like me, but the car was low on fuel and it was an absolute disaster. I got away from them for a bit, then they caught up, then I got away again, until finally I got up to a corner near Borden and the power in the car went completely. I dumped the car, my mate legged it one way and I legged it the other way, but of course I was the one who got caught. The copper walled me up and cuffed me.

'Where's your mate?'

'I was on my own, officer.'

'No you fucking weren't. Where's your mate?'

'I'm telling you, I was on my own.'

They told me that if I didn't tell them where he'd gone they were going to nick me instead, and that I was going to end up with at least a twelve-month ban for dangerous driving. But whatever he'd done, I couldn't give him up. It was one of those things you do for your mates and I just had to take it on the chin.

As if to highlight how naive I was at the time, I actually thought that a driving licence and a motorbike licence were different, and that you could lose one and keep the other. Also, I'm not going to lie, there was probably a part of me that thought, 'Fuck 'em, they'll never catch me anyway.' Either way, with no driving licence for the upcoming year, I decided I might as well get rid of the XR3i and take the cash down to Colwin's to spend on a motorbike.

I was still a regular down there and I knew they had just taken delivery of a Suzuki RGV250M. I'd been drooling over the advert for it in my *Performance Bikes* magazine for months, and even though this one was black rather than the factory blue and white colours in the advert, it was perfect. The guy who'd part-exchanged it had taken off all the gaudy decals that the black version came with, and it was in mint condition. I'd been lusting after one for so long, so I got the cash together and bought it. I was absolutely made up with the thing until five days later, when I was riding it home from work and the engine just blew itself to smithereens!

Right there and then, as I sat by the side of the road waiting for the van to come from Colwin's and pick me up, I had a moment of clarity. I knew I could carry on working on the Underground, turning cars around for a profit when I got my licence back and make a decent enough living. But that was never the future I had envisaged for myself. I thought, 'That's it. Enough messing around, I'm off to be a motorcycle racer!'

5

Captain Clueless

Racing on tarmac was something that I knew just *had* to happen, and I guess eventually that's the reason it did. There'd been a few people offering to help me get on track in the past before, but for whatever reason it had never materialized. Maybe I was waiting for this magical free ride that never came along, but blowing the RGV to bits was the trigger point: I realized that if I wanted it to happen, it was down to me to make it so. It was now or never.

My first plan was to rebuild the RGV and turn it into a race bike, until I added up how much it was going to cost to fit a new exhaust, ignition box, pistons, suspension and tune the thing. It made more sense to rebuild it as a road bike, sell it, and put the money into something that had already been converted for track use. Around the same time, a local club racer called Richard Dobbs brought his all-white Kawasaki ZXR400 race machine into Colwin's. It had been built by good people and was supposed to be a competitive little bike, so I rang Dobbsy and explained that I didn't have money to buy it off him outright, but I could offer him my freshly rebuilt RGV250 in part-exchange. Dobbsy took the offer and I had myself a race bike.

The next thing to do was to sign up for my race licence, and the people down at the British Motorcycle Racing Club (or BMCRC, better known as 'Bemsee') were absolutely brilliant. The club, based at a tiny little track just outside Dover called Lydden Hill, was run by a lovely couple called Dave and Bernadette Stewart, who just live, eat and breathe the sport. They were – and still are – the perfect first port of call for any budding racer, especially relative latecomers like myself. Dave and Bernie couldn't do enough to help me get in some kind of order, helping me with entry forms and any other little mess-ups I made.

Now all I needed was my kit. I borrowed a Wayne Rainey replica Shoei helmet from Dave Moore to see me through my first meetings, although I eventually took the plunge and bought my own. Whenever a customer was umming and ahhing about whether they could afford a more expensive helmet, I always used to say, 'Can you afford to buy another head? If so, buy this shit one for fifty quid. If you can't, then get an Arai or a Shoei.' Figuring I was going to be testing the helmet's capabilities to its full, I took my own advice on that and invested in an Arai RX-7 from Colwin's.

For the leathers, boots and gloves there was only one place to go, and that was Paul Smart's shop in Paddock Wood, just outside of Maidstone. Paul was bike-racing royalty, having famously won the Imola 200 for Ducati in

1972, and I would often drop in for a chat during my Friday morning jaunts over to the car auction just around the corner from his shop. I knew his son, Scott, from riding trials up at the farm, and I think Paul was pretty happy to see me making the switch to the tarmac. He offered to do me a big discount on this hideous, ill-fitting set of Frank Thomas leathers that I insisted on getting because they were the only ones that I could colour match with the boots and gloves. They were purple, white and black and they were way too big, but I thought they looked the absolute bollocks.

I was already very familiar with Lydden, because I'd spent many a day there as a kid with Colwin's, who would take the van down and use it as a recovery vehicle in exchange for a bit of trackside advertising. The boys even taught me how to drive the van, and there must have been more than one occasion when some famous bike racer like Ray Stringer fell off at Lydden and it was actually me – at around thirteen or fourteen years old – driving the recovery vehicle that picked him and his battered bike up and took them back to the paddock.

After spending so much time trackside, watching as the likes of Ray, Terry Rymer and all these other big names raced for the 'Lord of Lydden' trophy, it was exciting to finally be going back there to ride the track myself. The only time I'd come close to riding Lydden before was when I had been part of a trials display on the infield during a big Superbike event, so it was a big deal for me to go – with my race licence in my pocket and my very own ZXR400 in the back of the Colwin's van – for an open track day that basically served as a preseason test for club racers.

The conditions were semi-damp to start off with but, coming from motocross, I wasn't at all shy about getting stuck in, with the bike slipping and sliding around sideways underneath me on every corner. Some of the other riders weren't too keen on my approach and, after a few motocross-style block passes, which I thought were all fine and dandy, I was summoned to Dave's office, where it was made clear to me that a more considered approach would be required from now on if I was going to keeping riding on tarmac.

It wasn't just the other riders whose attention I caught on that first day on track, as unbeknownst to me a well-known local sports journalist called Kerry Dunlop from the *Kent Messenger* had been watching from the side of the track. When the following week's paper came out my phone went red hot.

'Have you seen the *KM*?'

'No, why?'

'There's a piece in there about you being sideways everywhere. It seems a few people were quite impressed.'

I did another track day at Brands Indy and had my first crash. I was getting my knee down at Clearways, a really long right-hander on to the front straight, from my second or third lap, and getting a massive buzz from it. Before long I had my knee on the floor in every corner, thinking, 'Yes! I am the bollocks!' I was Captain Clueless really, making it up as I went along, and it was only a matter of time before I tucked the front end at Surtees, a fast left-hander where the Grand Prix track splits from the shorter Indy layout and heads off into the woods.

I used to crash a lot in my early days of riding motocross,

and there was many a time, when the boys were shooting the usual shit in Colwin's, that I'd been told, 'You just wait until you jump off a road-race bike. You won't bounce so well on one of those!' I must have been doing 90 or 100 mph when I came off my ZXR400 at Surtees and, as I slid across the tarmac, those boys' words came back to me. 'Oh shit, oh shit . . . this is going to hurt!' I thought, bracing myself for a sudden almighty pain. I kept on sliding onto the grass, had a little roll and got to my feet. 'What a bunch of dickheads!' I thought. 'They ain't got a clue – I never felt a thing!'

By now I was brimming with confidence, and all set and ready for my first race meeting, which would be the opening round of the 1996 Bemsee Novice 400 and Supersport 400 Championships, back on the Indy circuit at Brands. I could hardly have been more pumped up as I prepped the bike and sorted out all my kit, but my world was completely torn apart just days before the race when my beloved nan passed away.

She had been ill for a while, but I'd only been to see her a week or so earlier, up at All Saints' Hospital in Chatham. Mum had got herself in a flat spin after receiving a call to say that Nan had taken a turn for the worse. I was panicking too and I jumped on the first train. I remember running all the way from the station, right up to her ward. I dashed in and she was sat in her chair, looking a bit down and – understandably – poorly. But as soon as she set eyes on me her face lit up and her big smile turned her thick wrinkles upside down. 'Ahh . . . Shaaaney boy!' It was the way she always greeted me.

'Nan!' I smiled back. I was so relieved. 'Mum said you're unwell . . . are you OK?'

'I feel so much better already, just for seeing you, Shane. How are you, my darling?'

That was typical of her. No matter how poorly she was, her only thought was for me. She had always looked out for me and treated me like the angel I definitely wasn't. Even though she got through that little scrape, it wasn't too much longer before she was transferred to a hospice on the Isle of Sheppey, and a few days later she was gone. I was absolutely devastated. Nan had plenty of other grandchildren too, but I was the only one who got left anything in her will – a little radio she used to keep in her flat. It was the first digital one I had ever seen, and she knew I loved it. To me, that just shows how special I was to her, even though we didn't share a biological bond, and the feeling was definitely mutual. I have still got that radio and I could never bring myself to get rid of it.

Nan knew my dream, she knew what I wanted to be, and she always backed me 110 per cent. She would tell anyone who would listen that her grandson was going to be a motorbike racing champion, so I was devastated that she wouldn't get the chance to see it happen. Nevertheless, I was sure that she was watching over me when I wheeled my ZXR400 out of the van on a morning that matched my mood – damp and grey – for the first practice session of my first race weekend at Brands Hatch.

It must have rained quite hard overnight because the track stayed pretty wet for practice, although it dried out as the day went on. I still didn't have a clue what I was doing and I only had dry tyres with me, but out of the three races that afternoon I ended up winning one of them and was given the award for 'Man of the Meeting'. I will never forget the cheers I got when I went to collect my trophies in the presentation ceremony up in the Kentagon Bar at the end of the day – the feeling was just unbelievable. The round of applause from the other racers and spectators made the hairs on the back of my neck stand up, and I knew I wanted more.

It just so happened that commentating on the racing that day was Scott Smart, who was just about to go off and race in the 500cc World Championship. Scott was a full-on rock star by this point; things were going great for him and I'm pretty sure he was hanging around Brands with his team clothing on just to make sure people recognized who he was. But he was genuinely interested to see how I got on, and after the races he and his dad came to see me.

'There will be plenty of people who try to bullshit you from now and tell you this, that and the other,' Paul said. 'But whatever happens, never, ever, let anybody try to tell you how to ride a motorbike. What I've just seen out there is probably one of the most natural displays of riding I've ever seen.'

For a legend like Paul Smart to say that about me meant the absolute world. I already couldn't believe what had happened that day, but at the same time it felt right and Paul's words just confirmed it. This was all part of my life's little maze, and now I was on the right path. I knew that one little victory at a club race didn't mean I'd won a World Championship, but I would have bet my life there and then that it was going to happen for me. If anything, I was angry with myself that I hadn't got my shit together a bit sooner, rather than dicking about in RS Turbos chasing girls.

*

Racing immediately became my way of life and I realized that I would need some sort of transport of my own to get me to the different tracks around the country. I was still banned from driving, but I always had a mate who was up for coming along to a meeting, so I went and bought an old Mercedes 508 camper anyway – out of the free ads off a guy in Rochester – so that we could get about and have somewhere to sleep overnight at the tracks.

The guy I bought it from had been using it to go to moto-cross meetings, so it was filthy and it wasn't in the best nick, but I cleaned it up and had it resprayed and then took it to a carpet warehouse and carpeted virtually every surface there was. My uncle Andrew was a diesel fitter and he showed me how to service it and fix the little things that were likely to go wrong. The 508 was our escape from the estate, and we drove it all over the place, even on the weekends I wasn't racing. The problem was, not all of my mates could drive legally, so sometimes it was a case of 'better the devil you know'.

One of those devils was an old pal from Sittingbourne called Steve Newman, and one weekend, between the two of us – along with another mate who was too young even to have a licence – we decided it was a good idea to take some girls we knew up to London and show them the sights. We took them up in the van and the evening went pretty well, one of us taking the wheel as we cruised around the big city while the other two had the crack with the girls in the back. We were making our way back home at about two in the morning when the diesel filter got blocked up, and we were just praying the police didn't see us because if they caught any of us driving without a licence we knew we were going to get nicked. We got down through Rochester, through Chatham, and crossed our fingers that we'd make it up the big hill that comes up past Gillingham Hospital. I'd had enough of driving, and Newman had just taken over when we saw a load of police cars by the side of the road, surrounding a bunch of lads. It was kicking off big time and we were already five minutes into a stint, and from previous experience we knew the van could stop any second. 'Just keep driving, Newman, don't look at them!' I said. 'Everybody, try and look calm!'

We crawled past the flashing blue lights and about twenty metres later the engine went *dur-dum-dur-dum* and cut out. The minutes felt like hours as we sat there, desperately waiting for the filter to clear itself, when the inevitable tap on the window came. I thought, 'This is it, we're done.' I opened the door and went with the only plan I had.

'Please don't start, mate . . .' I sighed wearily.

'Excuse me?' said the officer.

'All we're trying to do is get home from work in London and this fucking thing keeps conking out on us.'

'Well, what's the matter with it?'

'It's the diesel filter. I know how to fix it, I just need to get the thing home to Sittingbourne.'

The copper's radio was going mental and he obviously needed to get back to the real trouble.

'Right, well, you can't stop here. Just get the thing started as quick as you can and move along.'

'No problem, officer!'

I turned to Newman with a big, stupid grin on my face to see him gripping the steering wheel so hard his knuckles were genuinely white. I was crying with laughter as we eventually got the van fired up and back home. We got the diesel filter sorted out, and for the rest of that year the 508 became my home from home. I would go and work a shift with my dad on the Underground, get back home at three in the morning and jump straight in the camper and drive off to a test or a track day somewhere.

Unfortunately, I didn't see the end of my first season because that first win at Brands Hatch was soon followed by my first big injury. Back at Lydden Hill, I got flicked over the top of the bike and broke my scaphoid, a bone in the wrist that is notoriously difficult to heal as it doesn't get much oxygen to it. A broken scaphoid means that you lose strength and the full range of motion in your wrist, which for a motorcycle racer is clearly a big problem. I had an operation to fix it, and the doctor told me that if it didn't heal properly, I might not be able to race again.

My job on the London Underground was on a self-employed basis, so I had no choice but to turn up to work with my plaster cast on, or else I didn't get paid. I tried to look on the bright side and saw it as a form of physio-therapy – carrying all those big heavy generators, trollies and tools up and down flights of stairs – and just got on with it. I was convinced that all the physical labour would help get blood to the scaphoid and make it heal quicker, but when I went back to the hospital and got the cast off, it turned out I hadn't done myself any favours at all.

I told the specialist that I was going to be a professional motorbike racer; that this bone might be the most important one in my body and he simply had to fix it. 'Your motorbike career is over, son,' he replied. 'We can try another operation but it's unlikely to do any good. This wrist will never bend properly again.' I was devastated. Just one season of racing, and it looked as if my career might be over almost before it had begun.

Thankfully, the next break in my career was a lucky one.

6

Life on Track

Despite the surgeon's assessment, I never believed for one second that something as trivial as a broken wrist was going to put an end to my dreams. Any motorcycle racer will tell you that as long as they can get their body to operate the controls of a bike, they are as good as new. And one way or another, I was sure I could work around a dodgy wrist.

After a second operation, I managed to get back out on track again towards the end of 1996 at a semi-national event at Silverstone. I'd worked as hard as I could to get as much flexibility back as possible and, even though the joint didn't bend all the way, I got it to the point where I could just about twist the throttle open, and that was good enough for me. The slightly upright position I had to take on the bike to be able to do that would mark my riding style for the remainder of my career.

I was sitting outside the camper, meddling with my bike,

when I was approached by Mark Linscott, a top national rider who had won the British Superbike Championship before it was branded as such. Mark had officially retired through injury, but he was still racing in some support classes with a wealthy sponsor called Jim McNulty, who happened to live locally to me and knew of me from my junior trials and motocross days. Jim must have heard I was riding at Silverstone that weekend and asked Mark to keep an eye out for me.

I'd never been to Silverstone before and I didn't have a clue where I was going, but I was getting faster and faster with each session. Mark kept coming over, asking how I was getting on, and the faster I got, the more interested he got. He pointed out that the tyres I was using were complete shit, so he went to Avon and sorted me some new ones. Having put this new rear tyre in, I went so much faster, and even though I crashed out of the race, it seemed I had done enough to impress Mark.

Mark worked in telecommunications installation for a company called Cotswolds Communications, owned by a bike enthusiast and wannabe racer already in his late forties called Alf Cooper, who had arranged to buy the V&M Honda CBR600 machines that Dave Heal had just won the British Supersport Championship on. Over the winter, with some extra persuasion from my old friends Dave and Bernie Stewart from the BMCRC, Mark convinced Alf to let me ride one of his new bikes at the first Bemsee meeting of 1997 at Brands.

I got a couple of fifths and a third place out of the three races on that first weekend of the new season – my first time riding a 600 – and by the end of the meeting Alf offered to give me a ride for the rest of the year, as well as a job at Cotswolds Communications. The company I worked for on the Underground had just lost their contract, so even though it was a pretty dull job working for Alf, pulling and tagging cables ready for the engineers to come and connect them all together, it kept my head above water and got me back out on track, which was all that mattered.

Alf also agreed to fork out for a new set of leathers, since the Frank Thomas's that I'd bought from Paul Smart had been down the road a few times by now and the duct tape holding them together just wasn't cutting the mustard any more. Alf and Mark agreed that they looked horrendous and bought me a set of custom leathers, made by a small Dutch company called MJK. I actually designed them myself: blue and white – to match the corporate colours of Cotswold Communications – with a bright yellow stripe, and I was absolutely made up with them. I got some blue and white Sidi boots to match and thought I was the absolute Don.

With Alf on my side I started winning races from the word go. We entered the Bemsee Novice and Supersport 600 Championships, which was a step up in class, but I pretty much went unbeaten for the whole season, taking just shy of sixty race wins in total, and won both championships by a mile.

We also entered a couple of national races in the British Supersport Cup, which was a level below the British Supersport Championship but had sponsorship from *The People* newspaper, so there was plenty of interest in it. Our bikes were due a rebuild just before the first round we entered at Brands Indy, and with a tired engine I finished ninth. It wasn't bad for my first proper national race, but I still felt a bit gutted because I had become so used to winning at club level. We had the engines rebuilt by V&M up at their workshop in Rochdale and did another national round at Cadwell Park, which I absolutely smoked.

The next logical step was to try and have a crack at the British Supersport Championship, but because I'd not been racing long enough, I wasn't eligible to enter. The organizers were very 'by the book' about it, but we managed to get some kind of dispensation to do a round at Donington Park.

My good friend Richard Chesson arranged and paid for me to go up to the Ron Haslam Race School at Donington Park before the race, just so that I'd at least know which way round the track went. Richard had a company called Sittingbourne Motor Spares and quite often when I was heading off to a race meeting he'd give me a bunch of £20 notes to help me on my way. He'd raced a bit himself and, even though I was pretty confident about my abilities, he probably believed in me even more. Richard was and still is a top bloke – always calm, always ready with great advice, and always a source of support throughout my career.

My instructor for that day up at Ron's school was an ex-125cc British Champion called Steve Patrickson, who was really helpful, showing me the lines and teaching me the tricks of the circuit. Eventually, though, riding standard Honda CBR600s, we got to the point where he couldn't take me any faster. Every time it was my turn to lead he was struggling to keep up, and when we came back in he assured me I'd be just fine.

We went back to Donington for the race and I managed to bag a couple of points, which at the time was a massive result for me. There were too many riders and not enough decent seats in Superbikes, so a load of the top boys had dropped down – guys like Paul 'Marra' Brown, John Crawford, Howard Whitby, Phil Borley, Steve Plater and Jim Moodie. The depth of field in Supersport made it savagely competitive, probably even tougher than Super-bikes that season. And in that company I was delighted with whatever points I could get.

It was an incredible learning experience for me, and to see my name alongside theirs in *Motor Cycle News* and some of the magazines that I had pored over as a kid was a great feeling, and an indication of how far I'd come. In the same way that I had cut out pictures of my heroes and favourite bikes to stick on my bedroom wall, pretty soon my mum would be cutting out pictures of me and framing them to hang all around her house. For the first time in my life, I really felt that I was starting to find the right way through.

One of my favourite publications had always been *Fast Bikes* magazine. To me those guys were pioneers of the motorsport publishing scene in the Nineties. There were already plenty of mags around with photos of guys getting their knee down on exotic motorbikes, but *Fast Bikes* was the one that really pushed the boundaries. Instead of using journalists who could ride a motorbike a bit, they used established motorbike racers who could string a few words together. The articles might not have been the best written, but who cared about that when the pictures were so damn cool? More than that, the opinion of an actual racer on the latest Superbike to come out was way more relevant than that of a journalist who couldn't ride it anywhere near its true limit.

I guess you could say *Fast Bikes* was the 'fuck you' magazine of the motors section at WHSmith. A bit like *Loaded* and *FHM* were to the booming 'lads' mag' market in the Nineties, it was intended to be real, rowdy and on the limit, and I loved it. They had a section in the back called 'Race Riot', with little stories about the racers that the magazine was supporting; guys like Sean Emmett, Rob Frost, Andy Ibbott and Jamie Robinson. All of these guys were like gods to me, purely because they were in *Fast Bikes* magazine, and I wanted to be just like them. Amazingly, at the end of 1997, I got my chance.

One of the *Fast Bikes* reporters was a guy called Jimmy Miller, a really easy-going dude who came across more like a surfer than a motorbike racer. Jimmy was racing in a single-make Honda CB500 Championship, where some other promising young riders like James Toseland were making their name, and he was being sponsored by a track day company. When Jimmy's teammate got injured, the sponsor approached Alf to ask if I could step in. The CB500 would be a step down, machinery-wise, from Alf's Supersport bikes, but the series was running as part of the British Championship, so obviously I was mad keen to do it.

Alf was happy about it so I went up to Mallory Park in Leicestershire, excited because I was going to be teammate for the weekend to the great Jimmy Miller of *Fast Bikes* fame. I got put in the novice group initially, but I was much faster than anybody else, so they moved me straight up to the expert group and I turned out to be faster than most of them too, including Jimmy. I thought Jimmy was so cool, and I had studied pictures of him in the magazine for years. Now I was out on track, riding with him, but so much faster that I almost felt embarrassed.

I got a terrible start in the race, but I came right the way through to somewhere near the front – and then wrote the bike off. The exhaust on a CB500 exited from the rear on the right-hand side, and when I threw the bike underneath somebody into Gerard's Bend, the fast right-hand turn one at Mallory, the exhaust hit the tarmac and the thing absolutely obliterated itself. I had taken more than just the shine off poor Russell's CB500, but thankfully Jimmy was still laid-back about everything and said, 'Dude, that was so awesome! You should come up to the magazine and hang out and meet Colin.' He meant Colin Schiller, the owner of *Fast Bikes*. 'Mate, just tell me where and when!' I beamed.

A week later I got to meet Colin, who was really complimentary about my riding. It turned out he had actually already been to Snetterton to see me ride on a 600, having been given a shortlist of young riders he should check out to replace Sean Emmett, who they had already brought through into the British Championship. I had been so much faster than everybody else that weekend that I got protested three times, and had my bike stripped each time. Colin told me I'd been the last in and first out at every key corner on the track; he reckoned that if I could be that brave at Snetterton, I must have something special.

We had a look around the offices before Colin took me back to his house to chat about working for him. He sat me down in his kitchen and he was asking me all these quite deep questions, about what I wanted to do with my life. I guess it was a bit of a test to see where I was at, mentally, and whether I had what it took to be a success. At the end of the meeting he asked me to do some testing with them down in the South of France.

I couldn't believe it. Just a few weeks after trashing a CB500 at Mallory, I found myself riding some of the world's most exotic motorcycles around St Tropez. Let's just say I was keen to show them what I could do and, to be fair, I think I pretty much scared everybody stiff for two hours. They were trying to get this four-bike cornering shot of me, Jimmy Miller, Simon Mounsey and Rob Frost, who were all complaining to Colin, saying, 'This guy is trying to fucking kill us!' But Colin loved it and I was having an absolute ball, riding with my *Fast Bikes* heroes on these brand-new Superbikes on one of the best roads in Europe. It was a dream come true.

Of course, there was just one small problem: I didn't actually have a licence.

7

Cover Stories

By the start of 1997 my driving ban had actually expired, but I'd made a cock-up a couple of years earlier when I first did my bike test by not sending in the certificate to the DVLA. It meant my bike licence was no longer valid, but the opportunity to work for *Fast Bikes* was so huge that I hadn't dared mess up my chances by telling Colin about it. I decided I'd keep it to myself for a while, figuring that most of the riding would be abroad or on race tracks anyway, but just a couple of weeks after that first trip to France, I was already on the front page of the magazine, doing a fourth-gear stand-up wheelie on a Ducati 996 Biposto. A few more front covers later my conscience got the better of me and, reluctantly, I fessed up to Colin, thinking that I was probably going to get the sack straight away and lose my dream job before it had properly got started.

As it turned out, Colin was great about it, and all the boys had a good laugh. Colin loaned me his Ducati 996SPS race bike, which had about 145 bhp and was just about the best machine about at the time, and I redid my test with some poor instructor who must have thought he was Mick Doohan, trying to belittle me and show me how to ride a motorbike. 'Mate, let's go to a racetrack and I'll fucking spank you!' I told him, and when he passed me I celebrated with a rolling burnout – with the L-plate still on the front.

One of the bikes I brought home from the magazine was a Super Blackbird, which Honda brought out in 1996 to take on the Kawasaki Ninja ZX-11 as the world's fastest production motorcycle, and it was a huge success. This machine had 164 hp and was tested at 178.5 mph top speed. I picked the Blackbird up one evening from this place in Woking, just southwest of London, and rode it flat out back to Sittingbourne, right on the rev limiter, all the way around the M25 in about thirty-five minutes.

The following evening I was cruising around town on this thing, seeing who was about, when a guy pulled up alongside me at the lights outside the cinema on a ZXR750. He looked across and nodded – the kind of casual nod that bikers give each other when they're out and about. But by now I'm not just any old biker: I'm Shakey from *Fast Bikes* and, trust me, I am believing the hype!

I've got a cool set of leathers with my nickname written across the back, a custom-painted helmet with my own design . . . I am fucking *doing it*, as far as I'm concerned. But this guy didn't seem the least bit bothered! We pulled away from the lights and he pulled a little wheelie. I thought, 'Do you know who I fucking am, mate?' and stood the Blackbird up on the back wheel, pulling a massive stand-up wheelie all the way past him. 'Have a bit of me, sunshine!' I said to myself.

I carried on around the one-way system and then turned to go back towards town. As I was coming back, about two or three hundred metres up the road, I could see loads of youngsters hanging about outside McDonald's. I knew there was a speed bump there so, as I hit it, I popped the thing back up on the rear wheel and gave it a great big handful of 'check me out, lads!' What I didn't know was that these kids had been busy having a massive scrap and the Old Bill were absolutely all over the place.

This copper jumped out into the middle of the road in front of me and put his hand up for me to stop, but unfortunately for him I was already fully committed. There was no way I was putting this thing back down, so I just kept it lit and rode straight towards him, the front wheel spinning through the air at head height. To be fair to the copper, he stood his ground and didn't dive out of the way until the very, very last second and I was *gone*. I dropped the front wheel, cracked the throttle open and blasted down Sittingbourne High Street, flat out all the way back to my mum's. Without daring to look over my shoulder, I quickly dragged a cover over the bike, whipped my helmet and leathers off and slumped into the armchair in the front room, trying to catch my breath before the knock on the door. Thankfully, once again, it never came.

Thrashing other people's bikes around for fun had been a hobby of mine since I worked at Colwin's, so doing it for a living with *Fast Bikes* was an unbelievable perk of the job. However, by far the biggest bonus was that they were keen to support my racing career. For the upcoming 1998 season, I signed for a team based in Ashford, quite close to me. Two local businessmen – Graham Bromley, who had a lorry tipper firm, and Mark Hellier, who traded tractors – had been running a guy called Gary Weston in the European Supersport Championship; even though Gary had been doing really well, he had decided to retire. Richard Chesson knew them both and persuaded them that I was worth a shot.

Graham and Mark had arranged to buy these Yamaha YZF600 Thundercats from a Dutch team that had just run Wilco Zeelenberg and Jeffry de Vries on them in the World Supersport Championship. In the UK the Thundercat wasn't seen as the bike to race, since it was more of a sports tourer than a true Supersport bike like a Suzuki GSX-R600 or a Honda CBR600, but these had come straight from the World Championship and had been serviced by a well-known Dutch engine tuner called Jan Roelofs. I went over to Holland with Graham and Mark and picked the bikes up from Jan, who assured us that the engines were top spec. I tested one in a club race at Brands Hatch and sure enough it was an absolute weapon, especially compared to the Hondas I rode in 1997.

The British Supersport Championship was super-competitive again in 1998 so, as part of our preparations, Richard phoned our old friend Dave Stewart at Bemsee to get an ACU Start Permission to do the first round of the European Championship at Le Mans. It would be my first ever international meeting, and both Dave and Bernie were so supportive about the whole thing that they actually came out with us and joined the team for the weekend, along with a mutual friend called Richie Freeman.

Richie was a real character who had worked in the World Championship paddock for two years as a motorhome driver for a famous Australian rider called Daryl Beattie. He became well known for his stutter – which he would get in a right old pickle with sometimes – and his motorbike impressions. The guy could mimic anything from a Manx Norton to a 500cc Grand Prix bike, and he always had everyone around him in stitches doing so.

Richie's popularity proved invaluable at Le Mans, where I crashed both bikes in practice after getting caught out by a couple of damp patches. The boys had to work all evening to try and make one good bike out of all the bits, and when they came up short of a pair of forks and a fuel tank, Richie wandered off down pit lane with Dave at about 11.30 p.m., and was greeted like a long-lost brother by none other than Christian Sarron – the former 250cc World Champion – at Yamaha Moto France. Minutes later the pair of them came back with everything we needed to fix the bike.

I qualified eighteenth with what turned out to be a twisted swing-arm, so after another trip for Richie and Dave down to Yamaha Moto France to borrow a straight one, I was ready for Sunday. Now that the bike was pointing in the right direction, I went third fastest in warm-up, and I had made it to fifth within the first six laps of the race before I got caught out on the final turn by those little rubber bobbles the French used to put on the kerbs, and crashed again. When I got back to the pits I was in tears, thinking I had let everyone down, but Richie,

Dave and Bernadette, and the rest of the boys assured me that wasn't the case.

After my experience in France, once I had pulled myself together again, I felt really confident I could do much better back on home shores once the season properly started. We took part in a club race as a test and I cleaned up in that, then we went straight to Brands for the first race of the season. I did all right in practice, but the clutch was really hard to get it off the line, so I got a rubbish start and dropped back through the field.

Eventually, I'd got back up to about fifth when I found myself behind Phil Borley, a top rider who had won the championship a few years earlier. Phil had this wide, sweeping line down through Paddock Hill Bend and I just decided I was going to have him up the inside. Phil came sweeping back across and I just T-boned him and took us both out. He was not impressed at all and avoided any attempt I made to apologize.

After that rocky start the year got better, and we even won a race at Snetterton, but around halfway through the season Graham and I had a fallout. It was difficult because I appreciated everything they were doing for me, but the bike had some problems and, as far as I was concerned, they just wouldn't listen. The gearbox was so knackered, I argued it was getting dangerous, but Graham refused to replace it and instead came into the garage joking about the cost of his nice hotel and his bar bill.

We got to the tenth of twelve rounds at Silverstone in the September and I told Graham I didn't want to ride his bike any more. We had a massive shouting match in the middle of the garage, in front of everybody – not very professional, but it just happened. 'If you want to spend your money on beer, go spend it on beer,' I told him. 'If you decide to spend it on your bike then give me a call and I'll come back and ride it.' It was a bit of a scene, and we went our separate ways, although Graham and I get on well now and these days it always makes me smile with nostalgia when I see his 'Bromley Haulage' tippers rolling around the Kent streets. At the time, though, he never called, so I never went back. Luckily, Colin Schiller got me a ride on an ex-Ten Kate Honda CBR600 for the final round of the 1998 season at Donington, and had put an even bigger plan in place for me in 1999.

8

From Now On,
You're Twenty-Two!

As a young British Supersport rider, the one guy I used to love watching from trackside when the Superbikes were out was Troy Bayliss – a blindingly fast and aggressive Australian with an unorthodox style. Watching Troy come past was mesmerizing – the guy was just so unbelievably committed. There were places I remember watching him from, like the top of Cascades at Oulton Park – a blind-entry, fourth-back-to-third rollercoaster of a corner – where you could see he was so much more on the limit than everybody else. Everything with Troy was loose, yet the bike still looked under control.

In 1998 he was relatively unknown, having come over that year to ride in the UK for a friend of Graham's called Darrell Healey – who had a company called Groundworks Southeast and ran a really successful team called GSE Ducati – but Troy was already a hero in my eyes because of the way he rode. He would go on to prove his class, winning the British Superbike (BSB) title in 1999 before going on to become a triple World Superbike Champion, a MotoGP race winner and continuing to fight for wins in the Australian Superbike Championship into his fifties.

Troy's teammate at GSE Ducati in 1998 was Jamie Robinson, a brilliant little 250 rider from Yorkshire, who was only about my age but had been one of my heroes reading *Fast Bikes*. Despite his skill on a 250, Jamie didn't seem to suit the big Ducati; since he wasn't going very well on it, Graham spoke to Darrell and they offered to give me a test. We went to Knockhill, a short and tight little circuit up near Dunfermline in Scotland, and even though it was wet, I was instantly a lot quicker than Jamie, and also ended up only two or three tenths off Bayliss on my first day on a Superbike. To be so close to Troy's lap times so quickly, albeit in the wet, made me feel like some momentum was starting to build, but after a second test in the dry at Oulton Park I realized that I wasn't physically or mentally prepared yet for the onslaught on your senses that a Superbike is to ride.

When you first open the throttle on a Superbike, it feels like you've been fired out of a cannon, and when you grab the brakes it's as if you've hit a brick wall. Compared to my Supersport bike, it was like somebody had hit fast forward and every reference point had moved – even the straights were not straights any more. I was losing all my momentum in the corner and I didn't have enough time in one day to work out that with slick tyres, which I had never used before, I could carry so much more speed through the turn. Everything about the bike felt heavy, and just changing direction on the thing was a superhuman effort.

Colin Schiller was a fitness fanatic, and still a really strong runner even though he was in his fifties; he used to drill into me how important it was to train. His other mantra was to ride as many different motorcycles as possible, to train different aspects of your riding and have the broadest possible skill set to take onto a race bike. Some people don't see the point in riding around a track three seconds off the pace of a Superbike, but I have learned that as long as you are constantly on the limit of whatever you're riding, then you are preparing yourself well for the demands of the next level.

I had been running a lot with Colin since I had started working for him at *Fast Bikes*, so I thought I was fit until I rode that Superbike. Now I knew that I needed to step everything up to make sure I was in much better shape if and when the opportunity ever came up again. I joined a gym and started building some more muscle, and rode as much motocross as I could to get more bike-fit. At the time I was pretty green in terms of the structure of my training – I would keep going until I threw up, thinking that was the best way to measure myself. My motivation for my training often came from visualizing my biggest rival, telling myself, 'I bet he's not out running this early in the morning' or, 'I bet he can't cycle this distance in this time.' I felt that if I was training *more* than anybody else, then surely I was training *better* than anybody else.

Over the years, thanks to working with some top pro-fessionals like my long-term trainer Grant Breese and my cycling 'guru' Sean Dines, I have learned that having a structure to your training is much more important than how hard you push. Sean, who I first met in 2008 at a cycling show in London, would go on to become a huge influence – not just on my training but on my career and my life. We hit it off straight away and started going on structured training rides together. As a semi-pro-cyclist himself, Sean's dedication and positivity towards everything was off the scale and it rubbed off on me, to the point that by the time I was in my late-thirties I was slimmer, lighter and stronger than I'd ever been before. A funny example was when Alpinestars, my leather sponsors since 2005, measured me up for a new suit in 2015: ten years after they had first measured me, the only difference to my body shape was that my waist was smaller and my upper body ever so slightly bigger.

Essentially, the most important thing Sean and Grant did was make me start to see my body as an engine that needs to be looked after. If you run it to its rev limiter it will blow up, but if you're careful it can run for miles. Some days, a light session or a rest is all you need to improve your fitness and look after your immune system, which is crucial for keeping you going over the course of a season.

Back in 1999, I still had a lot to learn about the demands of being a professional motorcycle racer, but I had got myself physically much stronger for the start of the new season and my next opportunity to try a Superbike. Colin had agreed that *Fast Bikes* would buy some Ten Kate Honda CBR600s so I could run in Supersports again, but also struck a deal with two brothers called Lester and Steve Harris, who would give me some outings on a Kawasaki in the Superbike Privateers Cup. Colin knew they were big supporters of young talent, and he had built a good relationship with them when he was bringing Sean Emmett through in the early Nineties.

For the previous three years, from 1996 to 1998, Lester

and Steve had been running the Suzuki effort in World Superbikes, but they had just done a deal with Kawasaki UK to take over development of their BSB team, with Chris Walker and Steve Hislop signed up to ride the factory bikes. The Privateers Cup was strictly for non-factory bikes and I would be riding for prize money only, but that was cool with me. I had my *Fast Bikes* wages and a race win would be worth £1,000. With two races per weekend I could win a decent amount of money if I could pull it off consistently. I would be a professional rider at last, but more importantly we knew the Harris brothers would put a good bike together and give me the time to develop, without demanding results.

The first thing Steve asked me was how old I was. 'Twenty-three,' I told him, not thinking that it should matter too much. 'Not any more you're not,' said Steve, who had a charming way about him that reminded me a lot of the car dealers I used to hang around with at the auctions back in Paddock Wood. 'From now on you're twenty-two,' he grinned, filling in my entry forms for the 1999 British Superbike Championship. From that day on I have always been known to be a year younger than I really am. Believe me, though, I am not the only rider out there to have a 'racing age'. Honestly, I swear Chris Walker is eligible for a free bus pass!

The dominant rider in the Privateers Cup at the time was a guy called Paul Young, who was almost twenty years older than me. Youngy got his big break when he was already in his forties, at the time that the Yamaha R7 came out, when he did really well on it. In the first round at Brands we went out and beat Youngy and the reaction was immediate. Because Steve and Lester were running the official Kawasaki job, everyone assumed my bike must have been factory supported too, even though it wasn't, and there were constant complaints. Eventually they kicked us out of the championship, but Lester and Steve didn't bother protesting, because they didn't want to be falling out with the organizers when they had a Superbike title to try and win for Kawasaki.

To Lester and Steve, the Privateers Cup wasn't a big deal, but to me it was everything. I was gutted that we were kicked out, not least because no prize money meant no wages. Colin was paying me in dribs and drabs for the *Fast Bikes* job, so it was getting difficult to make ends meet. It had got to the point that one evening at Knockhill one of Colin's mechanics, Mark Hannah, a really good friend, asked me if I could pay for his dinner because he didn't have any cash on him. I had to say, 'Mark, if I pay for your dinner I don't have enough money to get myself home.' I had just enough to fill my car with fuel and drive it at 55 mph all the way back from Fife to Kent.

It might not have quite been paying the bills, but working for *Fast Bikes* was still my dream job and I was having so much fun doing it, even if we were pushing the limits of what was really acceptable. Colin was starting to get some heat from the police because we were making some pretty outlandish VHS videos, which they used to sell by mail order and at the various bike shows.

One of the videos that Colin got in trouble for was called *Mach* 2, which involved taking a Suzuki Hayabusa, a Kawasaki ZX-12 and a Honda Super Blackbird and getting them from Calais to Cannes in what was supposed to be the shortest time possible. We were doing mile after mile with the needle touching 210 mph on the speedo of the Hayabusa, pulling 150 mph stand-up wheelies up the hard shoulder of the French motorways, and ragging the bikes so hard we had to stop every seventy miles to refuel.

There was footage of us doing rolling burnouts and power slides through these sleepy French villages, and some of the footage actually ended up on *Crimewatch*, appealing for people to come forward and help them nail the hooligans involved. It was the best possible exposure for *Fast Bikes* at the time and I'm sure Colin loved it.

Steve 'Hizzy' Hislop and Chris 'Stalker' Walker were on the factory Kawasakis for that 1999 season, but Hizzy got the sack halfway through the year and, even though I had done well on the Harris bike, they tried a few other riders before finally giving me a shot in the last round at Donington Park. Stalker was fighting for the title with Bayliss, who was still on the GSE Ducati, so it was a massive chance for me to make a name for myself and maybe even help Chris out, which I knew would go down well with Kawasaki. Needless to say, I was super-keen.

I was even more excited when Spyke, who had agreed to sponsor me through the magazine with some leathers and gloves, sent me a new off-the-peg suit that they'd badged up especially for the weekend. Talk about full factory. The only downside to having new leathers is that they can be tight and stiff when you first put them on, so it is always advisable to wear them around the house for a day or two before you get to the track. Professional racers have four or five suits on the go at any one time, and the very top guys get a new set almost every weekend, which leads to some pretty inventive ways of getting them bedded in.

Over the years I have had teammates like Stuart Easton or Glenn Irwin, who would insist on pouring hot water on their leathers to loosen them up, or stick inner tubes inside the sleeves and pump them up to stretch the leather. Colin Edwards used to roll around on the floor in his, but I think this was more down to superstition, as if doing that got their first 'crash' out of the way. My personal thing was to take my leathers off the hanger, hold them by the shoulders and throw them out like a towel on a sunbed and let them drop on the floor. Later, when I was used to getting new suits regularly, I would never race in one without having used it for at least one warm-up session first.

The other 'tradition' I developed over the years, incidentally, was my race-day diet. I never had much breakfast but, between races one and two, I would always eat a packet of wholegrain rice with a tin of those baked beans you can buy with the little sausages in. It started off as just a cheap meal back in the early days, but actually it is so easy to make and it is full of carbohydrates and protein, so I stuck with it for the rest of my career.

Those tins also came in handy if I had problems with tight gloves, which can give you arm pump – a condition where your forearm muscles swell up and restrict the blood flow. I would grab a tin of beans and shove it inside the glove to stretch it out. Luckily for me this stopped being an issue from 2005, when I signed a deal with Alpinestars and had all of my kit custom-made. They even made me gloves with an extra-long thumb, so the stitching on the inside didn't feel like it was going to pull my nail off under hard braking, and special boots that narrowed at the toe so that they didn't rub on the ground, which my knackered-wrist-inspired position on the bike always seemed to make them do. Alpinestars racing suits are so accurate that it was ten years before I even needed to get re-measured.

But that first set of Spykes – as excited as I was about them at the time – needed a more traditional way of getting them race-ready. They arrived at our house on the Wednesday and I was due to drive up to Donington on Thursday, but I had to go out for the day, so I thought, 'That's all right – Dad will be at home, he can bed them in for me.'

As usual, my dad came home from his nightshift on the railways in the early hours of the morning, went to bed and got up shortly before lunchtime. Dad never did anything until he'd had two cups of tea while chilling out in his favourite armchair, then he'd walk into town to meet my mum and help her home with the shopping. 'Right then, Popeye,' I'd said before he headed out to work the previous night. 'When you get up in the morning, put these leathers on and just wear them around the house until you're going off to meet Mum.' He wasn't too happy about the idea but reluctantly he agreed, and the next morning when he got up and made his first cup of tea, he squeezed into them. After an hour or so sitting in his chair it was time for him to get sorted and go meet my mum in town. Now, as anybody who has squeezed into a tight pair of leathers knows, they are far easier to get on than off. And this particular set were *way* too tight for my poor dad.

Meanwhile, after an hour or so of hanging around waiting for him to show up in town, Mum finally got the hump and came stomping back home, laden with bags, only to find my dad rolling around on the floor like a beetle on its back, still with the leathers on, but unzipped down to the waist. 'What the bloody hell are you playing at?' she shouted at him.

'Don't you bloody start, I've been stuck here in these

stupid bleedin' leathers for the last two hours, haven't I? I can't get the fucking things off!'

By the time I breezed through the door a few hours later he was still wearing them, and he was absolutely fuming. 'You silly little bastard!' he shouted when I walked in.

'What's up, Dad? Are my leathers all nice and stretched?'

'I'll fucking stretch you in a minute!' he shouted. He was trying his best to give me a bollocking, but all I could do was piss myself laughing at the sight of him, rolling about on the floor like a fish out of water, trying to free his arms.

Between us, Mum and I prised my dad out of my nicely stretched Spykes and I took them up to Donington Park for the final round of the BSB season, where I did the ultimate job of bedding them in myself when I high-sided coming out of McLeans corner on intermediate tyres after about five minutes of a damp first free practice. The factory Kawasaki was a bit faster and a bit more rigid than I was used to and, to be honest, I struggled a little bit with it in the dry.

Thankfully, Sunday morning was completely wet, which meant that we had to go softer on all the settings anyway, and I had a good first race, nicking Bayliss on the last lap for fifth place. Stalker won to keep his championship alive, but unfortunately for him he crashed on a drying track in the second race and Troy took the title.

I finished sixth in that second race, ahead of a couple of big names like Niall Mackenzie and James Haydon, which was a brilliant result for me. It meant that – despite missing most of the season with no bike to ride – I would end the championship in fifteenth overall on 67 points, a number that would prove significant, for good and bad reasons, over the coming years.

9

What Happens
When You Crash

Here's a funny thing that happens when a motorcycle racer has a crash. As you're bouncing, rolling, sliding or even flying through the air towards the gravel traps and the tyre walls, you're already performing your own little medical assessment on how long each potential injury might take to heal.

You haven't even come to a complete stop before you're thinking about how quickly you can get back on your bike. 'That feels like a broken arm . . . might take a month or two. Maybe I can be back for Brands Hatch . . .' If you're not thinking that way, then the chances are you're in serious trouble. That was the case for me on not one but two occasions, during a disastrous second season in the British Superbike Championship.

The new millennium had started off in really promising fashion. Firstly, those 67 points I had scored in 1999 had convinced Kawasaki UK that it would be worth offering me a full-time paid contract to ride with them. However, the series organizers had announced they were bringing in some new regulations to help cap costs, introducing what were essentially dumbed-down 'kit' Superbikes.

Honda, as ever, were the quickest to react, and already had something that was good to go by the time the new season kicked off. The SP-1 was a purpose-built bike that complied with the new regulations, and Steve and Lester had wasted no time getting their hands on one. It seemed like a really smart move at the time, and they were both keen for me to stay with them and ride it.

Even though Kawasaki's offer was better from a financial standpoint, my loyalty to the Harris brothers and the opportunity to be competitive in British Superbikes was worth more to me than any short-term financial gain. It is an approach I have maintained throughout my career; I have always believed that riders who constantly chase a pay cheque above all else will not achieve their full potential and ultimately never maximize their career earnings as a result.

At the time of writing, for example, a good BSB team bonus is around £5,000 per win, whereas the factory Kawasaki team in World Superbikes pays something more like £30,000. It doesn't take a genius to work out that a young rider scratching around for a few extra quid in BSB could end up losing way more in the long run by making the wrong choices. That is the principle I have always worked to, although sometimes what seems like the *right* choice doesn't always turn out to be the *best* choice.

The way I saw it at the end of 1999, Steve and Lester

were the ones who had given me the chance to ride a Superbike in the first place – something that I'll be forever grateful to them for – and I wanted to stick by them. So I said, 'Thanks, but no thanks' to Kawasaki, and excitedly got myself ready to start the 2000 season as a full-time Super-bike racer with Honda.

What I could never have predicted at that point, and neither could Steve or Lester, was that these new 'kit bike' rules would get dropped almost immediately, handing the technical advantage straight back to all our rivals, and while Honda pushed hard for the World Superbike title that year with their full WSB spec SP-1, the development never filtered down to domestic level – other than a few extra rpm that they gave to Joey Dunlop at the TT, which his team was then able to pass on to James Toseland in BSB – and we were completely screwed. Meanwhile, as I tried to stay competitive, I rode the wheels off the Harris bike and smashed myself to bits in the process.

It all started to go wrong in the third round of the season at Thruxton, a fast, flowing, former Second World War airfield circuit in Hampshire that I usually love. I was running pretty well, battling somewhere near the front with John Crawford on the Crescent Suzuki, and in the approach to the final chicane I thought I had him covered, but John sat me up with a really late move into the corner and ran me straight on. The kerbs in some places at Thruxton are savage – they're designed for car racing, so they're way too high for bikes. It's a clear safety issue, but there seems to be some golden rule in motorsport about cars being more important than bikes and we often just have to take these things on the chin, sometimes literally.

As John ran me wide, I hit the kerb on the outside of the right-hander and took off into the air. My front wheel touched down on the back of the opposite kerb, on the inside of the left-hander, and I was flipped straight over the handlebars, landing heavily on my lower back. As soon as I hit the deck I got that feeling no rider ever wants to experience: severe lower-back pain and then complete numbness in my legs. I knew it was bad, and inside my helmet I started to scream. Boy, did I *scream*. I couldn't help but think the unthinkable.

For the next few hours I was floating in and out of consciousness, but I was vaguely aware that I had been taken to Andover hospital. The doctors told me I had broken some of the 'transverse process' bones in my back, which are the little bones that extend off your vertebrae and are surrounded by muscle. While it was massively painful, it was the best possible news, because fractures like that pose no risk to your spinal cord and don't require surgery because the bones can't actually move anyway, so even though it would be really sore to ride again, I knew it would be safe to do so.

I missed one round of the season but four weeks later I was back on the bike at Snetterton and feeling in good shape. Early in the first race I was in the middle of the pack as we all peeled in to turn two, a second-gear 90-degree right-hander. As I lined up my exit for maximum drive onto the long back straight, John Crockford, a top privateer, high-sided himself right in front of me. I hit the brakes and managed to dodge John, but his spinning Suzuki hooked my front wheel away from me and down I went again.

This time it was a relatively gentle landing and as I slid

and rolled down the track I thought, 'Cor, that was lucky – I got away lightly there!' A split second later there was another huge bang and I felt like I'd been run over, which funnily enough I had! Just a few weeks after helping me to break my back at Thruxton, an unfortunate and unsighted John Crawford had followed behind us and smashed right into me as I was rolling down the middle of the track. As I started to lose consciousness, I knew I was in a bad way again.

Two crashes inside a month – an unfortunate theme was emerging, although it never crossed my mind that this life wasn't for me. Nobody tried to talk me out of it, either, not even my parents. It wasn't that they didn't care, they just knew that I was going to keep doing it anyway and they knew there was no point trying to stop me.

Later on in your career, you start to understand a bit better: when to panic, when to take more risks and when to ease off. Lying there in intensive care after that second crash, on the first of too many visits to Norfolk and Norwich University Hospital, I didn't give it much thought. The crash had split my liver open and done a whole load of no favours to the rest of my internal organs, but my main worry was to plead with the nurses that I didn't need a catheter.

'Just give me a pot thing and I'll do a wee,' I assured them. They gave me a pot but nothing came, and in went the tube. I wasn't prepared for that. Nor was I prepared for what would come a few days later, when the codeine had me all blocked up and I was still waiting to do a first 'number two' since the crash. I was lying in bed with stomach pains, which isn't unusual for somebody who's just been run over by a Superbike, when this attractive young nurse comes in. 'Right then, Shane,' she says. 'I'm going to have to give you a suppository.'

'OK,' I replied, 'what's one of those?' She proceeded to explain what a suppository was – and where it had to go – and then pulled out what looked like a bar of Palmolive soap. 'Do you want me to put it in or would you prefer to do it yourself?' I explained to her in no uncertain terms that I didn't much fancy either option.

'I'm sorry,' she insisted. 'This has to go up there and it's either going to be you or me that does it.' I chose me and spent about half an hour squirming around, cursing and generally feeling disgusted with myself, until I had sorted the job out.

After a few more days of being bedridden in hospital, I had well and truly had enough. Anyone who has been to hospital as many times as I have knows that you spend the first few days and weeks doing as you're told, then all you want to do is to start getting up and about. You set yourself these little tests: you go from 'I can only lie down' to 'Maybe it's OK to sit up for a short period.' Then you want to sit up properly to eat, and before you know it you start to look at the chair by the side of your bed. Technically, before making that next move, you're supposed to get the nurses to help, as the first time you try getting to your feet after a week or so of lying down you go light-headed and it's easy to faint. But, as usual, I had my own ideas, and I figured that once I'd managed to make it on my own the nurses would chill out a little. What a shock I was in for.

A couple of days after my operation, I got myself out of bed, stood up and immediately almost passed out. Somehow,

I ended up slumping into the chair and found myself sitting there thinking, 'Fuck, how on earth am I going to get back into bed now?' Shortly after, the nurses came around with the doctor, who was doing his daily rounds. I was sitting there, proud as punch with myself, but he took one look at me and looked as if he was going to explode. He marched over and yelled, 'Shane, what on earth are you doing?'

'Making progress, doctor!' I grinned back.

The doctor pointed at an empty bed directly opposite mine and said, 'You see that bed, right there?'

'Yeah . . .'

'Last week there was a guy in that bed, a guy just a couple of years older than you, who got run over by a car and had exactly the same injury.'

'Right . . .'

'Can you see that guy now?'

'No . . .'

'That's because his liver was split open like yours and it never healed. I lost him on the operating table a few days ago.' He turned to the nurses and pointed. 'Get him back in that bed and chain him to it if you have to. I'm not losing two patients in two weeks.'

'Holy shit,' I thought. 'This is clearly more serious than I'd realized.' Of course, the whole episode did nothing to diminish my desire to get back on my bike, but it did convince me that a few more days laid up in bed might not be such a bad thing. In any case, like most racers, I had an insurance policy that paid out a set amount per night spent in hospital, so I decided to lie back and think of the money . . .

*

As a motorcycle racer you spend your entire time striving to be the best you can possibly be on the track, and there are two reasons for that. The first and most obvious is because you desire results – there is no feeling in the world like winning. Winning makes all the hours in the gym, all the cycle rides when you're freezing cold and piss-wet through, worthwhile.

The second reason is that, most of the time, a race paddock is like a snake pit. Whenever you're healthy and winning, everyone dances to your tune. 'You're the best rider, you're doing the best job, nobody does it like you can, no one's as consistent as you are . . .' Everybody is your best friend. However, have a crash, hurt yourself, leave your seat empty for a couple of rounds and see how quickly those comments suddenly turn into, 'Oh well, he's getting on a bit now. I can't see him coming back. The fire's gone out. I wonder who they're going to put on his bike. Do you think I should call the team?'

The only way to combat it is to get back out there as quickly as you can.

During those difficult times you also get to see who the good people are, and one of those during that nightmare second BSB season in 2000 was Chris Walker, who was easily the most popular rider in the paddock at the time. Chris was all-action – a former motocrosser with a spectacularly aggressive style who always raced with his heart on his sleeve, and the fans loved him for it. I had come back from my Snetterton injuries for the last-but-one round of the season at Brands Hatch in the September, and we were at an autograph signing session. Chris was leading the championship so he was the big attraction, but he actually turned to me and said, 'Do me a favour, buddy, sign one of your posters to me, please.' I laughed at him but he looked back with a completely straight face. 'I'm serious. You're going to be the man one day and I want a picture signed before you get too big!' I was blown away, and felt absolutely proud as punch as I signed a poster to the legendary 'Stalker'.

Whether it was Chris's little injection of confidence that did it, I'm not sure, but that weekend at Brands turned out to be my best of the season. The first race, which started on a damp track, was declared wet, but the majority of riders were on intermediate tyres, with a few of us deciding to run slicks, thinking it was going to dry out. In fact, it started pissing down again as soon as the lights went out and it turned into anybody's race, meaning I was competitive on the Honda at last. The conditions were treacherous but I was right up there with the leaders, the highest I'd run the whole year, when I got wiped out from behind by James Haydon going down into Graham Hill Bend.

Adrenaline's a funny old drug because, even though James had hit me from behind, he was angry and putting the blame on me. Meanwhile, I was furious that he was the one who had wiped the both of us out. It wasn't the best start to our relationship, but in 2006 we would become teammates and we have got on really well ever since. Later, we would get to work together again as television pundits on Eurosport, so I guess you could say we became teammates for a second time. James is an absolutely brilliant bloke – funny and intelligent, with a heart of gold – but we weren't best pleased with each other that day at Brands, that's for sure.

I came back in the second race to score my best finish of the season with fifth place, which was a decent end to an otherwise completely forgettable season. Riding that kit SP-1 Honda constantly over the limit for Steve and Lester had led to me hurting myself way more times than was healthy when, really, I could – and probably should – have been fighting for wins on a factory Kawasaki.

Saying 'no' to Kawasaki had proved to be the first big mistake of my career, so it was kind of ironic that my second big mistake would be to say 'yes' to them just twelve months later. But then, how was I to know that a former racer turned team manager – known simply to everybody in the paddock as 'Backmarker' – would be the next challenge I had to deal with?

10

From the Backmarker to the Birdman

Simon Buckmaster held his hand out to me at the National Exhibition Centre bike show in Birmingham in the November of 2000. Another chance to join the factory Kawasaki team, just twelve months after rejecting them to stay with the Harris brothers on the Honda, was exactly what I'd been hoping for, so I was delighted to shake on it right there and then with Simon and Kawasaki's marketing manager Martin Lambert. A moral approach is important to me and, as far as I am concerned, my handshake is my word – as good as any written contract. In my view, at least, the deal was done. The result at Brands had given me some confidence back, I was fully fit again and I couldn't wait to get started with my winter training and testing programme.

At the end of each season, *MCN – Motor Cycle News –* always did a test of all the Superbikes and Grand Prix machines from that year, and I remember eagerly buying a copy on my way home from the NEC and sitting in my car in Sittingbourne High Street, surrounded by Christmas shoppers, reading everything the magazine had to say about the Kawasaki.

I knew from working on *Fast Bikes* that the journalists writing these articles would be quite a way off BSB pace and it always amused me to read a review of, say, Mick Doohan's Honda NSR500 and how it compared to Max Biaggi's Yamaha, written by a guy lapping thirty seconds off their pace. On this occasion, though, I was just desperate to find out any information there was about the bike I would be riding in 2001.

Buckmaster, who in fairness to him had turned his hand to team management with more success than he ever had as a rider, had been calling me a couple of times a week to check how my training was going, telling me about the new parts we had coming for the bike, and about how hard they were working behind the scenes, detailing his plans to get me out to a test soon. So, a week or so before Christmas, I wasn't surprised to see his number pop up on my mobile.

'Hey, Simon, how's it going?'

'All good thanks, ace' – his usual way of greeting people – 'but I'm afraid I've got some bad news about your ride.'

'Yeah? What about it?'

'Look, I'm really sorry . . . I can't give it to you.'

It took me a few moments to comprehend what he was saying and I had to get him to repeat himself before my anger got the better of my manners.

'What the *fuck* do you mean you can't give it to me?' I raged. He started talking about Kawasaki pulling the budget, that they didn't have any money and a top rider called Michael Rutter had come along with a sponsor that could cover the deficit.

'Simon, we shook hands on a deal.'

'I know, but that's it. I'm sorry.'

I couldn't believe what I was hearing. I was absolutely livid and I made it clear to him in no uncertain terms. He knew as well as I did that by late December nearly all the rides for the following season were taken, and that this was my big chance gone. It's probably just as well he made his revelation in a phone call because I was so angry that, had we been face to face, I think all hell would have broken loose. I certainly wouldn't have been able to contain myself. This was my life, my dream that he was messing with.

*

Going through all that stress without anybody to look out for me was difficult, to put it mildly. I had always managed to deal with things myself up until that point, but I am a pretty straight guy so if I think there is something I need to say, I will say it. And in the corporate bullshit world of motorcycle racing management, that approach certainly wasn't the way forward. I was convinced that now was probably a good time to get myself a manager. I'd had some conversations a year earlier with Roger Burnett, a top former Grand Prix rider who was looking after James Toseland and doing a good job of it, so I wrote down a list of questions for Roger and gave him a call. Roger answered but said he was on a track day at Cadwell Park, so could he call me back later? With hindsight I am not sure I would react the same way now, but at the time it gave me the hump. This was a big thing for me and I thought, 'If he's more bothered about a track day, how important can I be to him?' In the end I turned to Chris Walker's manager Dave Pickford, who did a few small deals for me while I continued to fend largely for myself.

In a pleasant twist of fate, my split with Backmarker led me to one of the nicest guys in the paddock. Rick Cappella was a stocky, charismatic Italian who had been running the Suzuki GSX-R750 that John Crockford had wiped me out with at Snetterton, and also ran a car dealership with a motorbike tuning shop called Performance House down in Reigate in Surrey. I went down there to meet him and was really impressed by the set-up and his plans to make a bigger effort to win the Privateer Cup in 2001. The bike was going to be made up of James Whitham's old World Superbike, James Haydon's old Crescent Suzuki, plus whatever other bits and pieces they could throw at the thing to make it fast in BSB.

Rick was a warm, infectious personality and I agreed straight away to sign, convinced that with this guy's enthusiasm and a half-decent bike we could not only win the Privateers Cup but even challenge for British Superbike podiums. If I could do that on a privateer machine, it would prove a point to anybody who had ever doubted me.

We never quite got that British Superbike podium, but we came close, with a bunch of fourth- and fifth-place finishes, plus we managed to clock up twenty-two wins from twenty-six races in the Privateer Cup. I loved riding for such a close-knit little team who all just believed in each other. Rick was a typically flamboyant Italian who wore his heart on his sleeve; he was so madly passionate about the whole job that he'd often hug me so hard after a race he almost squeezed all the air out of me. On more than one occasion, after a particularly good result, I saw a tear roll down his cheek, and it meant a lot to me to see that kind of integrity and passion for racing. It made the whole job worthwhile.

That's why, when a sponsor failed to materialize and the team ran out of money halfway through the season, I agreed to ride the rest of the season for free so that Rick could use my wages to help keep us on track. We were having such a great year together, I saw it as an investment in my own future, and I'm so glad I did. I became the British Privateer Cup Champion, finished eighth overall in the main BSB championship, and my fan base took off, which was a bizarre experience in itself.

I can picture it clearly. I was at Mallory Park, on my out lap to the start of the race. As I was going up to Shaw's Hairpin, I could hear all these air horns going off. Figuring Stalker or Hizzy must be behind me, I got to the Hairpin and moved out to the left to let them through. But when I turned around, there was nobody there. I thought, 'Eh?' All the way back down the Bus Stop Chicane, the air horns and the cheering continued, until gradually I began to realize that it must all be for me.

That was the very first moment it clicked that I was actually gaining my own support out there on the bankings, and it genuinely made the hairs on the back of my neck stand up. I thought, 'Cor, blimey! How cool is this?' I had always dreamed of being a Superbike racer, and now it felt like I was actually being respected as one.

By this time, I had also gained a bit of notoriety from

those *Fast Bikes* videos we'd made. Once the fans started realizing that the guy doing the daft antics on the videos was the same Shakey as the one out there on track, I gained an extra level of support. Funnily enough, it kind of kicked off again more recently when the videos started to appear online and a whole new audience saw them for the first time. It makes me chuckle how many people come up to me nowadays on the pit-lane walkabouts and say, 'Oh my God – you're Shakey from the *Fast Bikes* videos!' – completely disregarding the rest of my racing career.

At twenty-six years old – or twenty-five as far as anybody else was aware, thanks to Steve Harris – it seemed like things were starting to come together. I was still a young-ster in BSB terms. I felt there was nobody else my age at my level in the paddock, yet it was still mission impossible to get a factory ride. The likes of Stalker, Hizzy, Sean Emmett and John Reynolds were all older than me, yet the factory teams seemed to favour these guys in their late thirties or even early forties with years of experience, who they figured would not throw their bikes at the scenery every five minutes. The opportunities just weren't available for the younger riders, and even the generation that came behind me – the likes of Jonathan Rea, Leon Camier or Cal Crutchlow – all had to wait around too long for a proper shot on the international stage.

Ever since I had first sat on a bike, my dream was to be a World Champion. Latecomer or not, with each season that passed I felt I was taking another step closer to fulfill-ing that dream. My big chance in BSB finally came along at the end of 2001. With the doors to the factory teams seemingly closed, it came via an unlikely source – an uncompetitive rider called Nigel Nottingham, and a backer of his called Mark Griffiths, the successful owner of a music publishing company.

Mark was also a registered FIFA football agent and was business partners with a famous ex-player called Tony Dorigo. I went up to their offices in Knutsford and demonstrated my serious lack of football knowledge when I was chatting to Tony. 'I don't know much about football,' I admitted. 'In fact, the only players I've heard of are probably David Beckham and that Mark Owen.' Of course, I meant Michael bloody Owen.

'You really *don't* know much about football, do you?' he laughed.

Mark told me he was putting together a new team with a big sponsor and a couple of brand-new Ducatis. It had all sounded a bit shifty to me when Nigel talked about it, but on this occasion it most definitely wasn't. Mark was legit and his big sponsor turned out to be Highland Spring mineral water. The bikes were a pair of brand-spanking-new 998s and my teammate was going to be Michael Rutter, one of the fastest guys on the BSB grid.

Even though he had 'nicked' my ride with Kawasaki the previous season, I couldn't help but like Michael – he has a really dry sense of humour and it is so easy to get on with him. Most importantly, he was established by then as a top, top BSB man – in my opinion, alongside Chris Walker he is still the best rider never to win the title – so having him on board meant that the whole business with Mark Griffiths was definitely serious.

*

Jumping on a Ducati was love at first sight. I had ridden them before on different road tests – not to mention my actual bike test – with *Fast Bikes*, and even had the chance to try Carl Fogarty's World Superbike at a magazine test a few years earlier at Misano. It was a day or two after the races there and Foggy was still at the track, so I'm sure I saw it as a chance to impress him, even though he will have thought I was just some dickhead journalist type wasting tyres and fuel on his bike. The track was so wet on the day that he probably had a point, but this was my chance to jump on the champ's bike and I wasn't passing on that. Within five or six laps I was already close to Foggy's wet lap times from the weekend, but by the seventh I was off the thing and sliding through the gravel on my backside.

I wrote off one of Mark's new bikes too in a preseason test at Guadix in Spain, which wasn't ideal, but by the time we rocked up for the first round of the British Superbike Championship in late March of 2002, there was not a thing out of place. Mark had been throwing money at the job like it was going out of fashion, and everything about the team was immaculate. He had promised me it was going to be a factory-standard set-up, which sounded hard to believe at the time, but that's exactly what it was: everything was brand new; every little detail had been taken care of.

I had trained harder than ever that winter – running, cycling and riding motocross – and we kicked off the season in decent form, with a couple of fourth places at Silverstone and Brands Hatch. Then Mark got us some new engines for the third round at Donington Park and suddenly my bike had turned into an absolute jet.

I qualified on the front row, and for the first time in my career there was a little bit of pressure to get a result. To make matters worse, it was freezing cold when we lined up on the grid and there were spots of rain in the air. For some inexplicable reason, I suddenly got this unexpected, overwhelming feeling that I didn't want to be there.

Craig Doyle was presenting the races for the BBC's *Grandstand* programme and he came up to me with a microphone as I sat shivering on the grid before the start of race one.

'Are you excited, Shane?' he asked.

'Fffff . . .' I instinctively replied, managing to stop the words coming out before I really made myself a household name by swearing on national television. 'I'm nervous, very nervous,' I managed, through my chattering teeth.

Over the years those nerves on the grid never went away, but I learned to turn the negative energy into positive energy. Richard Chesson always told me that being nervous before a race was good for me, and that the more nervous he'd seen me in the morning, the better I tended to ride. He even used to joke that if I had the trots in the motorhome before the race – a regular thing – then he knew I was in for a strong race.

Richard wasn't wrong on this occasion. As soon as the lights went out, I never looked back, and after a few laps a little three-rider breakaway formed at the front with me, Hizzy and Steve Plater. After Hizzy dropped back I had a real good scrap with Plater for the win. Steve was a British Supersport winner but neither of us had ever won a Superbike race before, so it was special to come out on top and take my first win.

The joy I felt at taking my first BSB win was massive when I crossed the line, but within a few corners it had started to fade. It was a strange sensation – almost as if I had a little monkey on each shoulder, one of them jumping up and down in celebration, and the other saying, 'Calm down, you plonker, how you gonna be a World Champion if you don't win a BSB race first?' It was a feeling I would become familiar with over the years. The excitement at ticking a box has only ever lasted a few seconds before my mind moves on to the next objective. When your life is spent racing against the clock, you don't ever think to stop and savour what's already in the past, no matter how recent it is.

The heavens finally opened for race two, and Rutter, who'd had a bike issue in the first race, came back to win it with me just behind him in second place, making it a perfect day for the team. Mark had a photo printed of me and Rutter laughing together on the podium that day, with the words 'Brothers In Arms' printed underneath. That's exactly what it felt like, and it was those little details that made Mark's team so special.

*

The other big breakthrough in my career that happened during that 2002 season was my World Superbike debut, as a wild card in the British round at Silverstone, before wild carding again at the so-called 'European' round at Brands. That was a bizarre experience for me because, only a few years earlier, in 1998, I had actually convinced the ticket staff at Brands that I was under fourteen by crouching slightly and keeping my head down while I paid for a junior ticket, because I couldn't afford a full-price adult one.

On that afternoon there had been a huge crowd out on the bankings to support Carl Fogarty, but the rider I really wanted to see was Noriyuki Haga, an exciting Japanese rookie the same age as me, who had just taken a win and a third place in the opening round at Phillip Island to share the championship lead with Foggy. Haga had shot to fame the previous season, taking a podium on his debut as a wild card at Sugo and then winning a race when stepping in for the injured Colin Edwards towards the end of the season.

Haga was a dude, and his riding style was spectacular, getting the awesome-looking Yamaha R7 dancing around on the front and twisting the bike into all kinds of shapes. I was so excited to see him close up and picked a spot on the banking on the outside of Clearways – the final corner – where I reckoned I could get a good view of him on the brakes, except that unlike all the other riders, Haga wasn't braking at all. I had to keep edging down the banking, further and further into the corner, until I could eventually pick out where he was getting the bike stopped. No wonder he was getting so out of shape. I made a mental note of it, planning to try and emulate Haga's braking marker the next time I was out there on track myself.

Four years later, Nori Haga was alongside me as I took part in the first practice at Silverstone for my World Super-bike debut. I just thought, 'What the fuck am I doing out here on the same track as *him*?' I had to give my head a proper shake.

I went all right at Silverstone and ended up having a good battle with Haga in one of the races, eventually picking up a ninth and a fifth, and then got a couple of tenth places at Brands. I went on to win a couple more British Superbike races for Mark's team that season, at Thruxton and Knockhill, and finished fourth in the championship. Meanwhile, Steve Hislop won the title, but it had become clear towards the end of the season that something wasn't quite right in his team, in particular between him and the MonsterMob Ducati team owner, Paul Bird.

My own first encounter with 'The Birdman' would spell bad news for Hizzy, and good news for me.

11

Chickens and Ducs

Paul Bird is a motorsport fanatic and a racing philanthropist – the flashy son of a multi-millionaire chicken farmer with a huge amount of disposable income, which he chooses to spend on motor racing – either driving his own rally cars or running his PBM (Paul Bird Motorsport) team.

'Birdy' has always been a fantastic asset to British Superbikes, although I think it's also fair to say that the status and attention he gets from being a BSB team boss means that he gets just as much out of the sport as he puts in. Essentially, his team is his train set, and he will only share it with people who play by his rules – otherwise the whole toy-box gets turned upside down.

In 2002 he had made a pretty astute signing in Steve Hislop, a brilliant rider and the 1995 BSB Champion, who had missed the majority of the 2001 season through injury. At forty years of age there were probably a lot of questions about whether Hizzy could come back at his best, but Birdy gave him a good ride on a Ducati 998R for a relatively small wage – something like fifty grand for the season. When it became apparent he was going to win the title, Hizzy started making some noises that Birdy had taken his pants down and that he wouldn't ride for that much again the next year.

My take on it is that it was Hizzy's way of starting a negotiation process to improve his contract, but I have learned in the years since that it is completely the wrong way to deal with Paul Bird. First, you have to gently sow a seed in his head. Then, you let it grow so that eventually he thinks it is his idea and then he comes to you with it, even though it is what you wanted in the first place.

Towards the end of that season, when Hizzy just about had the title wrapped up, Birdy started talking to me about taking his place. I felt awkward because Hizzy had always been good to me. When I was on the Harris bike and he was on the factory Kawasaki, he had always made a point of talking to me and seeing how I was getting on. Even if we didn't bump into each other in the paddock, he would come and find me, which was something I really appreciated. So, when Paul came to me with this offer, which was a typical Birdy-style 'Do you want it or not?' kind of deal, I didn't quite know what to say. 'But what about Hizzy? He's just about to win you a title.'

'Yeah, but I'm over it, he's going to go and do something else. He's too old anyway. He's the past, you're the future.'

The offer was a fantastic one: riding for the title-winning team with the possibility of moving up with them to World Superbikes in the future. It wasn't an easy decision to leave

Mark and his team, but I had learned my lesson about letting my heart rule my head when I'd stayed with the Harris brothers on the Honda, and I knew I would be an idiot to turn this chance down. By the time we got to the last round of the championship at Donington Park, I'd decided I was going to accept the offer from Birdy. As usual, he had a massive end-of-year party in his big hospitality unit and he treated me like a god.

When news got out that Hizzy had lost his ride to me, it went down like a concrete kite. Hizzy was such a popular rider and it was to be expected that fans would end up giving me grief in the letters pages of *MCN* for supposedly nicking his job. Even though Birdy was getting most of the flack, there seemed to be no shortage of bike fans who were keen to see me fail. I had big boots to fill and I knew there would be massive pressure on me to live up to the job.

One of the people most upset was Mark Griffiths. I felt sorry about that because he was a top guy and had done everything he said he was going to do, but at the end of the day I was out of contract and free to go. Mark ended up signing Sean Emmett to take my place alongside Rutter, and bought them a pair of F02 Ducatis, the factory World Superbikes from 2002. Meanwhile, Birdy went and bought brand-new versions of exactly the same bikes and a big rivalry immediately formed between the two teams. It was game on for the new season.

A tempestuous relationship between me and Birdy started early, before I'd even thrown a leg over his bike. Unfortunately, the start of our relationship coincided with me getting together with one of his ex-girlfriends. It had been ages since she had split up with Birdy, and it wasn't as if I did it to deliberately wind him up, but when he found out about it he went absolutely nuts and then refused to answer the phone when I called him to try and explain. I realized that the only way to resolve the matter and potentially save my Superbike future was to drive the 320 miles from Kent to Cumbria and knock on his front door.

I managed to sweet-talk Paul back onside, but it is fair to say that my relationship with my new team had started out on the wrong foot, and things got even more awkward when I turned up to meet the rest of the crew at Valencia for our first test together, only to discover that my crew chief would be Phil Borley – a former rider who I'd last seen skidding off his Supersport bike after I'd just T-boned him out of the race at Brands Hatch in 1998.

Thankfully Phil turned out to be a great bloke – really calm and considered – and the T-bone incident would become a bit of a joke between us whenever I needed taking down a peg or two over the years. In lots of ways he was the 'yin' to Birdy's 'yang' and he made the team tick. The other key team member was Stuart Bland, a brilliant technician and a willing whipping boy for Birdy, always prepared to take the brunt of the boss's outbursts in a way I could never understand, before passing the message on in a more diplomatic fashion to the rest of the crew. Between us all, the balance was just right and we clicked straight away, winning nine out of the first eleven races of the 2003 season – at least one at every round – until we got to Rockingham in Northamptonshire, where I finished second twice.

Top left: I never got to spend too much time with Grandad, but I worshipped the ground my nan walked on and the feeling was mutual.

Top right: Very early school pic. Butter wouldn't melt 😉

Above: Aged twelve or thirteen in the foothills of the Pyrenees in Spain.

Above: My first British Championship win at Snetterton, which was on a 600cc Yamaha Thundercat.

Below: With Lester (*left*) and Steve Harris, who gave me my first break in British Superbikes in 1999 – what a great pair.

Above: First factory ride with Kawasaki in 1999, final round at Donington Park. Those leathers fitted so well – just ask my dad.

Below: Riding the Harris brothers' SP-1 in a disastrous year. The bike smashed me to pieces.

Top left: With team boss and good friend Rick Cappella in 2001.

Top right: First win in BSB, at Donington Park in 2002.

Bottom: With my crew chief Chris Anderson, who helped me achieve it (*left*), and celebrating said debut BSB win in style (*right*).

Left: Celebrating my first British Superbike Championship. It felt almost surreal, but as I later realized I never took enough time to enjoy the success as I was always focusing on my next goal.

Above: The view most people got of me that year.

Left: 2004, running in MotoGP with Aprilia.

Above: Keeping good company at the press conference before the Malaysian MotoGP race with (*left to right*) Olivier Jacque, Max Biaggi, Valentino Rossi, Loris Capirossi and me.

2006 was a season of adjusting back into BSB after two years of MotoGP. Not a great year at all; (*below*) celebrating my only win which was at Knockhill.

For the 2007 season I joined back up with Paul Bird and his Stobart Vent-Axia team.
We had some success with the 1000cc Honda Fireblade and I placed fifth overall
as a privateer in the championship, being the only privateer to win a race.
Above: Leading the factory Ducatis at Thruxton.

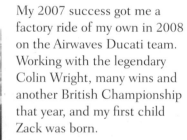

My 2007 success got me a factory ride of my own in 2008 on the Airwaves Ducati team. Working with the legendary Colin Wright, many wins and another British Championship that year, and my first child Zack was born.

Birdy has mellowed over the years, but at the time he was so savage, the dummy came out after race two at Rockingham and he practically wouldn't speak to me, just because I hadn't won a race. We ended up not speaking much for a few weeks, while I went winless for the next three rounds, but by that time we had built up such a big points lead that as soon as I got back to the top step in race one at Cadwell Park, it was enough to wrap up my first BSB championship with two rounds to spare.

*

In the middle of that run of victories in BSB came the breakthrough moment of my career, when Birdy entered me as a wild card for the World Superbike round at Brands Hatch. We'd actually been pencilled in for the Silverstone round earlier in the season, but Birdy decided to scrap the idea until we had built up a more comfortable gap in BSB, which made sense.

In the week before the race I was invited to attend a media day at the Sports Cafe in London, alongside some of the established names in World Superbikes. I actually turned up late after my taxi driver managed to get lost, but the journalists didn't care – the big draw for them was Neil Hodgson, who had his first chance to wrap up the championship on the factory Ducati, James Toseland, who had recently won his first WSB race, and the massively popular Chris Walker, who was looking for his first win at world level after picking up a couple of podiums. Whatever happened, it was going to be a huge weekend for the Brits, and there would be a bumper crowd of more than 100,000 people there to see it.

I hadn't been thinking about my WSB wild card much because I was so focused on BSB. It would be a good weekend for us to get more experience and keep ticking over, but I knew I had nothing much to lose. I went well in free practice, up near the top in every session, and then just before qualifying it started to rain. At Brands it is usually not until it's really wet that the grip comes and you feel fully in control, so I told Stuart Bland I didn't want to go out for a bit, and waited while the others posted some half-decent laps. When I eventually did go out, I realized I had made the wrong call. The track was actually still really slick and after my first run I was down in about eighteenth place. With around a minute to go, I took a gamble, knowing that I couldn't be competitive from that far back on the grid. Putting my head down with no real thought of the consequences, I set my fastest lap and ended up third on the grid.

The races themselves were strange because the WSB regulars like Hodgy were having some issues with the Michelin tyres, and I ended up in a battle with John Reynolds, my main rival for the BSB title, who like me was also running as a wild card on Dunlops. Really I wanted to bang bars and measure myself against the likes of Hodgy, Toseland, Haga and Rubén Xaus and, even though I got my wish for the first six laps of race one, JR and I pulled clear after that and it ended up being like a typical BSB race between two of us that season. When John broke down on lap twelve, I was able to manage the gap over Hodgy and won by almost six seconds.

I could hardly believe how easy it seemed to be, especially when it happened again in race two. This time John's

Suzuki held out and we had a battle to the line, which I was able to win by just over half a second. To be a double World Superbike winner as a wild card, especially when nobody had expected it, was an incredible feeling for me and a pretty big deal in general, since there were actually only two riders to have done it before and they were both Japanese – Hitoyasu Izutsu and Makoto Tamada, both at Sugo, in 2000 and 2001.

The World Superbike paddock had huge team hospitality units and there were always big parties on the Sunday nights after the races. Needless to say, I had an amazing night, strutting around like I was king of the world. The next morning I woke up in the motorhome, still thinking, 'Fucking hell, I can't believe I actually won two World Superbike races yesterday.' I rolled out of bed with a stupid grin on my face and opened the motorhome door to see that everybody else had gone. There were beer bottles and rubbish blowing around the empty paddock, but otherwise the place was deserted. It was an important reminder to myself not to get carried away by a single success. In racing it doesn't matter what you achieve, a moment is only a moment.

We were celebrating again at the end of August when I wrapped up that first British Superbike title at Cadwell Park, but this time the euphoria only lasted halfway around my celebration lap before I started to think about the next challenge. I will never forget the feeling of riding slowly along the Park Straight on the slow-down lap thinking, 'Oh my God, I've just become a British Superbike Champion.' I was super happy, but at the same time I wanted more, much more. This was cool, but it was like a decent starter in a nice restaurant. Now I wanted the main course, and I wanted to follow that up with a super tasty dessert!

Birdy had barely spoken to me for weeks because of that run of seven BSB races without a win, but a victory in race one and third place in race two meant that I had 129 points more than Reynolds, and the title was ours with six races to spare. But by the time I arrived back to the garage, amidst all the wild celebrations from the team, in my heart I was already thinking about moving on.

I was actually falsely quoted at the time by *MCN*, which ran a headline saying: 'WSB is too easy, I want MotoGP', but I had tasted success on the big stage and there was no doubt that, given the opportunity, I wanted to go straight to the highest possible level. The truth was that my double World Superbike win at Brands had moved the goalposts.

There was interest, and rumoured interest, coming in from all different angles and again I felt that I needed somebody to help me make the right choices. I also wanted to make sure that people weren't taking advantage of me, because in my head I was still just a kid from a council estate in Kent who didn't have a clue what he was doing. Since deciding not to follow up that phone call with Roger Burnett twelve months previously, I still didn't have a proper manager. Paul Smart, the legendary racer who had helped me early in my career, was now a close friend and he was great to bounce ideas off, but really I needed a more formal arrangement.

In the end I turned to Andrew Whitney, a friend I knew through Colin Schiller. Andrew had just left his job as marketing manager for Ducati in Italy and he was doing a bit of work for Dorna, which owned the commercial and television rights to MotoGP, so he was well connected at the top of motorbike racing.

I told Andrew that my first preference was to join the Ducati World Superbike team. Neil Hodgson had gone on to win the title for them in 2003, and he would now be stepping up to MotoGP with one of their satellite teams, so it made sense to me that I would be his ready-made replacement. I had just won the British title on a Ducati and proved that I could be a race winner in WSB. It was a logical career path, it made sense to me to aspire to that, but even though Ducati were definitely interested, they told Andrew they wanted me to hold off for another season.

To my frustration they had already agreed to sign Toseland to replace Hodgson, and their best offer for me was that I should go out to America for a year and try to win the AMA Superbike title, with the option of going to World Superbikes after that. The deal on the table was a good one, with sensible money, and it was exactly the path that Troy Bayliss had taken in 2000 before he came back to Europe in 2001 to win the Worlds.

I decided to go for it. Living the American dream for a while would be fun, I thought, and by October I had gone as far as looking for somewhere to live in California, with all the AMA dates safely in my diary, when suddenly Andrew called me and said to hold off. Dorna had told him they needed another Brit in MotoGP alongside Hodgson, to help sell their TV rights in the UK, and they were proposing that they would take me straight there and prop up a factory deal with Aprilia.

Aprilia weren't the most competitive factory on the grid, but still, this was MotoGP – the elite level of motorcycle racing, the two-wheeled equivalent of Formula 1. We kept Ducati hanging and headed down to Valencia to spend the weekend with them at the final round of the MotoGP season, all the while with a secret meeting with the bosses from Aprilia high on our agenda.

We sat down with Aprilia and they couldn't have been keener. They told me how impressed they'd been with my WSB debut at Silverstone in 2002, and that they had decided they definitely wanted me from the moment I did the wild-card double at Brands a few months earlier. They said they had a new MotoGP bike coming, that I'd have to test this year's bike a couple of times but then I'd get the new one. It would be a two-year contract – a year to learn the tracks and develop the new bike, and in the second year they would want some results – with the option of a third year after that. In the past, British riders in Grand Prix had been shoved on any old bike just to tick a box, and they'd been happy to take it. But this was a long-term project – a factory ride and a legitimate career path to the very top.

Unbeknownst to the Aprilia team, Andrew was fluent in Italian, although he didn't let on, so while they discussed terms with each other and came back across the table with their 'best offer', he made sure we came out of the meeting with their *actual* best offer. Once we had that, I phoned Paul Smart and explained the two options on the table – one from Ducati to go to AMA, and the other from Aprilia, for less money, to go to MotoGP – and asked what he thought. 'This is Grand Prix racing,' he said. 'It doesn't get any better than this. Once you're in, if you do a good job you'll stay there.'

I was still pondering my decision the following week

when I went up to an open evening at Ducati Manchester. Andrew had gone to Australia on business and he called me late at night to say that Dorna had put something together that made the deal financially sweeter, and it was up to me to decide. This was the kind of income that my parents could never even have dreamed of, but the question for me was whether or not it would be the right step towards my ultimate dream of being a World Champion. Plenty of riders have had their fingers burned by taking the wrong bike in MotoGP and never made it back again. I told Andrew that I would sleep on it.

The following morning, with a few hours to kill before I went home, I drove up from Manchester to the Blackpool Pleasure Beach to try out 'The Big One', the UK's highest rollercoaster. I sat there on my own in one of the carriages, still running through the pros and cons as it creaked and clicked its way towards the top of the huge first descent that gave the ride its name. Just as it tipped over the top, I felt the adrenaline rush kick in. At that very moment, everything came into crystal-clear focus in my mind.

'Fuck it,' I thought as the rollercoaster plummeted towards the ground. 'I am going to MotoGP.'

12

Mastering the Cube

Choosing a racing number is a really personal thing. There's a bit of pressure too; it's a bit like naming your kid. People are hopefully going to identify you by that number for the rest of your career and beyond, so it's got to be something meaningful, but also something you are still going to like in years to come. I've seen some riders chop and change numbers over the years, others who have gone for number 3 or number 2, and I've always thought, 'Why?'

Number 1 is fair enough. That means you're the defending champion and you earned the right to run that number by being the best the previous year. You are the man to beat. But why would you want to be remembered for being second or third? That's a weird one to me. A rider's number becomes like their calling card, a way to market themselves, and even a way to make money through merchandising and endorsements, so you want something that will stand out in one way or another.

Barry Sheene was probably the first rider to recognize the potential of this, bucking the trend of taking the number 1 plate as 500cc World Champion in 1977 and sticking with the legendary number 7, which he's still remembered for. Everybody remembers the 1993 champ Kevin Schwantz as the number 34 for the same reason, and then Valentino Rossi took it to the next level with the number 46, which has become a global brand all of its own, the bright yellow number recognizable around the world to people who have never even watched a MotoGP race in their life.

By the time I signed up with Aprilia for my first season in Grand Prix, Valentino had established himself as the sport's new Captain Cool. He had already won the 125cc, 250cc and 500cc titles, as well as the newly rebranded MotoGP World Championship on the 1000cc Honda V5, and at the start of 2004 he was about to attempt history by switching to Yamaha and winning the title back to back for different manufacturers. The man was setting new levels in the game, and having a number by which he could be globally recognized was just the start of it.

One of the first questions Aprilia had asked me as their new factory rider was what number I wanted to run. I knew I had to come up with something special to me but I didn't know where to start. I'd been number 4 when I won the British Superbike Championship the previous season, but that was already taken in MotoGP by a Brazilian rider called Alex Barros. Schwantz had been my hero, but there was no way a rookie could have the balls to run his legendary number 34. I was thinking about 40, which had been the first ever race number given to me back at the Bemsee Club races, when the light-bulb moment finally came – ironically enough, from my mate Jamie Ascott, one of those least likely to even be able to change the bulb.

'What about the big six-seven, Byrneard?' he said in his matter-of-fact way one evening while we were out cruising in one of our cars. 'It done you all right the last time you were in a World Championship race, didn't it?' It was a brilliant and simple idea. I thought, 'He's right!' I'd been allocated 67 for my WSB wild card at Brands Hatch and, as Jamie said, it had more than 'done me all right' with the double win.

I had convinced myself that the next task for a full factory MotoGP rider – after picking his number – was to get himself a full factory motorhome. After a little bit of research with my mate Chris 'Prof' Lambourne – so called because he was clever and wore glasses at school – we found just the thing. Prof was just as excited about me going to MotoGP as I was, and he had decided to take a year out from his job at a local motocross shop to come on the road with me. So the pair of us set off together to pick up a huge, blue and silver American motorhome from a dealer in Wolverhampton.

I could hardly believe the size of the thing. It was forty feet long with four slide-outs so big I could have fitted my old Mercedes 508 camper inside any one of them. It had a fully fitted kitchen with a washing machine and fridge-freezer, microwave oven and all the mod cons – I had ticked just about every extra option. Up front there were leather sofas, a satellite television, a surround-sound system and air conditioning, and at the back there was a separate bedroom with a double bed and an en-suite bathroom. It was a mansion on wheels and it cost me more than any of the houses I'd grown up in.

The salesman at the dealership started to give us the full induction on how everything worked, but it was so complicated that after about ten minutes I had to ask him to stop while I grabbed a notebook and pen and wrote all the instructions down. We drove back down to Kent, thinking 'this thing is the absolute bollocks', and no sooner had we got back home than we decided to set off in it again. The first official preseason test was scheduled for Jerez at the end of November, so we decided that we might as well get going early and have a steady run down to the south of Spain.

We set off all giddy with excitement, arguing about who was going to take the first stint of driving our mobile mansion. Even the driver's seat was like a leather armchair, but after a couple of eight-hour legs each, we were both so knackered and bored of driving in cruise control in the inside lane that the arguments quickly turned from whose turn it was to drive to whose turn it was to have a nap on the luxury bedding. The arguments got so bad as the season progressed that on one particularly long drive from Brno in the Czech Republic to Estoril in Portugal, when Prof refused to take his turn at the wheel, I just put it in cruise mode, got up and walked off to the bedroom. That made him jump behind the wheel sharpish.

While the motorhome might have been the last word in luxury travel, the Aprilia RS3 Cube was the polar opposite. The bike had a fearsome reputation, particularly after it famously burst into flames with Colin Edwards on board, and regularly threw Nori Haga at the scenery in 2003. It was famous for being one of the fastest bikes in a straight line, but corners were a whole different story for the mighty Cube – which was odd given it had been developed by a company that had won countless World Championships in the 125cc and 250cc classes, where very fast cornering is a prerequisite.

My teammate for the 2004 MotoGP World Championship would be Jeremy McWilliams, a tough, experienced Northern Irishman who wasn't just the last Brit to have stood on the 500cc podium – at Donington Park in 2000 – but also our most recent Grand Prix winner, having won the 250cc Dutch TT at Assen in 2001. Jezza was one of the guys I had looked up to ever since I first read about his exotic exploits in *Fast Bikes*, so I had a massive amount of respect for him and he would be a great yardstick for me to measure my progress against, but like everybody else on that grid, I was there to try and beat him. If I was going to become World Champion one day, that meant beating everybody.

It wasn't just the notorious Cube that was daunting about my first experience in MotoGP. The feeling when I walked into the hotel for breakfast was a little bit like that first day at school, when you don't know where to sit or who with. Thankfully I had Prof with me. We had picked our table and were sitting eating our cornflakes together when in walked Loris Capirossi, a former 125cc and 250cc World Champion, a proper legend, and now a factory Ducati rider; he was expected to push Valentino for the title in the top class. In my opinion there were a few guys in MotoGP at that time who were special, and Loris was definitely one of them. To this day, he is still one of my heroes.

Loris may have been tiny, but he had a big reputation for being aggressive – sometimes overaggressive – on track, so I was really surprised when his character turned out to be the complete opposite. He came over with a big smile, sat down with me and Prof and had just about nailed his fruit and cereals by the time I could think of anything to say to him. 'Fuck me,' said Prof as Loris left his empty bowl pretty much spinning on the table and headed for the door. 'If he's as fast on track as he is at eating his breakfast, you've got no fucking chance!'

I'd never been to Jerez before that first test, but I'd done thousands of laps on the PlayStation and felt as though I knew the layout like the back of my hand. My crew chief was Giacomo Guidotti, a great guy who spoke English very well and had worked with anybody worth working with in Grand Prix. In recent years he's proved it by working with guys of the quality of Dani Pedrosa at Repsol Honda. It was clear that he knew what he was talking about.

'The bike revs to 17,000 rpm,' Giacomo explained before I rode the Cube for the first time. 'It makes good power from 12,000 revs upwards and this is the band where you need to ride the bike. Everything is different from what you are used to, so try to think about everything, take your time and enjoy the bike.' With my hands gently feathering the throttle and the clutch, I pulled carefully out of pit lane for my first time on Michelin tyres, my first time on carbon brakes and my first ever lap on a MotoGP bike.

I knew which way the track went and everything was fine for the first few corners as I navigated my way round and let the tyres get some temperature into them. As I came around the long right-hander at turn five, I knew I was about to come onto the long back straight, and it was time to find out what MotoGP was all about.

The F02 Ducati I had ridden in 2003 had been a thing of beauty. It was really smooth, had lots of torque, and the power delivery was lovely. What I was about to find out was that my old Superbike was in fact a pussycat, and that what I was sitting on right now was a tiger. A tiger with a seriously sore head! As I pulled the bike upright onto that long, six-hundred-metre back straight at Jerez, I eased the throttle open and shifted quickly through the gearbox.

Paaaaah, paaaah, paaaah!

The palm trees and the blue and white rumble strips that I knew from the PlayStation game melted into a blur in my peripheral vision and I thought, 'Faaaaaackin'ell! This thing is *fast!*' I sneaked a quick glance down at the rev counter and couldn't believe my eyes when I saw the needle pointing to 10,500 rpm. Hadn't Giacomo said that it made good power from 12,000 rpm? When I looked up again I was already at the end of the straight. I grabbed hold of the carbon brakes for the first time and everything happened again in reverse. If hitting the brakes on a Superbike was like riding into a brick wall, this was more like going straight over the end of a cliff. And to think that I was nowhere near the limit of its potential.

I came around turn five on the next lap and built myself up to it again. 'Right, no fucking around this time,' I thought. 'I'm going to properly let this thing have it.' I ripped the throttle open and all hell broke loose. *Paaaaaaaaaaaaaaaaaaaaaaaaaah!*

The thing went *nuts*, like nothing else I'd ever ridden before or since. Each time I kicked another gear at it, it wanted another one. It was trying to wheelie and veer off track in every gear, added to which I was so busy looking down at the rev counter, making sure I was giving it full beans, that when I lifted my eyes back up to see where I was going, I had completely missed my braking point and the gravel trap was coming up fast. I grabbed the front brake and sent the bike into a rolling endo at 160 mph. Somehow, I got the rear wheel back down, made it through the corner and started to try and work out how I was supposed to control this absolute animal.

Once that terrifying first day was over, I had a wander down pit lane and spoke to a couple of the more experienced riders like Capirossi and Bayliss, who were kind enough to give me a few tips. Troy even walked me around the track, giving me some pointers and references. One suggestion he made was to squeeze hard on the brake lever on the way down pit lane and on the out lap, in order to generate some heat in the carbon brakes, which was something I made sure to do for the rest of my career. Troy's tips had an instant impact and the next day I got going about two seconds per lap faster – pretty much as fast as Edwards and Haga had been at the Grand Prix there earlier that season, and not far off where Troy and Loris were on the Ducatis.

When I came in after my first exit that second day, Giacomo's eyes almost came out on stalks when one of the mechanics showed him his clipboard and waved the lap time under his nose. 'Fackin'ell!' he said in his Italian accent. 'Yesterday was good . . . today . . . *fack!* This bike doesn't go any faster here!' I was excited and relieved. It meant I was actually able to give the guys some useful feedback about what the bike was doing, and how to improve it with a few adjustments to the gearing. By the end of testing we were pretty happy; with a brand-new bike due in the new year, I felt ready and excited for my first season as a MotoGP rider.

What nobody in the Aprilia racing department could have known at that time was that, in the boardrooms way above their heads, meetings were going on to secure the company's sale to Piaggio, a huge firm that specialized in small capacity motorcycles and scooters. At the time Piaggio had no interest in big sports bikes, and as such they had no reason to support such an expensive development programme in MotoGP. All we knew at the start of the 2004 season was that the new bike was going to be late, although in reality it had yet to even make it off the drawing board.

I managed to beat Jeremy at the opening round of the season in South Africa and score a single point in fifteenth place, but in the next race at Jerez I crashed on the first lap in the wet and broke some bones in my hand. I tried to come back for the next one a fortnight later at Le Mans, but the Cube got a bit feisty on the way into the awesomely fast turn-one kink during practice on the Friday, and I simply wasn't strong enough to catch it in time. I took a trip across the gravel at around 160 mph, which isn't an experience you'd wish upon your worst enemy, and after surviving that I figured the sensible move was to park the thing for the rest of the weekend.

I was in better shape for round four at Mugello, a race that started off in much the same way that most races did that season – with Valentino Rossi and Sete Gibernau taking off at the front and only Alex Barros and Max Biaggi able to be anywhere near them. I was having a decent race, chasing Neil Hodgson on his privateer Ducati and Alex Hofmann on the factory Kawasaki for eleventh place, when with six laps to go the heavens suddenly opened.

The race was immediately red-flagged, but by the time it was actually restarted as a wet race, the rain had backed off and the track was drying. It was clear that even with just six laps to run – the shortest race in the history of the championship – there was no way a wet tyre would last, so everybody went for slicks. Running full slicks on a damp track is dodgy at the best of times, for the simple reason that, unlike the road tyres on your car or motorbike, they don't have a tread pattern to disperse the water. As a result, slick tyres are about as efficient in wet conditions as a chocolate teapot is at holding hot tea, so all of the front guys were understandably a little cautious.

For somebody willing to take a risk, however, this was a chance not to be missed. I made some monumental manoeuvres on people early on, and for a brief moment I was up to fourth place and going forward. The next rider in front of me, occupying the final podium position, was none other than Valentino Rossi, who was aiming to win his home Grand Prix for the third year in a row in front of an army of loyal fans who had filled the bankings around the track with their yellow T-shirts and number 46 flags, the air thick with the yellow smoke from their flares.

Now, there was taking a risk, and there was taking the risk of wiping out a national hero in his own backyard. I was sorely tempted but, after thinking seriously about it a couple of times as I showed him a wheel up the inside, the track started to dry further and Valentino picked up his pace as mine started to drop. With every corner that went by, any attempt at a pass would have been ever more ambitious. I knew the game was up.

A couple more laps, a splash more rain even, and it could have all been so different, but as it was the track dried out completely and my race fell apart. I ended up dropping back all the way to tenth, and I was gutted, but when I got back to the garage the reaction from the team was as if I'd won the race. They were so ecstatic, and of course that made me happy too. I had experienced the Italians' passion for racing when I rode for Rick Cappella in the Performance House Suzuki days back in 2001, but riding for an Italian factory was another level – especially at Mugello.

I picked up points at most of the next few races but, with the Cube, the next disaster was never too far away. In my case, it came that August in round ten at the Brno circuit in the Czech Republic – one of the best tracks in the world. Set in a beautiful forest outside the city, the track is fast, wide and undulating, and I loved the layout from the moment I saw it. For my first visit I was going pretty well too, finishing twelfth fastest in the first free practice session ahead of a bunch of factory guys, but midway through the second free practice on the Saturday morning, I paid the price for getting too pleased with myself on a new tyre and once again the Cube showed me who was boss. Coming through the long, hanging hairpin at turn seven, the bike spat me so high out of the seat that I practically came down with snow on my helmet before hitting the tarmac and smashing my wrist.

As always, I needed to come back as soon as I could – if nothing else to gain experience of the tracks for the following season – and so it was that less than a month later I travelled to Japan. I felt excited to see the place for the first time in my life, even though McWilliams was insisting the best thing about the country was the runway out of there. I had to disagree with Jeremy, especially when I used one of those fancy hi-tech toilets for the first time. They have all these buttons down the side that offer you a jet wash from every angle you can imagine, which I can tell you is a blessed relief when you have a shattered wrist.

I went through a pretty gruelling medical, involving seemingly endless press-ups on my knackered joint, and somehow I was passed fit to ride, although as soon as I got out on to the track I wished I hadn't bothered. Motegi is the hardest-braking circuit on the whole calendar and my wrist was giving me grief just riding the paddock scooter around for a few laps on the Thursday, trying to get to grips with the layout. I knew straight away it was going to be aggro on the big Aprilia, and I wasn't wrong.

You approach turn one at Motegi on a MotoGP bike at about 170–180 mph, before grabbing those savage carbon brakes to shift back to second gear for an 80 mph entry to the corner, dropping to 50–60 mph as you throw the bike towards the late second apex. Being a second-gear corner, when you get back on the gas you are just hanging on for dear life, fighting a mixture of the front end wanting to wheelie and the back end trying to wheelspin all the way through the next three gears as you accelerate hard back up to 160–170 mph, then bang back hard on the brakes again, slightly downhill for the 50 mph turn four. A couple of corners later and your whole body is put through the wringer as you try to muscle through the fast changes of direction through turns seven, eight and nine, before you're hard on the brakes again for turn ten, a tight hairpin at the top of the hill. Then it's flat-out acceleration once again, touching 200 mph before you have to brake so hard for turn eleven that you feel as though your forearms are going to burst. The place is bloody savage.

Whenever I hurt myself and have to ride injured, I always try to do practice and qualifying with no painkillers. My theory is that if you can take the pain on Friday and Saturday and get through Sunday morning warm-up, a painkilling injection just before the race – the only bit of the weekend that really matters – will have the most profound effect on your performance. I was so sore I could only manage a lap or two at a time throughout practice and qualifying at Motegi, so I could only hope that the pain-killers and the adrenaline would pull me through the twenty-four-lap race.

I lined up on the back row of the grid, determined to hold on for as long as I could and learn as much about the track as possible for the following season. There was no pressure to try and score points and, even if I came last, at least I would know I had given it my best shot. As luck would have it, no sooner had the race started than Loris Capirossi went and wiped out half the field in the first corner. Six bikes went down in front of me, including all of the Americans – John Hopkins, Colin Edwards, Nicky Hayden and Kenny Roberts Junior – meaning that if I could just make it to the end of the race, I was guaranteed a good result. The first thought that came into my head when I saw the pile-up was, 'Bloody hell, Loris, that means I've got to stay on the bike now. Thanks a lot!'

The painkillers wore off far too quickly and as a result I honestly can't remember too much about that race, other than hanging on to the bike for the longest twenty-four laps of my life. I brought the Cube home in thirteenth place, good enough for three precious points, and again the Italians went nuts in the garage. Of course, they knew I couldn't manage more than two laps in practice, and they were all hugging me, until one of them grabbed hold of my broken wrist and ragged it up above my head in celebration. I screamed in agony. The poor guy was mortified, going: '*Scusa, scusa!*'

Even though it had only been a month since the crash at Brno, there was something that wasn't right with my wrist and my physio wasn't happy. He sent me for another X-ray, which showed that the scaphoid had snapped in two and the ligaments were so badly damaged that they couldn't even hold the joint together. I flew to the World Superbike round at Imola at the end of September for a meeting with Dr Claudio Costa, an eccentric old Italian with some notoriously alternative approaches, who was also the official MotoGP doctor, to have a look. Dr Costa confirmed the wrist had fallen apart and, on the following Wednesday, he and another old professor operated on me in San Marino, when they ensured the scaphoid would never break again by taking it out completely.

By that time, Piaggio had informed us that they were going to pull the plug on the whole Aprilia MotoGP project and that – for all the promises of a year to develop the bike and learn the tracks; promises that were made in good faith, for sure – my contract was effectively terminated at the end of the season. After just one year of what was supposed to be a three-year contract, my Grand Prix dream was in a worse state than my wrist.

13

A Dog Ran Out, Man!

Despite the injuries and disappointments on the track, becoming a MotoGP rider had completely changed my life away from it. For starters I had more money coming in each month than I'd ever seen before, and I wasn't afraid to spend it pretty much as it came in. With a bonus from the previous season I bought myself a brand-new Mitsubishi Evo, which I was so proud of. To be able to go out and buy a car like that from money I had earned doing something I love was a huge moment in my life.

It's fair to say my new status had also made me a more attractive proposition to the opposite sex, and from grid girls to high-profile glamour models, I wasn't the kind of lad to be saying no. I had company with such regularity that the joke in the MotoGP paddock was that my motorhome needed a revolving door fitting to it, and I eventually even ended up featuring in the tabloids having had a brief fling with Jodie Marsh, one of the top lads' mag models at the time.

Not long after that I had a full page in the *Sun*, when I accidentally nicked some poor bloke's girlfriend at a Bemsee presentation evening. My old friends Dave and Bernie Stewart had asked me back to hand out some trophies, and I rocked up in there in my latest new motor – a Porsche 911 Turbo that I'd traded the Evo in for after about a thousand miles. An attractive young lady told me she was there for her brother, who had raced at Bemsee that year, and while the party got going inside she came out with me for a look at my car. We were sitting there chatting when this lad came storming out and shouted at her to go back inside. 'My brother's very protective,' she said as she got out and scurried back to the party, although not before slipping me her phone number. I ended up taking her out a few times before somebody showed me a copy of this story in the newspaper with the headline: 'My hero stole my girlfriend!' I genuinely didn't have a clue.

Back in the MotoGP paddock, my teammate McWilliams must have been jealous of my extra-curricular activities, because he came up with a genius way of distracting me from the job at hand. Unbeknownst to me, he had hidden a remote-control doorbell somewhere in my fancy motorhome, and whenever he knew I was entertaining he would press the buzzer from next door. I'd be going around, checking the air con and the washing machine and the fridge, frantically flicking through my notepad trying to work out where the fuck this buzzing was coming from, and all along it was Jezza, peeping through his curtains and pissing himself laughing at the sight of me running about like a headless chicken!

The MotoGP paddock was a different world to British Superbikes, but some truths hold firm wherever you are. I have always believed that if you are genuine and approachable, then the chances are you're going to meet like-minded people, which is the way I found it with the likes of McWilliams, Colin Edwards, John Hopkins, Alex Hofmann and a very young Chaz Davies and Casey Stoner, who were just making their way in the smaller classes.

In 2004 while I was busy smashing up my wrist in MotoGP, Stoner was riding in the 125cc class and it was already clear that he was going to be something special. Everybody saw the moments of brilliance he produced on track, such as the first ever road-racing victory for KTM that he scored in Malaysia that season, but there were other things I saw in and around the paddock that impressed me just as much. For example, we'd often set up tracks of our own and have little races on our paddock scooters, and invariably Casey would be the fastest. We once took them over to this little rally circuit that they had at Valencia, and the kid was just so committed. You would just look at him ride and think, 'Fucking *hell*.'

Casey wasn't the only massive talent coming through at the time, Jorge Lorenzo was another one who really stood out for me. In 2004 he was riding a Derbi in the 125cc class and I was so impressed with the silky smooth way he rode that little bike. I studied him closely throughout his career as he moved up to the 250cc ranks, and there was never a doubt in my mind he would go all the way to the very top and become a MotoGP World Champion. As much as Jorge's skill on the bike, which was blatant to me from trackside, the kid just knew what he wanted and did everything he could in every facet of his life to achieve it.

In my opinion, though, Stoner is simply one of the fastest men ever to ride a motorcycle – an absolute phenomenon. As a motorcycle racer I always wanted to beat everybody, but as a motorcycle racing fan there are battles I would love to have seen. In recent decades we've been unlucky. We missed Mick Doohan against Valentino Rossi because of Mick's career-ending injuries in 1999, and we missed Stoner versus Marc Márquez because Casey retired. These guys are the true innovators of our sport.

Back when I first arrived in the MotoGP paddock, everybody was going bonkers for these little CRF50 pit bikes, buying trick little frames for them and putting different colour wheels on. I bought two and we used to keep them under the motorhome. If we got bored, or when Prof and I parked the motorhome up at a beach or whatever in between races, we'd get them out and mess around. There were regular wheelie competitions taking place and – needless to say – the competition got a little out of control. There was more than one occasion when one of us flipped off the back of our pit bike and sent it skidding up the middle of the paddock, which went down like a lead balloon with Dorna, and we eventually got banned from using them.

A bit like myself, John 'Hopper' Hopkins – a happy-go-lucky Californian with a constant, mischievous grin on his face – prided himself on his wheelies. He couldn't go anywhere without being on the back wheel of his scooter.

At the German Grand Prix at Sachsenring, we were hanging out in the Red Bull hospitality unit, a couple of us leaning out of the awning and most probably trying to chat some grid girls up, when John comes wheelie-ing into view and pulls up next to us.

'What's happening, dudes?' he grinned, half sitting on his scooter, half leaning with his elbow on the awning. We started giving each other a bit of shit and, for a laugh, spotting that his engine was still running, I grabbed hold of his throttle grip and twisted it open. The scooter shot forward from underneath him and John went with it, legs in the air as he tried to stop himself falling off the back, desperately reaching out for the handlebars, only to grab another big handful of throttle.

The bike lurched forward again, crashing straight into a row of parked scooters outside the hospitality unit next door; there was this almighty crunching of metal on tarmac, before poor old Hopper came to a rest in a massive heap of scooters and spinning tyres, people all around us turning to see what the fuck had just happened. I was absolutely doubled up laughing, I could hardly breathe, but Hopper did not see the funny side at all. He was raging, virtually foaming at the mouth, as he got up and came storming straight back over to me, winding up to throw a punch.

'John, fuck off!' I told him. 'It was a joke – get over it!' To be fair, he did, and we've remained good mates ever since.

John was living in England at the time and the two of us got on great. We'd do things like go and buy a pair of radio-controlled cars, the fastest we could get our hands on, and race each other with them. I suppose we did whatever we could to entertain ourselves without going out drinking, partying, and doing whatever else it was that other twenty-somethings with disposable time and income would do.

Any drinking and partying we did do – in my case, at least – was generally restricted to Sunday nights after a race, and after that crazy rain-affected race at Mugello, a few of us got a bit loose in the paddock. I had a good friend of mine with me, Jon Waghorn – better known as Wag, Waggy, Wagman, Fatty, Fathead or Foghorn, because he's got such a massive gob on him. Wag is a larger-than-life character who I had met a couple of years earlier at the motocross shop that Prof worked at, when he bought one of my old bikes from them, and we hit it off straight away. He would go on to become a really important person in my life.

That night at Mugello, for some unknown reason, Hopkins and Waggy decided it would be a great idea to set fire to some fuel. What can I say? It seemed like a good idea at the time. So the three of us went up behind the paddock to the car park on the infield between turns two and three with these big barrels of race fuel that had been left outside the pit garages, and started laying these long trails on the ground and setting them alight.

Hopkins was walking along, as he does, with his legs at quarter to three because of all his injuries, tipping fuel out of this barrel in an obscenely large circle. He finally completed his circle, and then for some reason known only to him he stood right in the middle of it as he bent down to set it alight. The last thing I can remember hearing before the mother of all fireballs went up was Waggy shouting: '*Nooooo!* Don't light it, you fucking div!'

The next thing . . . *Boom!* The hills of Tuscany were briefly thrown into a couple of seconds of daylight as this mushroom of fire shot skywards. I instinctively turned away from the blazing heat and started to run for cover. When I looked over my shoulder I saw those quarter-to-three feet running behind me through the smoke – like that scene in *Only Fools and Horses* when Del Boy and Rodney are running down an alleyway dressed up as Batman and Robin.

I was crying laughing, but poor old Hopper had smoke pouring off his hair and shoulders, his eyebrows had completely melted; he was an absolute state. We got him back to the motorhome and he was squealing and swearing in his high-pitched Californian accent, which just made the whole situation even funnier, as he assessed the damage in the mirror.

Hopper was a brilliant, funny guy with a vulnerability about him that was endearing, but that also meant he could be easily led and he was a bit prone to self-destruction. I don't know exactly what the triggers were, but sometimes he'd get this look in his eye and he'd set off down a particular path and then stick to it, even if it was the wrong one. You couldn't talk him out of anything.

He was a talented boy, though, that's for sure, and there came a point in time, at the end of a particularly strong season in 2007, when he became the most desired signature in MotoGP apart from Valentino, who was already tied in with Yamaha. At that moment he needed some proper guidance, but I guess it wasn't there for him; he went to Kawasaki to ride a brand-new – and therefore uncompetitive – bike for a load of money. It proved to be his undoing and, after a season of crashing his brains out, Kawasaki pulled out of the championship altogether.

Young riders are vulnerable like that, and in John's case I don't know if it would have made any difference to have somebody around. Dani Pedrosa, for example, came through at the same time and was the complete opposite. He had been discovered and developed through the smaller championships by a super-serious guy called Alberto Puig, who controlled Dani's every move. The poor kid wasn't even allowed to have a bright colour on his gloves because Alberto was so strict. He was there to race motorbikes and literally nothing else. Even the name on the back of his leathers was in Times New Roman font, for God's sake.

It is a hard balancing-act, but the person who always seemed to manage it best was Valentino. It was interesting spending a couple of years in the same paddock as him, seeing how he operates on and off the track, although I'm not too sure quite how many people can really say they know him. My mum's claim to fame is that – at a media day to promote the British Grand Prix that she and Dad came to – she gave him a kiss. That is the kind of effect he has on people of all ages and backgrounds, and I think the very best thing about him is that he clearly doesn't race for the money. He has more now than he could ever probably spend, but he keeps doing what he does for the love of racing. He's a truly global phenomenon, the best possible ambassador for our sport, and what on earth MotoGP will do when he retires, I have no idea.

Staying focused on your racing when there are so many distractions around you is not easy for anybody, but at the end of the day a happy racer is a fast racer. That was one thing you could see Valentino got right – keeping his closest, most trusted childhood friends around him throughout the madness. Personally, I found I always worked best when I was surrounded by a friendly, positive environment. If the job becomes too corporate, too stuffy, and nobody is having fun, what's the point in that?

Our other main source of entertainment throughout that 2004 season was Kurtis Roberts, riding that year for his world-famous dad Kenny – a three-time former 500cc World Champion from the Seventies and Eighties and a bona-fide legend, who later went into team management and was now running his own MotoGP bike and team. Kenny was a proper hero in our sport and Kurtis was the lesser known of his two sons.

The more famous one, Kenny Junior, was a really intelligent, well-spoken guy – calm, focused, and fast enough on a motorbike to emulate his dad by winning the 500cc World Championship in 2000. Senior, who was always happy to tell anybody who'd listen that he was down to one testicle after losing the other in a motocross crash, explained to me the difference between his two boys. 'I made Junior when I had two balls,' he drawled in his brash, all-American way. 'When I made Kurtis I only had one.'

Thanks largely to Valentino, the Italian Grand Prix is a huge national event and anybody who is anybody in Italy just *has* to be there. The local police force absolutely love it, and they swan around all weekend in their reflective aviator sunglasses and tight trousers, cruising up and down the paddock in their quick-response Lamborghinis and fancy new BMW motorcycles. So, when Kurtis spotted an unattended Beamer with a bobby's helmet resting on the tank – so to speak – he thought it would be a great laugh to jump on, turn all the sirens on and have it away.

For starters, the helmet was way too big for him, so it was hanging down over his nose, with just his scruffy ginger beard and his goofy grin poking out of the bottom as he wheelied off on the bike down the middle of the paddock. We were all doubled over laughing as this copper came running back to the empty spot where his bike had been, while his colleagues set about chasing after Kurtis. But Kurtis was so brazen about it that he just came skidding back, took the helmet off and placed it back on the copper's head. This poor policeman was so furious, yet at the same time so dumbstruck, that he didn't seem to know what to do, so Kurtis just said, 'Thanks, man, that was awesome!' and walked off.

For all the crazy stunts that Kurtis pulled that year, he saved his craziest for the final round of the year at Valencia where, on the Sunday night, as is tradition, pretty much everybody from the paddock went out for the end-of-season party. There were three or four car-loads of us lot – riders and their friends and girlfriends – heading to this nightclub on the outskirts of town, and I ended up in the passenger seat of the car being driven by Kurtis.

We were actually all due back at the track for a test session the following morning, so once the party was over, the obvious smart thing to do would be to head straight back to the paddock and go to bed. But this was Kurtis Roberts at the wheel and, instead of doing that, he decided that he wanted to play a game of real-life *Grand Theft Auto*.

Kurtis started driving this hire car like a complete maniac – one of those situations that is funny at first, but soon stops being funny when you realize the guy at the wheel could be about to get you all killed. I'd been in a few of these situations before, back in the day in Sittingbourne, and I told Kurtis to slow the fuck down. 'Fuck you, Shakey!' he laughed, with that stupid grin on his face again, so I just ripped the handbrake on as hard as I could. We were travelling at about 100 mph and the car went into a massive spin, three of the tyres exploded and we slid off the road into a ditch.

'Shakey, you fucking arsehole!' laughed Kurtis, completely enjoying the whole thing. 'What did you do that for? Look what you did to the bumper!' Sure enough, the bumper had ripped off and was lying in a cloud of dust, lit up by the headlights, but I didn't care – we needed to get this motor back on the road before the police came. Taking the spare wheel out of each of the other three cars, we started swapping them over onto ours. Each different wheel had a different stud pattern, so only a couple of bolts would fit in some of them, but we somehow managed to get them all on and got the thing mobile again.

With the benefit of hindsight, I know that the smart move at this point would have been to take over driving duties from Kurtis but – stupidly – I let him back behind the wheel. Maybe I figured this whole incident would have shocked him enough to make him calm down. But actually, since the car was fucked anyway, he decided to have even more fun with it. We got back onto the road but didn't stay there for very long, with Kurtis driving up onto the pavements, over roundabouts and all sorts.

Eventually we got to the slip road onto the motorway and he just let go of the wheel, folded his arms and let the car smash into the Armco barrier, railing the thing the whole way around. I was crouching for cover as the wing mirror smashed itself to smithereens, sparks flying off the side panels, but the crazy bastard was just laughing his head off. 'Kurtis! What are you *doing*?' I said.

'What the fuck, man?' he shrugged. 'You fucked the handbrake and ripped the bumper off! It's got the wrong fucking wheels on – what the fuck does the fucking door matter?'

We eventually pulled back into the Valencia paddock, where the security guard could hardly believe what he was seeing. He pulled us over – obviously – and signalled for Kurtis to wind the window down. '*Que pasa?*' the guard said, looking over the mashed-up hire car in total disbelief.

Kurtis just shrugged. 'Fucking dog ran out, man!'

The state of that battered vehicle was a pretty good metaphor for how my season had gone with Aprilia. Once Piaggio had halted development on the new bike, the old Cube was left to take a couple more victims in the shape of me and McWilliams before production was stopped completely. Jeremy described his experience of the bike really well a few years later. 'It wasn't that the Cube scared the shit out of you,' he said. 'It just wore you down until you gave up. It broke every one of my ribs, some vertebrae, partially deafened me and melted itself a few times. If we were reunited, I'd set it alight.'

Personally, I think if I ever saw the Aprilia again, I'd just give it a wry smile. Whether the new bike would have made the difference, who knows? I really believe Aprilia had the passion and the knowledge to make something competitive, but the decision had been made way above the heads of the racing department, and that was the end of it. It was a shame because I really enjoyed my time racing with those guys.

Andrew negotiated a decent pay-off and gained some assurances from Dorna that they would find me another ride to keep me in MotoGP.

14

Visual Flight Rules

I have always been fascinated with helicopters, which I can trace back to those evenings at Prince Charles Avenue, lying on the rug with my sister watching *M*A*S*H* on the television with our mum and dad. Early in my racing career I got into flying petrol radio-controlled helicopters between racing and training and got pretty good at it.

So, in 2003, when a chap called Ian Jarvis – a bit of a racing fan who eventually became a good friend – caught up with me one day at Brands Hatch and asked if I fancied a trip out with him in a Jet Ranger, I couldn't say yes quickly enough. The helicopter Ian flew was based at Manston Airport, just a forty-five-minute drive down the A299 from my house on the Isle of Sheppey. We went up with a fantastic instructor called Janet Garrioch, who runs a training school called Polar Helicopters at Manston, and I was hooked from the very first flight.

Once you're up and away, a helicopter is relatively straightforward to operate and, on that very first flight, as soon as we were cruising, Janet let me have my first go at taking the controls. A couple of years earlier I had done a few hours flying an aeroplane, a Cessna 152, at Rochester Airport. I got to the point where I could take off, fly around and land, but my instructor was one of those guys who seemed to love to make you feel inferior, just because they're being paid to teach you. I really didn't enjoy being made to feel so incapable and I didn't much fancy the idea of taking seven exams to get my licence either.

Initially I enjoyed flying the aeroplanes but, once you get up and select your heading, you can pretty much trim the plane so that there's not a lot else to do until you land. You're looking out and seeing what's going on, but I guess you could sit there and read the paper if you really wanted to. Flying a helicopter turned out to be the complete opposite. I'd compare it to putting a ball bearing or a marble on a piece of paper, and then trying to hold the paper flat so the ball bearing doesn't roll off. You know the saying: 'For every action, there's a reaction.' Well, that certainly applies to flying a helicopter. Every time it wants to go one way, your input makes it go the other, and because of that you're always busy – it's a huge challenge.

By the time we were on our way back to Manston I was convinced I had to get my licence and was already thinking about how I might be able to buy one of my own. In a helicopter you have to do a minimum of forty-five hours of flying before you can even think about doing your test. Flying a Jet Ranger for that amount of time was going to add up to a fair few quid and, even though I was riding in

MotoGP at the time and that was working out pretty well financially, it made much more sense to learn in a more cost-effective way, in a smaller helicopter.

I did a trial lesson with Janet in a Robinson R22, which is a really basic, light, single-engine two-seater – pretty much the reference learner helicopter. I remember getting in it for the first time and watching her turn a key to start it up. The noise of a jet engine is deafening, but this thing in comparison sounded like a bored-out Volkswagen Beetle. I remember thinking, 'Nah, this ain't a bit of me!' The Jet Ranger was properly cool, but taking off and buffeting around in the sky in this little thing with one other person on board was not my idea of fun.

In actual fact, you can learn far more about the principles of flying in a Robinson R22 – or an R44, which is the four-seat version – than you probably ever could in a Jet Ranger, because of the relatively minimal amount of power they have, which requires more skill to keep them in the air. I would liken it to riding a track day bike. Let's say you're riding at a long circuit, like Silverstone or Snetterton, on a 125cc bike. The straights are going to take forever to get to the end of and the lap time is not going to be so fast, so you'll have to work that much harder through the corners to keep your momentum and corner speed high, be late on the brakes and early on the gas in order to give yourself the best shot at a decent lap time. Jump on a Superbike and you'll eat the straights in seconds, you won't need to push so hard on the brakes or through the corners; you'll smoke your 125cc lap time with ease, but you won't have learned half as much about riding a motorcycle. You *really* have to fly a Robinson R22.

After my first lesson in the R22, I had one more go in the Jet Ranger and finally settled on a R44, which seemed like a good compromise, and signed up for the course. The weird thing about it was that this time around I really enjoyed the studies and even looked forward to the exams, which are in topics like air law, operational procedures, human performance and meteorology. I got right into it all and applied myself well, passing every exam. Ironically, considering that right now I'm paid to talk on television, the only subject I had to retake was communications – a practical exam where basically all you do is talk.

I took the test on my forty-fifth hour of the minimum forty-five. When you take your helicopter test, you get what is called a 'type rating', which means you are eligible to fly the specific type of helicopter that you took your test in. If you do it in a Jet Ranger, you are qualified to fly a Jet Ranger. If you want to fly a Squirrel, a Lynx, Sea King or a Chinook then you have to do another test in that 'type'. On top of that, you have to do a check flight every year for each type rating, so it's a massive ball-ache for anybody flying more than one helicopter at a time. I got my licence in the R44 and stuck with it for a while before I did a conversion to a Jet Ranger.

Generally, for your first ten, maybe twenty hours in a Jet Ranger, you have to go out with an instructor, who will oversee the start operation with you. Like any jet engine, if you get the start-up procedure wrong, within three to five seconds of pressing the start button you can literally melt the engine. It is so easy to allow too much fuel in, and the engine temperature rises so rapidly, that before you even know what's happening the whole lot has turned to mush.

It's called a 'hot start' and it's been done a million times – thankfully not by me, because if you hot start a Jet Ranger you can kiss goodbye to a hundred grand or more.

By the September of 2005 I didn't quite have my twenty hours in the Jet Ranger, but when I was invited over to Assen to meet with some teams and discuss a move back to World Superbikes, I knew exactly how I wanted to arrive. 'Go big or go home', as the saying goes. Arriving in the paddock in my own helicopter was bound to get a few people's attention, so I went down to Manston to borrow a Robinson R44 off Janet. I'd done over seventy hours in the R44 and would have been happy to fly around the world and back in the thing on my own.

'I'm going to the World Superbikes at Assen,' I told Janet, all proud of myself, when I turned up at Manston to collect the R44.

'Shane, you can't fly to Assen,' Janet replied, shaking her head.

'Why not?'

'Well, for a start, have you got a flight map?'

Me being me, I had just bought myself this really trick, top-of-the-range Garmin GPS. 'Janet, I've got a Garmin,' I said cockily. 'I don't need a map now.'

I told her how I'd plotted the route on the Garmin, knew exactly where I was going, knew exactly what headings I needed and what VORs – VHF Omnidirectional Ranges – I was tracking. I also knew exactly which airfield I was going to and where I needed to fill up. I knew the lot, or so I thought.

'Shane. If your fancy Garmin fails, what are you going to do?' She had a point, but I simply had to get to Assen, and by now there was no other way for me to get there in time. I needed a flight map, and fast.

'There's a Transair shop at Shoreham,' she said. 'Get down there and get a map; there is no way you're going all the way over to Holland on your first trip abroad without one.'

It was about an hour's flight from Manston to Shoreham, near Brighton, in completely the opposite direction to Assen. I got the right hump because that two-hour round trip meant I wouldn't be able to make the flight to Assen that afternoon, and would have to postpone all the important meetings until the following day. But, any excuse to go flying, I jumped in the R44 and headed down to Shoreham anyway.

When you're navigating using a flight map, you also need a thing called a 'whiz wheel', which is a flight computer. The whiz wheel allows you to calculate which track – or compass heading – to use for how many minutes and seconds before you change to a different track because the wind has changed direction. It covers every single aspect of your flight, and when you know how to use one it's pretty simple. But when you look at one for the first time, I don't care if you're a nuclear physicist, you think to yourself, 'What the fucking hell is *that*?'

Eventually I got hold of the map, planned it all out on the whiz wheel exactly the same as I had it on the GPS, and when I got back to Manston I told Janet: 'Right, Janet, I'll be back first thing in the morning. I *have* to be in Holland for this meeting.'

'OK, come down to the hangar for six o'clock and, if it's not too foggy I'll let you go. You'll still have to call

Rotterdam Airport, check they are VFR [Visual Flight Rules] and book in to get fuel. If Rotterdam are VFR, you can follow your map, get your fuel, get to Assen and reverse the route for the way back.'

Prof and Nick Shaw, a good pal who had been looking after my crazy bull terrier Max (the only dog I have ever known to get arrested) while I was travelling about doing MotoGP, had agreed to come with me, so the three of us headed down to Manston that following morning. I called Rotterdam who confirmed they were VFR, jumped in the helicopter and took on board Janet's parting words: 'Listen, Shane, I know this trip is important to you, but if you get to Dover and you can't see France, don't go.'

'Janet, you have my word,' I promised her.

It was a five- or ten-minute flight from Manston to Dover and, as the English Channel came into view, I radioed London to get clearance to cross. They said it was OK.

'Boys, are you happy?' I said. 'We can all see France, right?' It was hazy, but we all agreed we could make out the dark silhouette of Calais on the other side. I'd never flown over water before, and it's funny how vulnerable you feel when you're going across. It's only twenty-two miles, but when it is twenty-two miles of nothing but water underneath you and there's nowhere to land, it's unnerving.

I flew much higher than normal because I figured that if I had an engine failure, the higher we were, the longer we could spend autorotating and the more chance I had of keeping going and making it to dry land. Thankfully, that wasn't necessary, but as we finally made it to the coast of France, the ground below us was getting hazier and the cloud base seemed to be getting lower. We could still make out some fields and buildings below, but it was getting close to the limits of VFR. We had plenty of fuel on board, though, so I thought, 'Do you know what? We'll stick up here in this blue stuff and when we get to Rotterdam we'll have no problems as it's clear there anyway.'

Around fifteen to twenty minutes out from Rotterdam, I made my first radio call to approach.

'Rotterdam approach, this is helicopter Golf-Bravo-Zulu-Lima-Papa inbound to yourselves. Need fuel, three people on board, flying VFR from Manston in the UK, en route to Assen.' I gave them my altitude and a rough positioning and heading, and waited for their instructions to land.

'Helicopter Golf-Bravo-Zulu-Lima-Papa, we are sorry but the weather has closed in – we can't let you land here under VFR. You need to divert to Schiphol. They are currently clear for VFR.'

I turned to the lads. 'Schiphol? Where the fuck is Schiphol?' I'd never heard of it and neither had the boys – even Prof, who knew more than any of us. 'Must be a little airfield somewhere round here,' I thought. They gave me the frequency for Schiphol, but by now we had a bit of a different problem, which was that I couldn't really see the ground below at all.

Bearing in mind I knew we were heading up the coast of Holland, with the sea roughly to my left and the land to my right, I made a plan. 'Right, lads, we'll throw a left. Since there's not likely to be any skyscrapers in the sea, we can drop down and get ourselves below the cloud. Then we can come back in to dry land and sneak into this Schiphol place, wherever it is.' Only a couple of months beforehand, one of my final lessons had been on flying in inclement weather conditions. You have to wear special glasses called 'foggles', which simulate flying in cloud, as they block absolutely everything out of the top of your vision, so that all you can see are your dials and controls. The lesson is that whenever you get caught in inclement conditions, trust your dials and do not go on instinct because you'll almost certainly crash.

'Yep, sounds good,' the boys nervously replied. I think they both thought that this involved finding a gap in the clouds and gently lowering down through it. But actually, what you do is pick a heading, keep the helicopter and its tail in a straight line, then lower the collective – the lever that looks like a handbrake, which alters the pitch of the rotor blades and causes you to ascend or, in this case, descend. By this point we were dropping down over the sea, and as we were getting lower and lower through the cloud, all around us it was getting greyer and greyer, and darker and darker, and colder and quieter. I checked the pressure setting on the altimeter and I could see that I was now only a hundred feet above the water surface. Suddenly I started to feel very uncomfortable, but we carried on descending, desperately hoping that we would come out of the bottom of this cloud, but it just never happened. I knew now that I was really low, just about as low as I was prepared to go before I abandoned the idea, but Prof suddenly lost his cool and started screaming. I was concentrating so hard, that was the last thing I expected or needed: he frightened the living shit out of me.

In a helicopter, when you give it a load of gas by pulling

up on the collective, the front of the helicopter wants to yaw because all that power in the engine is going round in the blades and the helicopter essentially wants to spin around on itself. In front of you, there is a slip indicator, which is basically a piece of string that goes up the centre of the windscreen on the outside to indicate in the most basic way which way the helicopter is tilting. I pulled the power back in to do what we call a 'go around' and attempted to start climbing back up through the cloud. I was completely disorientated, but a quick check showed the slip indicator fully over to one side. I pulled all the power in, and the helicopter started yawing the other way. Meanwhile my ASI (air speed indicator) was showing that I was going too slowly as I was trying to climb vertically too quickly.

By now I couldn't see a thing. Getting yourself out of a pickle like this is probably the hardest thing you can ever do in a helicopter – and it's a situation you should never get yourself into. Schiphol, meanwhile, were talking to me on the radio, but I just couldn't hear them because Prof was still screaming his head off in the back. I was in a really bad place, literally, moving my mouth to speak to Schiphol but nothing was coming out. I was so involved with what was going on around me, I almost couldn't remember how to talk.

By now we were climbing, up and up and up – I'd lost all my air speed, but all I wanted to do was get the thing out of the cloud; I'd honestly never been so scared in all my life. But someone must have been looking out for me that day, and against all odds we suddenly emerged above the cloud, surrounded by nothing but blue sky. Prof had finally stopped screaming, the radio had gone quiet, and we all breathed a massive sigh of relief. 'Right,' I thought. 'Let's get back onto Schiphol.'

'I'm now back up out of the cloud,' I told them. 'Apologies for my lack of communication, but we're with you again, awaiting further instructions.'

They gave me a squawk number – a four-digit transponder code that allows them to identify each different aircraft on their radar, then gave me a heading and told me to report back in with ten miles to run to the airfield.

We were getting close to that when suddenly I saw this hole in the cloud and, for the first time since we left British shores, a clear view of the ground beneath it. I did the equivalent of a handbrake turn in the helicopter at around 110 knots, and spun it straight down through this hole. Now I could see the ground; the relief was immense and I was made up with life again. To stay under the cloud, however, I had to fly at two or three hundred feet, and you're not supposed to be less than five hundred feet above any manmade obstacle. I thought, 'Do you know what? I don't care, I'm coming in, and I'm not going anywhere near that cloud. They can take my licence, I don't give a fuck!'

I got back in radio contact with Schiphol and did everything they said, but I still couldn't see the airfield. The next thing I knew, me and my two daft mates in this Robinson R44 came buzzing in over the top of a load of jumbo jets on the runway at Amsterdam's main airport. I had no idea they called it Schiphol!

It was too late now. I carried on towards the control tower, still at about 300 feet, before the radio burst back into life again.

'Helicopter G-LP, you are heading towards the wrong tower! You're at the wrong end of the airfield!'

Now I'm the one screaming. *'Aaaaaargh! I just want to get out!'*

Eventually I got myself to the right location and taxied down the correct taxiway, but I then got a call to hold. They held me on this taxiway while manoeuvring another aircraft and left us hovering about ten feet off the ground while a crosswind bounced the R44 all over the place. I seriously started to think about what the penalty would be if I just dropped it on the deck and left it there. Would it be prison? Or would it just be a fine? I was past caring, but I hung on long enough and finally they let me continue to my landing spot.

In fact, the staff at Schiphol were really nice to me once we were on the ground, giving us a cup of tea and refuelling the helicopter while they showed us around a little museum they had there just next to where we had landed. I stayed for a while, sipping my tea and looking out of the window at the R44, trying to pluck up the courage to get back in and continue the flight on to Assen.

The feeling of relief was totally unreal. I had just managed to keep my head in what was literally a life-or-death situation, one that I am not sure too many people would have escaped. That's not because I'm some super-hero helicopter pilot, because if I was, I wouldn't have got myself in that situation in the first place. But I do believe it takes something pretty special to cope under such extreme stress, and I was proud of myself for doing so.

I knew right there and then that I would never, ever make that mistake again. There is no question that setting off that morning had been a huge error of judgement. I thought I had to fly to Assen that day, but I didn't. I put myself under so much pressure, pressure I didn't need to be under. I fucked up by deeming something to be more important than the rules, and the result of that decision put me in a position where I have never been so frightened in my life. Just two years previously, Steve Hislop had crashed a Robinson R44 in heavy cloud and died. I didn't need anybody to tell me how close I had come to doing the same thing to myself and two of my friends.

Sometimes people joke about never getting on the back of a bike with me, but as Petra always says, who could be safer on a motorcycle than the guy who has won the British Championship six times? In theory you can't get a better person. But in a helicopter I am so respectful and so careful now, and I am also very proud that I have a licence. Of all the things I've done my life, other than being a husband and father, becoming a helicopter pilot is probably the thing I am most proud of.

As it turned out, the whole trip to Assen proved to be pretty pointless anyway, because for all the interest in World Superbikes, there was one major force set on keeping me in MotoGP. As the rights holders to the series, it was in Dorna's interest to have a competitive Brit on the grid, especially now they had just done a new television deal to show live mainstream coverage on the BBC. With young British talent being a bit thin on the ground, Andrew made out like they were begging me to stay; because it was Dorna, he insisted, there was no way I could end up without a decent ride.

There was talk of a factory Kawasaki, a factory Suzuki,

various decent satellite Honda rides – any of which would have given me half a chance, but none of which came to fruition. In the end we signed a contract with KTM, a hugely successful Austrian factory in the off-road world who were now venturing into road racing. Joining a new project would be a risk, but I'd worked so hard to get to MotoGP and I didn't want to leave it now. It was the pinnacle of the sport, and I knew this could be my only chance.

KTM had built a new V4 MotoGP engine designed by this ex-Formula 1 guy called Kurt Tribe, and come to a kind of co-operation agreement with Kenny Roberts. Team KR were proven to be brilliant chassis builders, and the Austrians had done a great job of assuring Kenny and his team that this motor was the dog's bollocks. Altogether, the whole package looked like it could be a really good option on paper.

The problem was, we don't race motorcycles on paper.

15

Getting the Hump

Team KR were a well-established and very professionally run outfit. They'd had some success running their own chassis with a Proton engine in the 500cc days, but when MotoGP switched to four-strokes in 2002, it had been disastrous for them because they had to start again from scratch. Developing a new engine was easy for a major factory, but for a small team working out of a workshop in Banbury, it hit them hard.

Nevertheless, typical of Kenny Roberts, they were working hard to try and upset the odds. Kenny always said that his ultimate goal in life was to work out how to make a motorcycle go faster, and I liked that simple ethos. The fascinating thing about motorcycles is that no matter how trick or fast they are, they can always be improved on. It's a never-ending quest.

So, after spending the 2003 and 2004 season running

various incarnations of Proton's four-stroke V5 motor, which Kenny famously described as being perfect if you needed an anchor for a ship, the team had done this deal with KTM. Chuck Aksland – a lifelong confidant of Kenny's – was a hugely experienced team manager, and my crew chief would be Tom Jojic, a calmly spoken Canadian who was always keen to listen to me and translate my feedback into a plan. There was full support from the factory, with an army of Austrian technicians on board, and – of course – top of the pile was the legendary 'King' Kenny.

From the word go, Kenny and I got on like a house on fire. Essentially, the guy doesn't care what anybody thinks about him, which leaves him totally free to say and do whatever he wants. He is brutally honest and savagely funny, with great comic timing, and he loves to offend people. He doesn't mean it badly, he just likes to see if he can get a rise out of people and test how they react. I loved that about him and never took it personally. There was never a dull moment in his company.

Kenny is one of the guys I most respected in racing, firstly because of what he did as a rider, coming to Europe as a relatively unknown dirt-tracker from the USA and revolutionizing the way Grand Prix motorcycles were ridden on slick tyres. Then, towards the end of his career, he brought other American dirt-trackers through like Wayne Rainey, Eddie Lawson and Randy Mamola. These guys all became legends of the sport and it couldn't have happened without Kenny's influence.

They say you should never meet your heroes, but that notion couldn't be further from the truth in my experience of Kenny, and I was so grateful that I got to spend time under his guidance. It made me wonder what kind of relationship I might have had with another of my heroes, Barry Sheene. I only met Barry once, when I was twelve years old, at Brands, and I told him that one day I was going to be a racer like him. I remember Barry saying something like, 'Well, best of luck, kid.' I was already a cheeky little bastard and I replied, 'If I do half as well as you I'll be doing pretty good – but I want to be better!' That made him smile. I was sad that I never got to know Barry better, but determined to make the most of having another of my heroes in my corner.

Kenny's imaginative, instinctive approach to racing was completely at odds with KTM, who were run by a British former professional motocross racer called Kurt Nicoll. This guy was so arrogant, I honestly think he reckoned he would be faster on the MotoGP bike than I was. What Kurt probably didn't want to know, however, was that despite their massive investment, his factory had commissioned an engine that had turned out to be a complete heap of junk.

They were telling me how much horsepower it had, how linear the torque curve was and everything else, so I was really looking forward to riding the new bike after getting off the complete animal that was the Aprilia Cube. They told me it was completely different to the Aprilia, and I suppose in that respect they were absolutely right. I opened the throttle at the first test and where the Aprilia had screamed *Paaaaaaaaaah!* and tried to pull my arms out of their sockets, this thing just went *Wuuuuuuuuuuuh* . . . This motor would have had trouble pulling the skin off a rice pudding. It had no grunt, no push – it was like a massive elastic band that just kept on stretching but never pinged back.

I hadn't been fast enough on the Aprilia to threaten the points on a regular basis, but it was going to take a long time to get up to anywhere near the same pace on the KTM. I complained and gave them feedback about their expensive new engine that they weren't prepared to hear. They got Randy Mamola to test it, and Randy did me a whole load of no favours by telling the Austrians he didn't think it was so bad, and then admitting to Kenny and Chuck that the thing was a steaming turd. As good as he was in his day, I'm not sure why KTM thought Randy's feedback was of any relevance at all when the guy was four or five seconds off my pace.

Either way, by the time we got to Mugello for the fifth round of the season at the start of June, we hadn't even come close to scoring a single point, and KTM arranged a big crisis meeting with Kenny, Chuck, me and all the Austrians. Kenny was the kind of man who walks into a room and commands respect from everybody immediately. He has this aura around him and – besides anything else – this was his project. His reputation was on the line and he was not happy with how it was going. Diplomatic as ever, he gave it to them straight. 'Your fucking motor is a pile of shit,' he said.

The Austrians were essentially not feeling this idea, and suggested that maybe the problem was with the rider. 'Listen, you motherfuckers,' Kenny replied. 'I've been out trackside all weekend and I've watched Shakey, and I've watched Valentino. I saw Shakey brake where Valentino brakes, I saw Shakey turn where Valentino turns, I saw Shakey release the brake where Valentino releases the brake, and I saw Shakey take the gas where Valentino takes the gas. You want to know the difference between the two?'

The Austrians were like, 'What's the difference, Kenny?'

'The difference is that when Valentino takes the gas, *his* bike goes forward. The problem is *not* the fucking rider. You can put anybody you like on that bike and they won't go any faster than Shakey.'

I was so proud at that moment, I was almost in tears.

As well as having the worst bike on the grid, Kenny's team also had the shittest paddock scooters. They were battered and tatty – basically an embarrassment to ride around on, which was great for Kenny because he just found things like that hilarious. After the first race of the season at Jerez in April, when the KTM had conked out after two laps, a bunch of us – including Hopkins, Hofmann, Chaz and Casey – all shot off to cause some mischief on our scooters.

At Jerez there is a huge banking surrounding the last sector of the circuit, the bit they call the stadium section, with a gravel track that goes up into the hills. We all shot up there as fast as our scooters would go. I was standing up on mine, its little two-stroke engine singing away, flat out up the banking where just a few hours earlier thousands of Spanish fans had been sitting cheering us on during the races. There was rubbish blowing about everywhere – plastic bags, tin foil and beer bottles from their packed lunches – so I leaned back to pull the front wheel up to avoid all this debris, a load of which just happened to be wrapped around a concrete bollard, which I piled straight into at around 40 mph, wearing nothing but flip-flops, shorts and a T-shirt.

With no helmet on either, I went flying over the handle-bars and landed headfirst in a heap of gravel, dust, tin cans and glass bottles, knocking myself clean out. I don't know too much about what happened next, but evidently one of the boys put me on the back of their scooter and took me back down to the paddock to see a medic. I had cuts and bruises all over my body, my hands were ripped to pieces and the scooter was completely written off – I'd hit the bollard so hard that it snapped the headstock out of the top of the suspension. 'Thank fuck for that!' Kenny said when I gathered my senses and told him the bad news. 'We've been trying to get rid of those fucking scooters for years!'

It wasn't just the scooters Kenny was keen to see the back of, and at the Czech Grand Prix in the August – by now with at least one point next to my name, thanks to a fifteenth-place finish at Laguna Seca – the team had another big crisis meeting with KTM. Despite Kenny's backing for my riding, the Austrians still weren't convinced, and even though Kenny had told them what to do with the engine, they hadn't listened and were insisting on going their own way with it. That clearly didn't sit right with Kenny, and when they all sat down together just before first practice at Brno, he told them to go fuck themselves.

Anticipating this scenario, the team had brought some of their old Proton V5 motors to Brno but – since my contract was with KTM – there was no way I would be allowed to ride them. Effectively, I now had a contract with a factory that no longer had a bike, so while Jeremy McWil-liams stepped in and threw his leg back over the Proton he'd ridden for them the previous season, I went out and partied the whole weekend. I was gutted because Kenny,

Chuck and the whole team had made me feel like one of their own, but even they couldn't do anything to help me. I put on a brave face, hit Brno town centre and tried to make the best of a bad weekend.

I spent the summer on the Costa Brava in Spain, where I had sorted myself a house to stay at during the season, training, cycling and bobbing about on a little speedboat I had bought myself. I was out on the boat in late September, when I got a call from a well-spoken English guy introducing himself as Malcolm, who worked as a marketing manager for the Camel Honda Pons team, informing me that Troy Bayliss had broken his wrist and they wanted me to take his place for the next race in Malaysia. I thought it was some kind of wind-up, but it turned out that Malcolm was serious and here was my big chance.

The Honda V5 had been the bike to be on ever since it had been first revealed at the start of the new four-stroke MotoGP era in 2002, winning all but two of the races that season and every race in 2003, mainly with Valentino, before he had famously switched to Yamaha for 2004. Even then, by the middle of the 2005 season, no fewer than six other riders had also won races on the V5 – Tohru Ukawa, Alex Barros, Max Biaggi, Makoto Tamada, Nicky Hayden and Sete Gibernau. Like I said, this was my opportunity to finally make a name for myself at the highest level.

Such is the life of an unemployed MotoGP racer, I went from putting my flip-flops up on a boat in the Costa Brava to pulling on my race helmet on the other side of the world in the space of two days, ready for action at the Malaysian Grand Prix at Sepang. As first free practice started it was pissing down with rain and I was waiting for the mechanics to say to me, 'Come on then, let's go.' I sat there with my helmet on, excitedly waiting to ride this factory Honda V5, but everybody else was also sitting around, doing nothing. All the other riders were rolling past the front of the garage, the thunderous sound of MotoGP bikes on their pit-lane limiters heading out onto the track, and I kept thinking, 'Come on, lads, get on with it! I want to go and ride this bike!' The boys all came around at the end of their first lap, roaring down the front straight in front of the huge grandstand, then Barros had gone out and I was still sitting in my chair, thinking, 'What the hell's going on? Why aren't they letting me go?' I'd never experienced anything like that before.

In the end, the team owner Sito Pons came over to me and said, 'Shakey, don't you want to ride the bike? What's wrong?'

I was like, 'Course I do, I'm waiting for the nod from the mechanics.'

'You are the rider,' he said. 'You tell *them* what to do.'

I jumped straight to my feet. 'Get the tyre warmers off then, let's fucking go!'

In that respect I was being treated like a factory rider but, in reality, Honda weren't really interested in anything I had to say about the bike. Camel Honda were a satellite team, paying to lease their bikes from Honda Racing Corporation (HRC), who weren't too interested in getting feedback from satellite riders – especially one who was a stand-in – and the team weren't about to break the bank to make the bike more suited to me. For instance, in Superbikes I always liked to ride with a thumb brake, which is an effective manual anti-wheelie device when you don't have sophisticated electronics, but they didn't have one and they weren't going to spend time and money on making one. I'm not making excuses, but just a few small changes like that would have made a big difference.

One of the most amazing things about the Honda was that it never actually felt that fast. The power was so linear, it was like a V2 engine even though it was a V5. The thing was so smooth to ride, but without a thumb brake on it, I really struggled with wheelies and generally keeping control. I like to throw a bike in on the front tyre, scrub my speed off by trail braking on the way in and then point, turn, run some corner speed and fire the bike back out of the corner. With the Honda it was like you could only really stop it while straight – what we call 'up and down braking'. You had to virtually park it, then use the engine's torque to turn it and fire back off the turn.

Changing your riding style overnight is not easy for any rider to do because so much of it is automatic, but I couldn't have asked for better support that weekend, with five-time 500cc World Champion Mick Doohan – a true legend – on hand in an advisory capacity for HRC. Mick came into the team office and sat with me for ages, talking through things, encouraging the engineers to listen to me, pointing out that their laptops didn't ride the motorcycle, but I did. Even if he didn't realize it at the time, he was such a calming influence, assuring me that various riders had spent full seasons on the V5 and still not cracked it. The problem for me was that I didn't have a full season on it. In fact, if I didn't show some progress quickly, then I might not even have another Grand Prix.

I had no idea what to expect over race distance – how

the rubber would hold up, where was the limit of the front tyre, how I might adapt to the lack of thumb rear brake – but, for whatever reason, the race was a disappointment. I ended up in a battle with Rubén Xaus on a Yamaha, eventually pipping him at the last corner to finish fourteenth. I wasn't at all happy, although the team seemed pretty made up and they promised a thumb rear brake for the next race at Qatar.

I immediately felt much better on the bike at Losail, a circuit in Qatar which I hadn't got to ride the year before on the Aprilia because of my wrist injury. I was getting faster and faster throughout the weekend, and in morning warm-up on the Sunday I was running on the cusp of the top ten when an experienced Spanish rider called Carlos Checa punted me off at the last corner. It was the first time I'd crashed the bike and I was devastated. I thought the team would figure I'd been a dickhead and crashed because I was pushing too hard, but thankfully it had been caught by the television cameras and they'd seen everything in real time.

I felt like I had a lot of potential for that race. I had started to gel with the bike and, after qualifying seventeenth, I got off to a decent start, running with the pack until I made an early mistake and lost the tow. I ended up riding around on my own, with no rider in front of me as a point of reference to make up for my lack of track knowledge, and eventually crossed the line in thirteenth. I felt gutted, contemplating what might have been, but again the team were encouraged – insisting that they wanted to see progress, not results, and pointing out that my average lap time was actually less than 0.3 seconds off that of my teammate Barros.

Sito was happy, too; he could see I was making improve-ments, and with Bayliss ruled out for the remainder of the season, he told me he wanted me to finish the year with them. The last few rounds would be at circuits I knew – Phillip Island in Australia, Istanbul and Valencia. 'This is my ticket,' I thought. 'Now I can really show everybody what I can do.'

At the same time, a twenty-three-year-old Australian called Chris Vermeulen was riding for Ten Kate Honda in World Superbikes and doing really well, fighting with Troy Corser for the title. Chris had already won the World Supersport Championship for Honda in 2003, and under-standably he was being touted for a move to MotoGP. HRC wanted to keep him for at least another year in WSB before bringing him over to Grand Prix, but with some rumours surfacing that he was already some way down the line with Suzuki, they tried to offer him the sweetener of taking Bayliss's place on the Camel Honda for the MotoGP round at Phillip Island if he stayed loyal to them. Of course, Chris jumped at the chance of making his Grand Prix debut in his home round – who wouldn't? – and to be fair he did a good job, qualifying fourteenth and finishing eleventh, but it all happened above Sito's head and he wasn't happy. It was even more frustrating for both of us when Chris later went and signed a MotoGP deal with Suzuki anyway.

Sito was as good as gold with me about the whole thing. He rang me up to explain and insisted that I come to Valencia to ride for him again at the final round of the season.

'I'm so sorry this has happened, Shane. Come to Valencia, you will ride there.'

'Are you sure? The motorhome's back in England. I'm not going to drive it all the way down there to watch.'

'Sure, sure. You will ride there, Shakey.'

'OK, Sito, if you're telling me it's going to happen, I'll come down.'

We drove the motorhome all the way from Sittingbourne to Valencia, and no sooner had we pulled up in the paddock on the Wednesday afternoon than I bumped into Ryuichi Kiyonari, a young Japanese rider and HRC protégé who had just enjoyed a strong first season in BSB, finishing runner-up to Gregorio Lavilla. Kiyo had some MotoGP experience from a couple of years previously, when he stepped in for the late Daijiro Kato, and clearly Honda had decided that his performances in BSB were deserving of another chance at the top level. Once again, they went over Sito's head to offer Kiyo what was supposed to be my ride for the weekend.

Having recognized Kiyo in the paddock, it didn't take a rocket scientist to work out what was going on, but I was still fuming when Sito came around to see me.

'Shakey, I am so, so sorry . . .' he muttered when I opened the motorhome door.

'You're fucking kidding me, Sito. We had this conversation . . .'

'I know, I know. I am sorry, really.'

That weekend would turn out to be my last in MotoGP, which in theory should make it a sad memory. But, as fate would have it, the end of one avenue on my life's maze would direct me to probably the most important one yet.

16

What Will Be

To me, if you're not dreaming of being a World Champion, there is no point putting your leathers on. What's the point in doing anything if you don't feel the need to do it to the best of your ability? By the end of 2005 I was a British Superbike Champion, a World Superbike race winner and I had spent two seasons competing at the very highest level of motorcycle racing in MotoGP but, somehow, my ultimate dream felt to have died. I felt like I had spent my whole career trying to take the next step up the ladder, and then suddenly it had been pulled from under my feet.

I spent pretty much the whole of that last weekend in MotoGP at Valencia hanging about and feeling sorry for myself, in the motorhome or in the Alpinestars' hospitality unit, which is where I was sitting, gazing absent-mindedly out of the window, when I saw this absolutely stunning girl walk past. I didn't know who she was, where she was from or what she was doing there, but I knew that she was like no one I had ever seen before. With no racing to focus on, she became my mission for the weekend.

I did some digging and found out that she was there working for the factory Kawasaki team as a grid girl for a Japanese rider called Shinya Nakano. I spent all weekend making a plan to speak to her, and then backing out. For some reason, my usual confidence with women was completely gone.

It was a feeling I'd not had since I was eleven years old, when I had fancied a girl called Hayley from the all-girls' school next to mine. Somehow or other, through mutual friends, Hayley had agreed to be my 'girlfriend', and she would often call by my house after school, but she was so pretty that I knew I wouldn't be able to talk to her, so I'd make sure I was already out. One day she saw me sneaking out of the house and rightfully passed on the message through a friend that I was now dumped, before we had even so much as exchanged a word. I definitely deserved it, but I suppose I had put her up on such a pedestal that I felt as though I wasn't good enough for her. Twenty-odd years later, here I was in Valencia and having that same feeling all over again.

It turned out this particular grid girl wasn't being exactly receptive to me either, because of the Kawasaki team boss, Harald Eckl, who had been warning her off me, telling her about my reputation as a womanizer, which was ironic given that every time I set eyes on her, I turned into an eleven-year-old boy who couldn't so much as open his mouth to speak. In the end, she herself decided to go against Eckl's advice and approached me.

On the Sunday evening, after the race had finished, I was trudging through the paddock when she came up to me and asked for a photo. 'Yes!' I thought. 'You're back in the game!'

'No problem,' I grinned, and slipped my arm around her waist. 'So, you're English then?'

'No, I'm from the Czech Republic but I live in Greenwich.'

I still don't know why she said that, because she didn't live in Greenwich at all. But she did live on the outskirts of London, and she knew exactly who I was. Her name was Petra, and it turned out she was originally from Brno, just eight miles up the road from the track where they hold the Czech GP, and she was massively into motorbikes, having first gone to watch them as a little girl with her dad. My confidence came flooding back and I turned on the charm, and when I saw her again at the party later that evening, I convinced her to give me her number.

She told me she was jetting off straight from Valencia to Jamaica for a modelling job, but we agreed to text each other and stay in touch. While she was away I was at a car dealership back home in the UK, looking at a Ferrari – a car I had dreamed of buying ever since I realized that the RS Turbo was not the be-all and end-all of high-performance motoring. This thing was a black F430, which had just come out, and I sent her a picture. She texted me back and said, 'Don't buy a Ferrari, buy a Lamborghini – they're much better.'

I couldn't believe it. Here I was thinking, 'I'm going to get my Ferrari and she's going to be all impressed,' and this girl I'd only met once is telling me to get a Lambo instead!

As it happened, they had a beautiful bright yellow Gallardo in the same garage that was only a couple of months old, with about a thousand miles on the clock. I traded in my 911 there and then and texted Petra back to tell her I'd bought the Lamborghini on her advice. There was no way she couldn't agree to a date after that, was there?

We arranged the date for 18 November and it was absolutely mega. *Get Rich or Die Tryin'*, 50 Cent's album, had been out for a couple of years but I still had it on repeat, and I had it blasting out of the Gallardo when I went to meet her by a roundabout just up the road from a new house I had bought on the Isle of Sheppey. She followed me back to mine and, as soon as she jumped into the car, I reset 'In Da Club' to the beginning, that famous first riff booming out of the speakers: *Den den! Den den! Den den!* I loved that song and so did Petra.

'Right then,' I said. 'I guess seeing as you've driven here and I've got you to myself for the day, I'd better make this a good date. We'll go for a blast about in the car, grab a coffee somewhere then we're going flying. Did I tell you I fly helicopters?'

'Are you serious?' she said.

'Yeah! Come on.'

I picked up a Jet Ranger from Manston, took her for a buzz about, showed her Leeds Castle and the Kent coastline and landed for lunch at a posh spa hotel near Ashford called Eastwell Manor. After that we flew back to Manston and I took her back to my new house. Exactly five years later, on 18 November 2010, we flew back to Eastwell Manor in a helicopter to get married.

Meeting Petra just at that time was the best thing that

could have happened to me, because it happened to coincide with the most difficult period of my professional life. The 2005 season had petered out in MotoGP without any offers coming in for the next one, and even though I had some conversations with Yamaha about going to World Superbikes, which would have been a good opportunity, a proper offer never materialized.

The most attractive proposition that did come in was from Paul Denning, an ex-BSB racer whose dad John owned Crescent Motorcycles down in Verwood near Bournemouth. Paul had given up riding to concentrate on running the Crescent Suzuki team, who had won the BSB title with John Reynolds in 2004 and had now been entrusted to run Suzuki's factory MotoGP effort. The deal the team were offering me included the possibility of doing some testing on the MotoGP bike, if I rode for them in British Superbikes.

I really didn't want to give up on my World Championship dream and come back to BSB yet, but with the possibility of a test on a factory MotoGP bike, I decided to take it. James Haydon would be my teammate. It turned out to be a complete disaster for both of us, and to this day I find it hard to put my finger on exactly why.

For a rider to be fast and successful, there are so many components that need to fall into place, starting with the bike itself, of course. Suzuki had a brand-new GSX-R1000 out and, like any new Superbike, it needed some work to get it up to the speed of the old one, before we could even think about taking it forward. My crew chief was Les Pearson, a good engineer and a good man, but I think he just tried too hard for me, and every time I got on it I felt as if I was riding a completely different machine. For example, I'd mention that the bike was not turning enough, or that it was running wide on the exit of the corner. Les would do his thing and fix whatever was wrong, but it would completely alter the bike in other areas. Finding a set-up that worked was elusive, to say the least.

The other thing a rider needs is a strong team around him, but while Les and I struggled to make the bike work, I was overhearing comments from other team members about us being quickest through the speed trap at the end of the straight, so how bad could the bike really be? Once you have guys doubting you in your own garage, that always spells bad news for a rider and leads to disharmony within the team. I am putting my life on the line out there, and the very least I expect is to win together and lose together. Even though we did bag a victory at Knockhill, when we switched back to the previous season's machine, for too much of that season we were losing.

It didn't help that Paul Denning was off running the MotoGP job full-time, and the BSB effort was being run by a big South African guy called Robert Wicks, who had come from power-boat racing but frankly had no idea about motorbikes. I felt I wasn't being listened to, people within the garage started pointing the finger at each other and there was no clear direction. Paul was the kingpin of that team; without him around, it seemed that nobody else knew what to do, and I ended up taking quite a lot of the flak when things didn't work out. Niall Mackenzie – a successful former Grand Prix rider who had won three consecutive British Superbike titles during the time I had been starting my career in the late Nineties – was brought in to the team in a kind of a consultancy role to try and steady the ship, but by this point the ship had taken on too much water.

Some of the criticism of me was justified, because I probably did come back from MotoGP as a bit of a prima donna. The thing is, I knew what I needed and I knew how I felt. I came back to BSB, looked around and thought, 'What the fuck are you lot doing?' In MotoGP everybody is working for the rider, and whatever the rider says goes. Yet in BSB it was the other way around. Even the tyre man in the team could make a decision and the rider had to follow it. I voiced my opinion and it didn't always go down well.

The last time I had been a BSB rider, I had cleaned up – winning twelve races and only finishing off the podium three times out of twenty-four races. But by the end of 2006 I had just four podiums from the same number of races and finished sixth overall, a massive 224 points behind the champion Ryuichi Kiyonari. The opportunity to test the MotoGP bike never materialized, which was probably a good thing considering the form I was in, and the whole shit show ended in forgettable fashion – literally – when I knocked myself out in a crash at the final round.

Understandably, there weren't exactly many options on the table for 2007, and I started feeling really down. I spoke with Petra and told her I'd had enough. I wasn't enjoying racing, wasn't feeling it at all, and when that thought creeps into your head, it is a very difficult thing to cope with. Jorge Lorenzo has said that he was in a similar place at the end of 2018 when he left Ducati, contemplating retirement, and the thought of it made him depressed. I can certainly relate to that. I didn't want to retire from racing because the thought of it made me sad, but then I wasn't getting any enjoyment out of it, so how could I carry on?

It's hard to say what I would have done without Petra at that point. Prior to meeting her my only focus had been on racing and, when I wasn't doing that, I was pretty loose. I moved from girl to girl, flash car to flash car, flying around all over the place in the helicopter, wasting a load of money doing a bunch of pointless shit with people, most of whom I would later realize weren't important to me. Now I had somebody I wanted to build something with. We bought a house in Spain together, started growing our family with a pair of dogs and a pair of cats, and suddenly I had something to go home for.

I absolutely love dogs, and I went in head first with a handsome 'little' Presa Canario pup – also known as a Canary Mastiff – that we called Tyson, who appropriately grew into a heavyweight, although he was a real gentle giant. Petra and I were head over heels in love with our boy, and very shortly after getting him I agreed to a kitten we'd seen in an advert in a pet shop window – a cross between a Siamese and Burmese. We called him Divvy, and he was a bloody cool cat, an absolute savage. I mean, most people get gifts from their cats like a mouse or a baby bird, but Divvy was so loose he would bring back half-eaten snakes, lizards, rabbits, you name it. Shortly afterwards we added to the pack with an American Staffordshire Terrier called Missy, and then finally Shelby, a little rescue tabby cat that must have been fed growth-stunting pills as a kitten as she never really grew up.

Petra could listen to my issues with racing, but she

couldn't do anything about them. Finding the motivation to rebuild my career from scratch, when I was already in my thirties, would have to come from somewhere else. Thankfully, the one positive to come out of that season with Crescent Suzuki was the relationship I built with Niall Mackenzie.

We were together at a press event at the end of the season and I was asked by a journalist about my greatest achievement in racing. It was the first time I had been forced to reflect on my career at a time when it looked as though it might have run its course. I was just taking a couple of seconds to digest that scary thought when Niall cut in. 'He hasn't had it yet,' he said in his calm Scottish brogue. 'There's too much more to come.' Niall was a person I had always looked up to, both on and off the track, so for him to say that about me when I was at my lowest ebb meant the world. I filled with pride and thought, 'Maybe he's right. I don't want to retire yet, what am I thinking?'

Even with that kind of encouragement, I didn't really know how to go about picking up my career again. It's not as if the offers were rolling in, and motorcycle racing can be a cruel old sport at times. Just a few years previously I was being hailed as the next big thing, likened in the national press to the great Barry Sheene, and now it felt as though everyone thought I'd forgotten how to ride a motorbike altogether.

I ended up speaking to a mate of mine, Paul 'Midlife' Rooney – so nicknamed simply because, unlike the rest of my pals, he was already in his forties – who worked at Sparshatts of Kent, a big Mercedes dealer that had been a personal sponsor of mine back when I first rode for PBM in 2003. When I'd left to go to MotoGP, Birdy had done his typical thing and approached Sparshatts to keep the sponsorship for his team. But I guess business is business, and as well as using their trucks to cart the team trailers around, his dad probably bought up about fifty-odd trucks for the poultry firm.

'Why don't you jump on one of Birdy's Hondas?' Midlife suggested. At first, I wasn't that fussed about the idea. PBM were running privateer machines by now, with backing from the massive Eddie Stobart haulage company, but even with two strong riders on them in Michael Rutter and Michael Laverty in 2006, they'd had an even worse season than me – and that was saying something. Plus, Birdy still owed me money from the last time I rode for him.

With Birdy you always have to wait for your money, always. He jokes around about it but eventually you have to get serious and – in my case – refuse to speak to him until he coughs up. 'Ah sorry, driver, I didn't realize!' he'd laugh. This time, with Midlife acting as a mediator, between Sparshatts and PBM they came up with a package worth considering and I thought, 'You know what? Last time I rode for Paul it was all right. We'll have a go.'

As soon as I signed for PBM, it felt like coming home. Birdy and I were always in touch, not just because he owed me money, and we always had good crack together. Like me, the team were coming off the back of a bad season, but I still believed in them and I knew Birdy would do whatever it took to help me be competitive.

We knew it wouldn't be easy because the BSB grid in

2007 was absolutely packed with top international talent and factory machinery to rival the level in World Superbikes, in particular the Honda, which would be ridden by the defending champion, Ryuichi Kiyonari. I had been impressed by Kiyo from afar when he'd finished runner-up in 2005, and I had seen him close up, albeit not close enough, when he won the title in 2006. It was hard not to be impressed, but as a rival at the time I had to try. My instinct was more to justify his superior performance by putting it down to his bike, which was being run directly out of HRC in Japan, or his Michelin tyres, which were being shipped over for him from France. It wouldn't be until a few years later that I truly appreciated the guy's mercurial talent.

Kiyo's teammate on the factory Honda would be a relatively new kid on the block from Northern Ireland by the name of Jonathan Rea, while there was another hot young talent called Cal Crutchlow teaming up with Chris Walker on the Suzuki, and the likes of future champions Leon Camier and Tommy Hill in there too. Gregorio Lavilla, a top former World Superbike rider who had come over from Spain and won the BSB title himself in 2005, would be back on the factory Ducati alongside Leon Haslam, while my teammate on Birdy's privateer Honda would be another top youngster by the name of Tom Sykes.

When you look back now and consider what those guys have gone on to achieve – numerous World Superbike and Supersport titles between them, and even MotoGP wins in Cal's case – that was a seriously talented field. Add in experienced names like Rutter, Haydon and Plater, and the competition was tougher than I had ever known it in BSB, but that was exactly the motivation I needed.

The year started well, and after the dramas with the Suzuki the previous season, I was relieved to click with the bike and the team – including Sykesy – straight away. We probably got more preseason testing done than anybody else, and I even managed to secure some factory Öhlins front forks from the factory Yamaha World Superbike team; they immediately felt good from the minute we bolted them into the Honda.

In the very first race of the season at Brands Hatch, I was already up there near the front, mixing with the factory boys and eventually beating Stalker to fourth place after an epic battle. I remember my overriding feeling after that race being, 'Thank fuck!' I had been longing to be competitive again, and now I knew I could be there from the very first round of the season.

Every one of that crop of young British riders was good, as they have gone on to prove, but in my opinion Jonathan was the best. I'd had some close races with him the previous season when he was on the Red Bull Honda and I knew he was going to be fast. Coming from a strong motocross background, he had the full skill set, and his ability to adapt in riding the bike at different kinds of tracks, in any conditions, was amazing. Added to that the fact he was so young and so fit, I knew he had all the attributes to be a top rider. So, even from the start of 2007, he had become that rival I kept in my mind when I was training, using him as the focus to keep me motivated in the gym and on my pushbike.

Jonathan actually took his first ever BSB win during that 2007 season, in the sixth round at Mondello Park in Ireland – a tight, undulating track full of second-gear hairpins and short straights packed into a relatively small piece of land just west of Dublin – which also happens to be one of my fondest memories of that whole year. I liked Mondello, and had set the lap record the last time I was there in 2003, but it was a wet weekend throughout practice so nobody really knew what to expect on race day. We took a little gamble with our gear ratios after warm-up for the first race, and I got a good jump from sixth on the grid, sneaking up the inside of Crutchlow and Karl Harris into the tight first turn, before settling into fourth behind Jonathan, Kiyo and the early leader, Leon Haslam. After getting past Kiyo at half distance, lap nine of eighteen, I eventually made a move on JR on lap twelve – through one of the left-handers where he was taking a more open line than me – and quickly reeled in Leon, setting a new lap record that was two and a half seconds faster than my old one. I piled the pressure on Leon for the last few laps but he had the edge on his Ducati and we had to settle for second place.

I got an even better start in race two, jumping up to third place by turn one, and when Jonathan nudged Leon out of the way in front of me on the fifth lap, I took my chance to dive through too before quickly nipping underneath Jonathan for the lead. Another lap record on the following lap stretched the lead group out and, as some of the guys battled away behind us, Jonathan and I went faster and faster at the front and opened a gap.

It was a fantastic battle, but with five laps to go Jonathan's pace was stronger than mine and he made a move that I couldn't respond to, beating me fair and square to take the win. When we stood together on the podium, I told him to soak it up and enjoy it, because it was sure to be the first of many. I know it's easy to say now that he's gone on to become a multiple World Superbike champion, but I could tell he was the real deal and I meant every word that I said.

I would have preferred to make Jonathan wait a bit longer for his next wins, but they duly came next time out with a double at Knockhill, and then we were back on the podium together again in the following round when he took another win at Oulton Park. Finally, in the ninth round of the championship at Mallory Park at the end of July, it was my turn to take the top step. Once again, I had to start from the second row of the grid but, after making up a few positions on the first lap, I was able to nick Walker for third place when he edged slightly wide on the exit of the famous Shaw's Hairpin – the tightest corner in the whole championship – at half-race distance. A couple of laps later I did a carbon-copy move on Jonathan, and when Kiyo crashed out of the lead in front of me, I was left to manage the gap over Jonny and take one of the most memorable wins of my career.

That was PBM's first win in over two years, and their first ever as a privateer team, which made it extra special. It also proved to be our only win that season, but we eventually finished up with ten podiums, which was way more than the team had managed the previous season. Everybody was made up with it, but I wanted more, much more. My ideal scenario was to go back to World Superbikes, maybe even with Birdy, but when he insisted they couldn't do it, it became pretty clear that it would be in my interest to start looking elsewhere.

The other funny thing about that win at Mallory was that Birdy wasn't actually there because he was off competing in a rally event somewhere, but applauding me under the podium was the GSE racing team boss Colin Wright. That wasn't unusual, given that his rider Leon Haslam was up there too, but I noticed Colin giving me a smile and a wink and then he even started turning up to clap me at the podium when Leon and Gregorio weren't there. It was Petra who noticed it first because she'd worked for Colin before as a grid girl and got to know him pretty well. She was convinced he was lining up an offer.

I didn't think too much about it until the end of the season, when Petra and I had already headed out to Spain for the winter, and the phone rang. 'The new 1098 Ducati is coming out and I want you to come and ride it for me,' Colin said in his no-nonsense style. Colin was a notoriously difficult guy to work for, by all accounts, known for taking zero shit from anyone, but I already liked his directness and – obviously – I was interested.

It was around this time that a good friend Terry Rymer – a former British Superbike Champion, World Superbike race winner and World Endurance Champion – had offered to start helping me out a little on a management level. 'Too Tall Tel', as he was known due to his six-foot two-inch frame, was a fellow native of Kent and we had always got on great, so I suggested he tried to broker a deal with Colin and he ended up looking after me for a couple of seasons.

The newly launched Ducati 1098 was going to be the new greatest thing, famously boasting the highest torque-to-weight ratio for a production sport bike at the time, and was a massive step forward from the outgoing 999 model.

It was absolutely stunning to look at – a proper Ducati, the Ferrari of motorcycles – and the lap times being posted by Troy Bayliss in World Superbike testing suggested it was going to be every bit as fast as it looked.

To jump off a privateer Honda onto this weapon was an amazing opportunity but, knowing what Birdy was like, I was really worried about telling him. I told Colin that I needed a little time, and I spent a week or so building up to it before eventually calling Paul, deciding I would just be upfront about the whole thing. The fact was that he couldn't match my ambition and take me to World Super-bikes, so surely he couldn't be too bothered about me jumping onto a more competitive bike in BSB?

'Listen, mate, I've been offered another ride,' I told him.

'Oh, right. And what the fuck makes you think you're going to go better on somebody else's bike?' It was typical Birdy.

'Look . . . we've had a good year, we've beaten the factory HRC boys a couple of times, we ain't done too bad. But this is a chance to ride the new 1098, Paul. I'm planning to accept it but I wanted to tell you first, before I call Colin back.'

'OK, driver, no problem. See you later.'

Petra had been watching me talk. 'Well? What did he say?' She was expecting me to tell her it had been a total disaster. To be honest, I was too, so the way he'd just accepted it caught me a bit by surprise. Could it be that the Birdman was actually maturing at last? I phoned Colin and told him I was happy to go ahead. 'Great,' he said. 'Come over to England and we'll sign the contract, get a story in *Motor Cycle News* and get cracking.'

I met Colin at Stansted airport, shook hands and signed the contract, and a few days later the story was in *MCN*. A week or so later there was another big Superbike story in the paper, only this time it was a huge spread announcing that Paul Bird Motorsport had signed Gregorio Lavilla to replace me and they were going to World Superbikes as a privateer Honda team.

I honestly couldn't believe what I was reading. There were these quotes from Birdy saying I was too old, too demanding, too overrated. He said he had no intention of going to World Superbikes with me, and told everybody how much I had been paid and how much he was going to pay Lavilla; that I was just all about money and Lavilla was twice the rider I was. He put the boot in, basically, and it was completely out of order. By that point I'd won him a championship and however many BSB races. I thought, 'You arsehole! Why would you do that? When I am being straight up and honest and trying to act like a gentleman, why would you do the complete opposite?'

But I took it on the chin and thought, 'Fuck it, what will be will be.' Besides, I had bigger things to worry about.

17

Strong to the Finish

My dad had been having problems with his throat and voice box for a few years and, even though he'd never been diagnosed with anything as serious as cancer, in 2003 he was told by doctors that if he didn't stop smoking it was going to kill him.

By then he had been coming towards retirement age, and his work on the railways had been drying up for a couple of years, so he'd actually started coming to watch me race a bit. All I'd really known him do was work his nuts off to keep a roof over our heads, so having him around felt a little unusual at first, but I quickly got used to his little ways around the motorhome and I came to love having him around.

Dad had always been incredibly proud of my racing ever since I started out in motocross, and would talk the hind legs off a donkey around anyone that displayed even the slightest hint of interest. He and my mum used to sit down together on the sofa to watch my races on the television, although Mum would often get so nervous she'd have to tape them and wait until I was sitting next to her in the house before watching, just to make sure I was definitely back safe.

Despite what the doctors had told him about his throat, Dad was still sneaking in the odd crafty fag, which really made me angry, and at Brands Hatch, when I won the World Superbike double, it all kicked off. As I came back from the podium on my scooter with the winner's trophy, I came up through the paddock tunnel and saw him. I stopped to have a quick chat and to hand him the trophy to bring back to the motorhome for me. We were both absolutely made up with life but then I looked down and saw a cigarette in his hand. It wasn't one of his roll-ups, but a conventional cigarette, which he never normally went near.

I couldn't believe what I was seeing. This man who I loved so much, who had cared for me and brought me up, had been told, 'Don't do that again because it's going to kill you,' and yet here he was, doing it anyway, on the most special day of my life up to that point. I absolutely lost my shit with him and ripped the trophy back out of his hands. 'You might as well keep walking all the way back home from here,' I told him. 'If you're prepared to throw your life away over one fucking miserable cigarette, then I don't want you around me.'

That conversation is the biggest regret of my life. It took six months before we spoke to each other again – six months I would do anything to get back now. In fact, I

Above: Celebrating second place in Misano in Italy, which is as good as it got for my debut season in World Superbikes in 2009.

Below: 2010, racing against Jonathan Rea in Valencia for the World Superbikes. I didn't know it at the time, but it would be my last year in World Superbikes. To date, Jonathan has won five back-to-back World Superbike Championships!

I spent 2011 with HM Plant Honda, putting to bed all the naysayers who said I couldn't win on a four-cylinder bike.

Above: Celebrating a win with Zack during the 2012 BSB Championship.

Below: This time the Showdown rounds went in my favour
and I won my third BSB Championship.

2013, I needed a bit of help to get on my bike (*left*) at Silverstone after injuring myself in a practice lap. Me and great friend and rival Alex Lowes won a race apiece that weekend (*below*) in two of the closest races BSB have ever seen.

Above: Celebrating the 2014
BSB Championship.

Right: Sharing a
moment with my
2011 teammate,
great friend and
2014 championship
rival Ryuichi Kiyonari,
the second most
successful BSB
rider ever.

Left: I started the 2015 Championship well, but by mid-season Josh
Brookes turned into Josh Rossi
and was practically unbeatable. It
bugged me so much we ended up
changing manufacturer for 2016.

Above: Boring my good mate John McGuinness by the looks
of things during the 2016 season.

Bottom left: Taking the race win and the championship in 2016.

Bottom right: TV interviews after sealing the championship
with my two kids by my side.

Above: Leon Haslam came out to congratulate me after
I unexpectedly took the 2017 BSB Championship.

Below: Celebrating with circuit boss Jonathan Palmer (*left*) and race director
Stuart Higgs (*right*), both dripping wet after I filled them in with champagne.

Above: As it stands, my last and eighty-fifth race win in BSB,
only three weeks before the crash.

Below: One of the best days of my life. I'd literally just flown home
from hospital to surprise the kids after they returned from school.

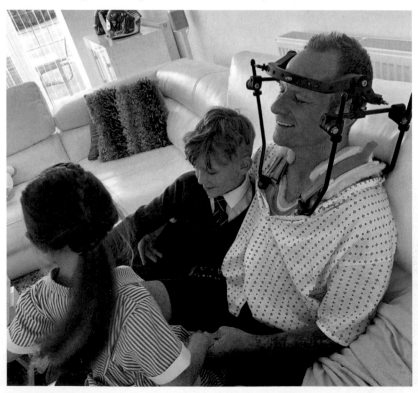

wouldn't even be greedy and ask for six months. Just enough time to tell him how much I love him and to show him my children, that'd do me. That's how much I miss that man.

By the time we did make up he had officially retired from the railways, and I got him a little part-time job at Sparshatts as a groundsman – cutting the grass, trimming the hedges and generally making the place look tidy – and he loved doing that in the week and then coming away again with me at the weekends to watch me race.

One day I caught him sitting in my car, looking in one of my cycling magazines. 'What you looking at that for?' I said. 'I don't recall ever even seeing you ride a bicycle. It's not like you're ever going to ride one now, is it?' His voice had gone all funny because of the problems with his throat, but he grunted something back at me.

'You want a pushbike?' I said. 'All right then, I'll get you one.' I bought him this new bike, a helmet, and all the bits and pieces that went with it, and he was absolutely delighted – he pottered about all over the place on that thing. I've still got it now at my house in Spain, fitted with the kids' seats from when they were little. Even now, it's always a little treat for them to go out on 'Grandad's bike'.

I got to know my dad more in the last couple of years of his life than I ever did before that, yet still most of what I know about him has come from Petra, believe it or not. She used to spend hours chatting to him and he opened up to her about all sorts. He even told her that before he met my mum he'd actually got engaged to a girl in Hong Kong while he was stationed there in the army. He'd had to come back to England but promised her he'd return one day and they'd get married. He knew, really, that he could never make it back out there and it broke his heart. When he came back to England he met my mum and the rest is history.

It's funny, because he always used to go on about wanting to visit Hong Kong, and I never knew why. When he was eventually diagnosed with cancer, in 2005, I even promised him I'd send him out there. I didn't know anything about his nearly bride, but if either he or Petra had told me the full story at the time, I would have understood. Dad was a good man and I could see him wanting to go back to find this woman and say sorry, to put the thing to rest. Unfortunately, the illness would get to him more quickly than even the doctors had predicted, and he never got the chance.

Petra and I had started trying for a family, and I was doing absolutely everything I could to give my dad the motivation to keep fighting. Part of his lung had collapsed because of the cancer and he'd got an infection. I was telling him, 'Come on, Popeye, it's not time to give up now – Petra and I are trying to make you a grandad! Stick around, you old bastard!'

Towards the end he started getting really grumpy and impatient with my buoyant, never-give-up attitude. I would try dragging him from pillar to post to keep him out and about, but sometimes he just wasn't well enough. I wanted my dad; it wasn't time for him to go.

Everybody who knew my dad liked him – you couldn't help it, he was such a character. It's hard to describe but he just had this unique way of making the best of situations and bringing an air of calm with him. He'd become a proper part of the Stobart Honda team in 2007, but he was laid up in Medway Hospital for the final round of the year at Brands Hatch, so the whole team came down to see him, including my teammate Tom Sykes, which Dad absolutely loved. Dad always said Tom reminded him of Shaggy from *Scooby Doo*, so the boys brought him a little toy Shaggy figure as a gift. Bless him, he nearly pissed his bed laughing when they gave it to him. I will always be grateful to Tom and the boys for that.

Unfortunately, there was no amount of spinach in the world that could save my Popeye from 'the big C'. On 7 February 2008, my mum, my dad's sister Pat, Petra and I were gathered around Dad in their bedroom at home. Dad hadn't so much as opened his eyes for days and it was so tough to sit there looking at him, trying to be chirpy and keep everyone's spirits up, knowing that the inevitable was going to happen soon.

Every second felt like an hour, every minute a day, and by nine o'clock that particular evening I felt like I'd been sitting with him for a lifetime. During one quiet moment, when the others went out and I was alone with him, I broke down. I started welling up and begged him to go off to a proper sleep, to just slip away and get away from the pain he was riddled with. I just wanted him to be at peace. I took his hand tightly and leaned into him. 'Listen to me, Popeye, listen to me,' I kept saying. 'Stop being such a stubborn old bastard now, enough's enough.'

I heard my mum, Petra and my aunt Pat coming back up the stairs and pulled myself together before they got to the room. 'Come on, you,' I said to Mum, clearing my throat. 'Let's take you to get some shopping, you've not left the house in days.' Aunt Pat said she'd stay behind and watch him. 'Right, Popeye,' I piped up again. 'Mum needs some shopping. I'm going to take her and Petra to get you a few beers and some milk – I don't want no playing up or clearing off over the pub while we're gone.'

Mum and Aunt Pat laughed. It had broken the sombre atmosphere a little, and then all of a sudden Dad opened his eyes. It was as though he'd heard the laughter. He stared at me – not blinking, not moving, just staring. At first, I was absolutely over the moon. 'There you are, you sneaky old bastard.' I smiled at him. I repeated what I'd just said to him about taking Mum out, and he just stared straight back, his eyes not diverting to anybody else in the room. He kept looking, and I just about got to the point where I couldn't take any more, I was about to fall apart. 'Right,' I said. 'Stop staring at me now, I'm off to get Mum sorted. We'll be back in half an hour or so – behave yourself.'

It can only have been a quarter of an hour later that we were wandering around the supermarket, throwing some bits into a trolley for my mum, and my phone rang. It was Aunt Pat. 'He's gone to sleep, Shane, he's resting now.' I broke down. I'll never forget those words.

He was a good dad, old Popeye. Now, half the reason I act the way I do with my kids is because of the way I miss him. I want them to be close to me, I want them to be my best friends. I want them to argue over who comes with Dad and who stays with Mum. I am so hands-on with my kids and I wouldn't want it any other way. All I knew was my dad working to make ends meet. British Superbike racers don't get paid millions, but what I do have is a lot of free time and much more money than my parents ever had.

Over the last few years I have loved nothing more than racing on a Sunday, smashing out a couple of wins with my family by my side, seeing them all proud, and then no matter what time we get home, I am up at 7.30 a.m. to do the school run. Nothing makes me happier than that, and even when I come back from a weekend covering World Superbikes with Eurosport – it might be two or three in the morning when I arrive home – but, sure as eggs are eggs, I'll be taking the kids to school later that morning, spending every waking moment that I can with them.

Only the good die young. That's what they say, isn't it? Well, Popeye was 67 years young when he died and the irony of his age wasn't lost on me. From that moment on, there could definitely never be any other number on the front of my bike, and even though I would never run the number 1, I was more determined than ever to earn the right.

In 2008, I would get the chance to do so, with one of the best team managers I ever had.

18

The Wright Stuff

It may not have looked this way after the results I'd posted in 2006 and 2007, but I knew I had come back from MotoGP a better rider. When you have ridden the most advanced prototypes in the world, you get an understanding of how good a motorcycle can be, so when you get onto a production bike you know what you should be aiming for. It could be a double-edged sword because I could never really have what I wanted, but at least by aiming for it I could get the absolute maximum out of what I had.

All I needed was a machine with potential, and the new Ducati 1098 was that bike. Being a new model, ours came quite late from the factory and I could barely handle the anticipation after I watched the first round of the World Superbike season in Qatar, where Troy Bayliss won the first race from Max Biaggi, with Rubén Xaus in fourth place – each of them riding a 1098. Our debut with it was at

Almería and, even with the base setting that my Italian engineer Luca Ferracoli fired in to the bike, I immediately felt at one with it. Our lap times were incredible and the bike just didn't seem to do anything wrong; it was as if it was created purposefully for my riding style. We had to run control-spec Pirelli tyres, which I'd never tried before, but even then it was like the bike and I spoke the same language.

The best example I can give is the third corner of the track at Almería, a downhill left-hander that you approach in third gear at around 110–120 mph before braking hard, back-shifting to second and then throwing the bike in to the turn. The change of direction was fast but the bike was so stable, it was as though I was completely connected to it. I had so much feel for the front tyre through the handle-bars that I found myself running in to that corner faster and faster with every lap. The electronics package enabled me to rail the turn on a high amount of partial throttle, and the side grip and feel from the rear tyre when transitioning towards the exit of the turn was just amazing. In that one section of track alone I was a full second per lap faster than my new teammate Leon Camier. I couldn't believe Ducati had built a chassis that felt like a prototype in terms of agility, grip and stability, while still managing to incorporate the forgiveness and flex you get from a street bike. I was in love with the thing and I knew this was going to be a good year for us.

The first round of the season at Brands Hatch in April was actually snowed off, bizarrely, so the first races ended up being round two at Thruxton. Despite my misfortune there over the years, I still loved the place, and the twin-cylinder 1098 was purpose-built for the kind of fast, flowing track where you don't need that four-cylinder grunt to get you out of the corners. Riding a Ducati at Thruxton I could always conserve my tyres and be strong at the end of the race. Everything I was good at, the 1098 was good at too.

I won the first race quite comfortably by a couple of seconds from Cal Crutchlow on the Honda, and then the second race was red-flagged following an incident after about five laps and restarted over a shorter distance. This time I got held up for the first part of the race by Tom Sykes on his Suzuki, and by the time I got past him Cal was away at the front for his first win in BSB.

Seeing Cal close up at that point in his career, it was clear that he was talented and he was going somewhere, but I was never convinced he quite had the ability to back up the amount of confidence he had in himself. Saying that, I'm sure that as Great Britain's only MotoGP race winner of our generation, he might beg to differ! Cal has gone on to have a fantastic career and I'm delighted for him because I got on with him so well; he was often in and out of the motor-home asking me for advice, and as a friend I was more than happy to give it. But in terms of natural talent, I honestly didn't rate him as highly as Jonathan Rea and, as such, I didn't see him as a rival in quite the same way.

We did the double at Oulton Park and should have had another one in the rescheduled 'round one' at Brands Hatch, when I won the first race and felt I had the measure of Cal in the second one, only for the red flag to come out with a lap to go and hand him the win with me just 0.1 seconds behind him. Still, altogether I had four wins and two second places from the first six races, and the organizers reacted by imposing a ten-kilo weight penalty on the 1098.

I was fuming, but I channelled my frustration into my training, and for the first time in my life I went on a diet. By the time the next event came around at Donington Park I had lost a couple of kilos off my bodyweight and we went out there and smoked another double win, beating the local favourite Leon Haslam twice. It was turning into that kind of year.

Colin Wright ran a tight ship and his most important quality from a rider's perspective was that he always had my back. He was honest and to the point, and if anything needed doing it got done. In people like Colin – or the Harris brothers earlier on in my career – I found like-minded professionals with the same goals and drive that any top racer must have. Every rider understands that it is impossible to win every race, but these are the kind of guys who back you up on the days when things aren't going well, not just on the days you smoke a double. A good team wins together and loses together, and when a rider has that kind of support it means they can continue to work to the best of their ability, without the undue pressure that the odd bad result or setback can bring.

Take the fifth round of the 2008 season at Snetterton, for example, when race direction black-flagged me for dropping oil during practice and reckoned I'd ignored them and continued riding. When I got back to the pits I was summoned to race control – a tiny little building at the top of pit lane – to be disciplined by the race director, Dave Francis.

While I was getting changed I got a one-word text message from Colin that simply read 'Meeting.' Ask any rider in the paddock who has worked with Colin and they'll tell you: that word usually means bad news. 'What's your fucking story?' he demanded when I stepped into the team truck. 'I saw the black flag so I pulled over to the side of the track,' I explained. 'I looked down at the bike, checked the belly pan and there was no oil. I couldn't see a problem with it so I rode the bike on the inside of the track to the end of the back straight, stayed off line, done my bit and got back.'

'Right. That's it, is it?'

'There's nothing else to it, Colin.'

'OK.'

Together we went marching up to race control and Colin barged straight in ahead of me, giving them my version of events and saying that he stood by my decision, which they eventually accepted. I really respected the fact that he'd asked me for an explanation, listened to me, took it on board and then went in and stood up for me. Colin was great to work for like that, and I was thrilled to be riding for him.

That weekend at Snetterton I finished second to Leon Camier by 0.092 seconds in race one and beat him by 2.5 seconds in race two. Another win and a second place at Mallory Park in round six meant we had eight wins and four second places from the first twelve races, and at the halfway point of the season I was leading by almost a hundred points over Crutchlow. By that point, we had such a strong lead that it made sense to start riding with my head, score some consistent podiums and top fives and let the championship take care of itself. As a result, the wins suddenly became harder to come by.

To be honest, the fact that Troy Bayliss had announced he would be retiring from the sport and leaving a vacant ride in the factory Ducati World Superbike was also playing on my mind. I had probably started to think too much about that and about making sure of the championship, rather than just winning races, but eventually we got the title boxed off with a pair of podiums in the penultimate round at Silverstone. Again, I probably rode a little bit too conservatively that weekend, but it got the job done and I was over the moon. A double win in the final round at Brands capped off a perfect season, finishing 117 points clear of Leon Haslam, who had put together a really strong second half of the season to edge out Crutchlow for the runner-up spot.

Meanwhile, our success on the 1098 had rekindled some serious interest from the factory World Superbike Xerox Ducati team for 2009. Troy was keen for me to get the ride, and the deal I so desperately wanted was almost done, but things went a little quiet until we eventually got the call to say they'd signed Nori Haga instead. Nori had won a bunch of races that season on the Yamaha and finished third in the WSB championship, but to say I was gutted to miss out on a factory seat with Ducati would be an understatement.

Even though they'd signed Nori, Ducati were keen for me to go to WSB and said that they'd back me in a satellite team instead, run by an Italian ex-rider called Marco Borciani and sponsored by Sterilgarda, a huge Italian milk and dairy produce company. In 2008 it had been a well-funded team, running Max Biaggi and Rubén Xaus, who took a win and a bunch of podiums between them that season.

Max had agreed a switch to Aprilia, who were reigniting their interest in big sports bikes with a brand-new, trick-looking Superbike called the RSV4, so the idea was that I would slot into his side of the Sterilgarda garage and everything would be great. Terry did the deal again but I told Colin Wright what was happening myself and I was really straight with him. Another crack at World Super-bikes was something I could not turn down and he knew that.

I was so pumped to get another shot at my dream of being a World Champion. I'd just beaten the likes of Crutchlow, Haslam, Sykes and Camier to a BSB title, and I knew I was as fast as anyone on a Superbike. In MotoGP, where all things aren't equal, achieving my dream had proved impossible, but with a competitive ride in World Superbikes, I felt this had to be my time to finally shine.

Three weeks after the BSB season had ended I flew out to Portimão, a brand-new track on the Algarve in Portugal, for a post-season test with my new team, just a couple of days after the final round of the World Superbike season had taken place there. That weekend had been the first time the track had ever been used, and I had watched excitedly on television at home as Troy Bayliss officially signed off from his amazing WSB career with a double victory on the factory 1098.

Meanwhile, Rubén Xaus had crashed his brains out all weekend trying to learn the track on the Sterilgarda bike, and just about totalled every fairing and spare part the team had. They cobbled something together for me to test, but the bike was completely crash-damaged – it had gravel rash on every panel, there was barely a straight bit of metal on the thing and it was practically held together by duct tape. Colin Wright's GSE bikes had been absolutely immaculate – probably the smartest and best-prepared machines that I ever got to ride – whereas this thing was probably the worst-looking pile of metal I'd ridden since I started club racing. Borciani opened his palms and gestured towards the bike. 'I am sorry, this is not my normal standard of motorcycle, but Rubén has crashed everything we have. We will be getting new bikes for the new season and they won't look like this, don't worry.'

I couldn't help but look down pit lane at Ben Spies – who had signed for the factory Yamaha team after winning the AMA title, basically America's version of BSB – on his brand-spanking-new, carbon-shod YZF-R1, wondering where I had gone wrong.

On television the track had looked like a nightmare of a place to learn, with so many blind crests, cambers and drop-offs – the kind of thing that you usually can't appreciate properly on TV – but as soon as I rode the place for the first time I absolutely fell in love. It is hard not to, from the moment you charge flat out between the huge grand-stands either side of the long pit straight at 190 mph before plunging steeply downhill and grabbing hard on the brakes for turn one. All the way around the rest of the lap you are fighting wheelies and wheelspin through fast changes of direction in third and fourth gear, diving into downhill hairpins that change camber in mid-corner, before dropping off what feels like the edge of the world through a steep

downhill third-gear left-hander that has since been appropriately named after one of the bravest riders our country
ever produced – the late Craig Jones, an incredibly talented
young lad who tragically lost his life in a crash during the
World Supersport race at Brands Hatch in 2008, when he
was riding for a team owned by the Portimão circuit
owners.

Fighting to keep the front tyre in contact with the track
through Jonesy's is an absolutely unreal rush, and it is
followed by another steep climb back uphill before more
blind crests, drops and cambers, all the way to a final
corner that you drive through in fourth gear, the bike
slightly sideways and pinned to the apex as you try to pick
it up off the edge of the rear tyre and gain drive grip
without running out of track on the exit – something you
really don't want to be doing at 140 mph. Another crest as
you snick fifth gear over the start-finish line makes the bike
want to wheelie again as the needle creeps back up towards
190 mph, and then the whole rollercoaster ride starts all
over again.

I was in my absolute element around that place, and
after something like twenty-odd whirlwind laps on Borciani's patched-up 1098, I went faster than Spies, faster
than Xaus and even faster than Biaggi had managed over
the whole race weekend, and by the end of the test I was
the outright fastest rider there. Borciani promised me
everything would be rebuilt over the winter and, with
backing from Ducati, we would come back brand new
after Christmas.

The money wasn't great with Marco, but it was OK and
the deal was done; it was announced that I was finally

going to World Superbikes. I was super-proud because I had come back from losing my ride in MotoGP, spent a couple of tough years in BSB, and turned my career around. The absolute cherry on the 2008 cake was becoming a dad for the first time. Petra gave birth to our son Zack on 20 November in Figueres, the birthplace of the famous Spanish artist Salvador Dalí. Little did I know how much that bundle of joy would help me through the next two seasons of my career.

I worked hard over the winter break and when we came back for the first preseason test of 2009, also at Portimão, at the beginning of the new year, I ended that on top of the timesheets as well. Now I was really buzzing about the start of the new season, feeling convinced I was ready to challenge for my first world title.

The next test would take place just a week before the first race of the new season at Phillip Island, a beautiful island just off the coast near Melbourne. It is one of my favourite tracks in the world because of its insanely fast, flowing layout. If you mixed the twists and elevation changes of Brands Hatch with the flat-out speed of Thruxton, you'd get Phillip Island. It was a track I couldn't wait to race at, having missed the opportunity in MotoGP in 2004 because of my wrist injury and also in 2005, when Honda made the late call to give Chris Vermeulen my ride on the V5.

Phillip Island also features one of my favourite corners of any track in the whole world, since named after the MotoGP World Champion Casey Stoner, who had come a long way since the days of our paddock scooter races. As you approach turn three in third or fourth gear, the track drops away with a little bit of negative camber, and to get the bike to turn well through there you have to make the rear wheel spin, like a speedway bike. That is not easy on any motorcycle, especially in fourth gear, but Casey did it better than anybody, so you can fully understand why they named the corner after him. Getting Stoner Corner right – spinning up on the lock stop in fourth gear – is the biggest buzz you could ever imagine on a motorcycle.

Most significantly, having the final preseason test at the venue of the first race weekend gives all the teams a chance to make use of the warm conditions in the Australian summer, and to save money by avoiding the logistics of holding a separate test somewhere else. So, when Borciani called me just a few days before we were due to fly to say that he didn't have the budget to do the test, the alarm bells started ringing.

19

Losing My Milk Money

It turned out that when Max Biaggi had left Borciani's team, so had all the cash. The series organizers at the time, the Flammini group, had been subsidizing the team to run Max – in a similar way to Dorna's deal with me in MotoGP – so they had pulled their funding, and most of the Sterilgarda milk money went with Max too. My new teammate was supposed to be an Italian kid called Alex Polita, the previous year's European Superstock Champion, but his sponsor pulled out at the eleventh hour and the team were left without a pot to piss in.

Borciani managed to cobble together enough of a budget to run me as a single rider, but we were on the back foot from the start and clearly weren't going to have the resources to compete with the factory teams. We finally got to Phillip Island in time for the first round, but effectively two days behind everybody else in terms of track time. I rode my nuts off but the bike was so lacking on top speed down the long Phillip Island front straight that it felt as if it had a Superstock engine in it, not a Superbike one. I ended up crashing out of both races trying to make up the deficit.

Physically, apart from a hand injury, I was all right, but that whole experience was mentally damaging. How could things have turned to shit so quickly, when just a couple of months beforehand I had been dominating at the Portimão test and gearing myself up for a crack at the World Superbike title? I couldn't get my head around it.

It didn't help that it was also our first time leaving Zack, our beautiful little boy, who had come along and changed our lives just a few months before. It was hard to justify leaving him at home for the week with Petra's parents while we went to the other side of the world for me to race a motorbike, and then to come back with literally nothing to show for it. This was not in the script.

Phillip Island had gone so badly that I couldn't help but doubt myself and everybody around me, but we went to Qatar for the second round and I qualified on the second row, which was a relief. I had a big battle in the first race for fifth place with Carlos Checa, who was teammate to Jonathan Rea on the factory Honda, which was not where I wanted to be, but pretty good under the circumstances. Some of the other Brits would joke about how easy it was to slipstream and pass my bike compared to other Ducatis, and one even commented that my bike sounded so flat and lazy it was as if I was constantly in the wrong gear.

Unfortunately, other than a second place in mixed conditions at Misano and a couple of fourths at Donington Park and Brno, that was about as good as it got for the rest of the season. Because Borciani had no money, early in the season he decided he couldn't afford to continue using Brembo brakes, which were the best, although at the time we weren't even getting the top-spec ones that the factory guys were using. My 2008 GSE bike had had the top-spec Brembos and braking had never been an issue, but in 2009 I would often have complaints about their consistency and brake pad feeling.

Marco decided to change to a manufacturer that would supply their products for free, but for the rest of the season we had issues with the front brakes binding. So many times when the front wheel went light on the exit of a corner, the brakes would bind so much that it would lock the front wheel and nearly cause me to crash. In my home round at Donington we found a decent feeling with the bike, and I was running in the lead pack with ease – on for a podium at the very least – but halfway through the race the binding got so bad exiting the Melbourne Hairpin that it was hard to stay upright.

The mechanics were also grumbling because we had no new parts to work with, and every weekend was a massive effort for everybody, with no real reward at the end of it. A situation like that soon leads to disharmony in a team, and even though it wasn't really anybody's fault, people inevitably ended up pointing the finger. I myself had a big fallout with one of the crew chiefs at Brno, where I lost out on another certain podium to Carlos Checa because I simply didn't have the horsepower to make any kind of move on him. This cheeky bastard had the nerve to ask me why I hadn't tried to make an overtake on Carlos. 'You give me a bike that can even get alongside him and I'll make a pass – I'm not a fucking magician!' I ranted. 'You're a mechanic, so you concentrate on fixing the bike and don't ever try telling me how to ride it!'

I was annoyed because I wasn't getting what I'd been promised. I knew that the bike was a pile of shit; on top of that I wasn't getting paid. Nothing was going to plan. I was riding on the limit but not getting anything for it. Every time I went out to race I felt like a boxer going into the ring, fighting his heart out, but then getting knocked out by one lucky punch. It was completely demoralizing.

At least for the European races I had Zack with me and Petra in the motorhome. He was at the age where he was just starting to smile and gurgle, and nothing meant more to me than seeing his little face at the end of each day. I could have had the shittiest day – an oil leak and a crash, ended up fifteenth, whatever – but it didn't matter: Zack didn't know about it. When I walked into the motorhome, closed the door behind me, and that little bundle of fun smiled up at me, none of it mattered. Prior to Zack, I would have brought all that stress back in with me, putting a strain on me and Petra.

Becoming a father meant that my family's happiness became more important to me than anything in racing, though that didn't mean I lost any of my drive. I could remember coming up through racing as a young single lad, thinking I was the most focused rider on the planet, ready to attack and take no prisoners. I would look at my rivals – the likes of John Reynolds or Steve Hislop, who had families – and wonder how they could possibly be as committed as I was. They had mouths to feed, other people to worry about, but my daily focus was 100 per cent on making myself a better, fitter, stronger rider.

I knew people would be looking at my performances in World Superbikes and assume it was fatherhood getting in the way. But, in reality, my experience of having Zack was that life just got better in every way. If anything, it made me stronger, more determined than I had ever been, and the fact that I had that little mouth to feed was one of the reasons I stuck it out as long as I did in World Superbikes. I truly believed I would be a World Champion one day and that it was only a matter of time before everything clicked into place for me to do that.

Giovanni Crupi, who would later become my crew chief in BSB, was my data engineer that season; he was one guy who I felt was always in my corner. The last race of the season was at Portimão, and Giovanni did something with my engine control unit that gave me the same rpm as the factory team. I qualified second behind Spies, finished fourth in race one and then led race two for the first ten laps.

Jonathan and I got away and had a fantastic battle, passing each other for the lead, but I kept losing the front and towards the end I could barely steer the bike. Trying to force a motorbike to go where it doesn't want to go when you are fully leaned over in the middle of a corner is a really good way to fall off the thing.

I was determined to hang on in there, to finish the season with a win and show the whole world I couldn't be broken, but the problem with the front got worse and worse, to the point that I seriously contemplated pulling in. With a couple of laps to go, a podium was still on the cards, but Biaggi was lapping a lot faster than me and he nicked it off me right at the end. It later turned out that I had a cracked front wheel that was causing the tyre to slowly deflate. I was devastated to miss out on the podium because of something so fundamental.

Ben Spies was absolutely brilliant that year. Fair play to him – he cleaned up, winning at circuits he had never been to before and taking the championship by six points from Haga, earning himself a deserved move to MotoGP on a really competitive satellite Yamaha. The guy was focused, dedicated and professional in his approach, and I truly rated him as a rider, but did I feel he was better than me? Absolutely not. With the might of the Yamaha factory team behind him and a brand-new R1, what chance did I have against that? You don't take a knife to a gun fight – especially not with a Texan!

Towards the end of the season I was approached by a friend of Borciani's called Genesio Bevilacqua, the owner of a big ceramics company in Italy called Ceramica Althea. Genesio was going to run a proper satellite Ducati team in 2010, and he pretty much came into the Sterilgarda garage at the end of the year and said, 'I want you to ride for me.'

'OK,' I said, 'let's talk about it.' We exchanged numbers and I felt happy that I had another option on the table for the following year to try to make things right. However, it turned out I wasn't the only rider Genesio had his eye on, and when he went worryingly quiet for a while, it transpired he'd gone all in to get Carlos Checa's signature after Carlos had left the factory Honda team.

Genesio is a wealthy man, but like all wealthy men he's

very careful with his money. Carlos wouldn't have been cheap, and Genesio had a budget that he wasn't prepared to shift on, so when he decided to run a two-man team built around Carlos, it became clear I would have to accept a massive drop in wages if I wanted to be a part of it.

Genesio's offer was a base wage of just €30,000, which at the time equated to about £20,000, out of which I had to cover my own travel. It was difficult to justify doing it at all, given that I could probably have earned ten times more back in BSB, but to be fair to Genesio, he was pushing the extra mile to make it a two-man line-up and I truly believed this was a good opportunity. A new team, new bikes, plenty of budget to run the bike . . . I thought that was fair enough. Plus, Borciani still owed me €65,000 from the previous year, so I figured I could muddle through and pick up some bonus money from podiums and wins.

At the start of the season I was fast again, riding well. We did the test at Phillip Island and I was on the pace, but in one of the qualifying sessions before the race I had a monumental third-gear high-side at the second-to-last corner, the long left-hander, and it flicked me so high I virtually got an aerial view of the whole island. I tried to race but I'd had a bang on the head and I wasn't really with it, plus you don't land from that kind of height and speed without some pretty severe bruising.

It scrambled my brain, and in hindsight I probably shouldn't have been passed fit to ride. I went out there and everything felt as though it was happening in fast forward. At the time of the crash I had been the fastest rider on track, but now I was going around a second or two off my previous pace, yet feeling as though I was going ten seconds per lap faster. It was such a strange sensation and eventually, almost inevitably, I crashed again.

It is good that in other sports the dangers of playing through concussion have been highlighted in recent years, but I think motorcycle racing in general remains a little way behind. Plenty of times a rider will get knocked out in a crash but by the time the dust has settled and the medics have arrived on the scene, he is conscious again, and either doesn't know he's concussed or knows it and doesn't want to let on because of the consequences.

A rider will always want to race. I have been there and I would never back out, but riders need protection. Right at the top level of MotoGP, all the way down to the British Championship, you can see a guy break his leg and be riding again two weeks later. Is that normal? Should a guy with a broken leg be jumping on a 200 mph motorbike just to try and score some points? Is he physically capable of avoiding a situation, should a situation arise? Should there even be that level of pressure on a rider to return so quickly?

MotoGP fans will remember Jorge Lorenzo famously crashing at Assen in Friday practice, jumping in a private jet to Barcelona to get fixed overnight, and then returning to finish fifth two days later in the race.

One thing about MotoGP is that the pressure to rush back is perhaps slightly less, given that there are so few riders available of a good enough quality to stand in. The ones that are, generally they're tied into a contract in Moto2 or World Superbikes. Like Lorenzo that time, the injured rider also gets treated properly, with the best doctors on hand, and they're earning enough money to pay the best insurance companies. The best insurance companies find you the best surgeons, the best surgeons find you the best physios, and everything is done in the correct way.

The problem at BSB level is that there isn't that level of care. People might think that sounds like me biting the hand that has fed me for many years, but it's a fact. If you are injured in BSB and aren't able to get back on your bike at the next race, some ambulance chaser will phone up, maybe with a sponsor on board, and he can be on your bike for the rest of the season.

For example, during the 2019 British Superbike season, just two weeks after breaking his leg at Knockhill, Christian Iddon appeared at Snetterton with a splint he'd made himself, fashioned from some kind of resin-based glass fibre they use for car bodywork repairs, which he slid down the side of his boot. Christian is a particularly tough lad, but that just demonstrates the lengths most riders will go to, to make sure nobody else gets their backside on their bike – especially at BSB level. There is something not right about that.

I had unscrambled my senses in time for the second round of the 2010 World Superbike season at Portimão and I was really looking forward to it, but again I had another massive high-side at the last corner. We'd gone from the Borciani bike, which had a conventional throttle cable, to a 'ride-by-wire' system on Althea's new Ducati 1198 that electronically controls the delivery of power with no cable at all. In my view, the technology was nowhere near ready. It felt really light to touch and not consistent at all. You asked it for 10 per cent throttle and it gave you 70 per cent. It just wasn't accurate, and for any rider coming from a mechanical throttle, it just seemed all wrong. Even hitting a bump mid-turn would see you give the bike a blip of throttle that you really didn't need. It was bloody hard to ride like that!

We raced Portimão, didn't do very well and then went on to Assen. At the end of both races I was going backwards, which was strange because my strength had always been over the last few laps. Generally I am quite smooth and kind on tyres, but when you have no throttle feel or connection, all you can do is pin it and hope that the traction control will take care of things. Eventually you use too much tyre riding in this manner and the traction control starts working overtime, cutting power, hindering your ability to accelerate and costing you lots of time.

Genesio sat me down and said, 'Look, I think what we need to do is make your bike like last year's. We'll give you a conventional throttle; you'll have a lot more feel for where you are with the bike and we'll go from there.' I was happy to give it a try and immediately it felt better. What we lost was the ability to map the engine power delivery from corner to corner, which was the big step forward that this new 'fly-by-wire' technology offered.

Kyalami in South Africa was one of the next races, and while Carlos's crew chief could tailor the power delivery from his engine to each individual section of the track, which made the whole set-up less of a compromise, my bike performed exactly the same in every corner. All of a sudden, when they started to get on top of the new system, it became a big problem for me. Carlos was doing well, I was starting to struggle, and naturally all the good stuff went to his side of the garage. The fairings looked the same but essentially after a few rounds we were riding completely different bikes. Maybe it was all his years of experience riding and getting flicked off 500cc Grand Prix bikes that gave him a more delicate throttle hand, I don't know, but to his credit Carlos persevered with the ride-by-wire system and made a fair bit of progress, widening the gulf even further.

Meanwhile, away from the track, money was getting tight. The Althea wage wasn't doing much to cover my costs, and there was still no sign of the €65,000 that Borciani owed me. I'd heard when I rode for him that he'd owed Max Biaggi some money from the previous season, and my understanding was that Max had come along and told him in no uncertain terms that he was taking one of the race bikes to cover the debt. I decided I was going to have to take similar action.

The rider who'd taken my place with Borciani was my old hero Nori Haga, riding an Aprilia, so I put together a plan with some people I knew from back home to go to the British round at Donington Park and forcibly remove one of the bikes from the track. We had a couple of ideas on how we might do that – one slightly shadier than the other – but €65,000 wasn't an amount of money I could just let slide. I figured paying a small percentage to some people who might be able to recover some of that debt was far better than not getting anything at all.

The only problem was that a week or so before the World Superbike round at Donington, there was a big earthquake in Japan that killed thousands of people, and Nori made a statement before the weekend saying that he would be racing for the honour and pride of his country. He was paying tribute to his people, and there was clearly no way I could bring myself to take his motorcycle, not even for my missing €65,000.

I never expected the 2010 season to be my last go at World Superbikes, and at the end of the year I had no reason to think it was. In the penultimate round, at Magny-Cours in France, I shook hands with the Kawasaki boss Ichiro Yoda and the team manager of PBM at the time, Paul Risbridger, on a deal that would see me ride a factory ZX-10R, under the umbrella of a satellite team. Birdy had been in World Superbikes since moving up with Gregorio Lavilla in 2008, and I was a little sceptical about signing for him again after he'd overlooked me the first time, but the bike was going to be the brand-new model and with factory support, so I was really excited to get going.

As far as I was concerned, the deal with Kawasaki was done, but the contract had to go through Birdy and I started to get a little nervous when nothing materialized. After several days of ignoring my calls, he finally answered, only to tell me that something had changed, that my deal was off and he'd re-signed Tom Sykes instead. 'But we all shook hands,' I told him.

'Yeah, with Yoda and Risbridger you did. It's my team and I've signed Sykesy now.' It was typical of him, but what more can I say about Paul Bird? Sometimes his whimsical ways worked against me, sometimes they worked in my favour. There was nothing more I could do about it. As I've said before, Paul's team is his train set and ultimately he decides who gets to play with it.

After I'd left MotoGP at the end of 2005, I felt sorry that I hadn't really taken any pictures, captured any memories, or stopped to think about where I was in life; it came as a shock when I realized I was never going to get the chance to go back. I kind of wished I'd stopped to smell the roses a little more, and I didn't want that to happen in World Superbikes. Not for one second did I think that this was the moment.

It hadn't been the season I'd wanted, but I'd finished it ahead of Sykes on Birdy's Kawasaki, ahead of a double World Champion in Troy Corser on the factory BMW and ahead of Leon Camier, who had stepped up onto the factory Aprilia after smoking the BSB title with Colin Wright's team in 2009. I was only a few points behind James Toseland on Spies' 2009 title-winning factory Yamaha. All of those guys got rides for 2011, but I didn't. I thought, 'How the fuck has this happened?' I wanted to be World Superbike Champion, I felt strongly that I would do it as soon as I got the right package, and I was convinced I deserved at least another shot.

I simply wasn't ready to come back to British Superbikes yet, but I was also struggling with earning such pitiful amounts of money for putting my life on the line week in week out. It made no sense to hang around riding for peanuts any more. There were options to stay in WSB, but I still hadn't been paid by Borciani and I had spent a year earning next to nothing with Genesio, so vague promises that they might be able to find me some travel budget and a small wage were no good to me. 'Fuck that,' I thought, 'I'm off.'

I'd left BSB at the end of 2008 as champion, and had been offered a far more lucrative deal to stay on in 2009 and defend my title, so I knew where my value was in that paddock, which was ten times more as a base than I'd earned with Althea. Plus, my travel expenses would obviously be a damn sight cheaper. I went to Oulton Park and had a chat with all the BSB teams, but it was HM Plant Honda who made the first move, offering me a good package. It didn't take long at all to get everything agreed, with a car and some motocross bikes thrown in, and I couldn't wait to get started.

I wasn't going to be a World Superbike rider any more, but at least I could say I was actually going to be a professional motorcycle racer again.

20

Better the Devils You Know

A bit like when I came back from MotoGP in 2006, those two really difficult seasons in World Superbike – which might have looked like a waste of time from the outside – had actually been hugely valuable and improved me again as a rider. I'd had to push so hard, so on the limit, so often, that I had become a better rider for it. I'd felt as if I was having to push harder than my rivals to achieve the same result, and even then it hadn't been good enough. If anything, I actually felt as if I was over-performing, pushing to the limit in every aspect of my preparation and on every single lap on track. When you're trying to find time, a natural instinct is to brake later because you think it is going to make you go faster. In fact, letting go of the brake and getting the drive out of the corner is much more important. I could ride the front of the 1098 and 1198 really hard, so I was forever trying to make up the time I lost on the straights in corner entry, but I was actually losing more time on the exit. It took two years of hard graft to make me realize what I was doing wrong, but eventually I learned how to rein that in, to control the urge.

A term I hear a lot from riders when things aren't going to plan on a Friday or Saturday is that they are 'Sunday men'. They reckon it is all going to come together on race day, when they give that last few per cent of effort. What a load of bollocks! If you do your job properly on a Friday and Saturday, then Sunday takes care of itself. When the lights go out, we're all Sunday men. You've got twenty laps to do, and you do them as fast as you can.

The Fridays and Saturdays during my two years in World Superbikes were about extracting every last little thousandth of a second that I could out of the bike because I knew I would need it all on a Sunday. When I came back to British Superbikes in 2011, my approach was the same, and it often meant that by the time the first race came around on Sunday morning, I had a couple of tenths in my pocket if I needed them.

Although I hadn't expected to be coming back to BSB so soon, this time I got my head around the idea pretty quickly. I was actually feeling really excited about it. Riding a Honda again would be a fresh challenge, an opportunity to show people who thought I could only win on a Ducati, and I was looking forward to riding at circuits I already knew like the back of my hand, where I could focus on going fast from first practice rather than spending two practice sessions trying to learn my way around.

As a young rider I had always looked forward to one day swapping tracks like Oulton Park, Cadwell Park and

Knockhill for exotic locations like Phillip Island, Motegi and Sepang. But racing around the world against riders who knew the tracks, riders on better machinery – in some cases riders with more talent – meant that one way or another, the odds were always stacked against me. Now these quirky, tight British circuits felt like old friends that I couldn't wait to see again. They were more dangerous, for sure, but I'd found ways to injure myself at some of the 'safest' tracks on the planet, so you could say it was a case of 'better the devils you know'. That would also be true in terms of the riders I would be facing up against in 2011.

Before the season started we had to go to Bedford Auto-drome for a press launch and photo shoot. We were out on the tarmac, in a freezing cold gale in the middle of March, when who comes prancing over, his feet still pointing outwards at quarter to three, but my old MotoGP rival John Hopkins, wearing a set of spanking-new Crescent Suzuki leathers. 'Ah, Hopper!' I said. 'Fancy seeing you here!'

I gave John a bit of stick that he'd had to 'lower' himself to BSB standards, but I was genuinely pleased to have him there, not just as a mate. The guy had been through a hard time in his personal and professional life but there was still no questioning his talent. Only a couple of years previously he'd been the most in-demand rider in MotoGP, and I knew that nobody could question the validity of winning a British Superbike title against a rival like him. My attitude was, 'If I can't be World Champion, then I want to beat as many guys from the World Championship as possible.' That way, nobody would be able to say I hadn't earned it.

My achievements hadn't come because I had a silver spoon up my arse. They came through hard work, dedication, focus and belief. For me, the more people who came to race me in BSB the better. I would have loved nothing more than to race Scott Redding in 2019 for all the same reasons. Did I look at Scott during that season when I was injured and think, 'I'm glad I'm not racing him'? Of course I didn't!

The first person I had to beat in 2011, though, was my HM Plant Honda teammate Ryuichi Kiyonari, which promised to be no mean feat given that he also happened to be the defending and now three-time champion. Kiyo is somebody I have a lot of respect for – he is a humble, funny guy who never has a bad word for anyone. Young riders could learn a lot from the way Kiyo conducts himself off the bike and he was pretty sensational on it too.

But I jumped on the bike for the first test and couldn't understand how much quicker I was than him. My crew chief Chris Pike was telling me, 'This is testing Kiyo – race Kiyo is very different', and he was absolutely right.

Of all the teammates I ever had, Kiyo was the one I felt I had to keep a sneaky eye on. I could never let my guard down around him because – no matter what happened in practice or qualifying – if he turned it on, he could easily win from the back row on his day. He had that raw talent, which must have been what HRC saw in him when they brought him straight into MotoGP as a young man to replace Daijiro Kato in 2003. That was probably all a bit too much too soon for him, especially in such difficult circumstances, but on his day, if his head was in the right place, Kiyo was a special rider, and he had proved it by winning a bunch of World Superbike races in 2008, as well as his BSB titles.

From the outside, the factory Honda team was generally viewed as being too serious, because nobody looked to be having any fun. But I have to say that the team manager Havier Beltran, Chris Pike and all the guys there were absolutely brilliant from the start. Going back to that old adage that a happy rider is a fast rider, they definitely created the right environment for me at the start of that year. The bike, of course, was a Fireblade – an inline four-cylinder 1000cc engine that I was determined to show any doubters I could win on, having enjoyed most of my success up to then on a V-twin Ducati.

The bike was so competitive from the start that for the first time in a couple of years I could actually work on different aspects of my riding – try new things and experiment without losing ten places every time I made the tiniest mistake. On the Honda a small mistake was just a small mistake, so it gave me the confidence to push to the limit when I needed to but also to be more consistent the rest of the time. We started the season with a win in the first race at Brands Indy, and we were hardly off the podium for the rest of the season after that.

The only issue I had with the team was when they asked me to do an event for the main sponsor – HM Plant – up in Darlington or somewhere, but I was away on holiday in Spain. I spoke to Hav and asked if there was any way I could get out of it.

'Sorry, mate,' Hav said. 'It's a pretty big deal. HM Plant are a really important sponsor. You'd be doing us a massive favour.'

I agreed to come over from Spain for the day, flying directly into Durham Tees Valley, but the flights the team had booked meant I had to return via Bristol, with an over-night connection. Suddenly this quick trip over from Spain had taken two days out of my holiday, so I wasn't best pleased about it, but I let it slide.

A couple of months later, the team principal Neil Tuxworth called me in to a meeting with him and Hav. 'How's things, Shane?' he said. 'Everything all right?'

I told them I was happy, I thought the team was working well, there were a couple of things I thought we could do with but they were fixable and everything was cool. The year was going well and I was leading the championship.

'Good, good . . .' Tuxworth said.

The conversation tailed off into an awkward silence. I looked at Havier as if to say, 'What the fuck's going on?' Hav gave me a pained look back, like he knew what was coming.

Eventually Neil pipes up and says, 'Right, there is just one more little thing we'd like to talk to you about.'

'Oh yeah, what's that then?'

'The HM Plant day, up in Darlington.'

'Oh right, yeah, the one I took two days out of my holiday to attend.'

'Yes. So, we said we would pay for your return flight from Spain.'

'Yeah.'

'Well, I'm looking at the invoice here and we've ended up having to pay for three flights and a hotel.'

'Yeah, because that's the way you booked it.'

'Right, well, all that we agreed to was one return flight, so we'll need to give you a bill for the extra flight and the hotel in Bristol.'

I couldn't believe what I was hearing. I looked at Hav, who was covering his eyes, and then I lost my shit.

'Fuck off!' I laughed. 'No fucking chance. You're not getting a penny out of me, you're lucky I even came. Seriously, Neil, go fuck yourself.'

Neil was one of those team managers who sign a contract with you to race a motorbike for twelve rounds of a BSB season, but their interpretation tends to be that they essentially 'own' you for the full term of that contract. Clearly, that's not the way I see it at all, and I stormed out of Tuxworth's office with a bad taste in my mouth. It didn't affect my relationship with the rest of the team, or my results on track, though, and by the time we got to the tenth round of the season I had scored a win or a podium at all but one round and was leading the championship by twenty points ahead of Tommy Hill.

Rounds ten, eleven and twelve – at Donington Park, Assen and Brands Hatch – would be my first experience of the 'Showdown' format that had been brought in for the 2010 season after my old GSE teammate Leon Camier completely cleaned up in 2009, winning fifteen of the first eighteen races and effectively ending any interest in the outcome of the championship long before it had actually finished. The organizers decided to do something to keep the interest up right to the end – a bit like the play-offs in the NFL – and the Showdown was their baby, with the points essentially reset for the top six riders ahead of the final three rounds (plus podium 'credits' accrued during the regular season).

If I'm honest, I thought it was a shit-box idea – and with my rider's head on, I still do. Kiyo, for example, had been a massive 138 points behind me after nine rounds, but now he was just fourteen points adrift and right back in contention. Along with the two of us, Swan Yamaha riders Tommy Hill and Michael Laverty, Crescent Suzuki rider Hopper and Tyco Suzuki rider Josh Brookes were the other riders in the Showdown, all six of us having won races over the course of the season, and all with our own reasons to be confident about winning the title.

Out of the six, it was kind of funny that it was Laverty – usually such a calm, calculating rider – who came at the first round at Donington Park like a man possessed. In the first race, I had a massive dice with him at the front, along with Hopper and Tommy, but over the last few laps my tyres started moving around on the rim and I lost a second per lap, dropping back to fifth behind Brookes.

In the second race, 'MLav' came charging up the inside of me off the start and wiped us both out in the first corner. His bike ended up kind of stuck underneath mine, so I managed to keep the Honda running, got back in the race in last place and came through to finish eighth. I couldn't be angry with Michael because I had actually done the exact same thing to him at Silverstone in 2006. On that occasion it had been completely my fault, I ran straight over to him and picked him up, apologizing like mad. He wasn't happy but Michael, being the gentleman that he is, accepted the apology right there on the spot and we moved on. This time, the boot was on the other foot.

We went back to Silverstone for the second round of the 2011 Showdown and I struggled like mad with the most unbelievable chatter. Chatter is a sensation you get from the bike, which happens at different frequencies. If you can imagine the amount of vibrations that go through a motorcycle that is being ridden on the edge of grip, sometimes the suspension and the tyre become out of sync with the tarmac and start to flex at a different rate and never recover.

This is a racing team's worst nightmare, because it can appear out of nowhere and fixing it is a long process of elimination that you rarely have time for over the course of a race weekend. We hadn't really struggled with it before on the Honda, but at Silverstone I could barely ride and I knew from the Friday morning that we were fucked.

I had chatter so bad around some of those long corners that I reckon the tyre was only in contact with the ground for about 10 per cent of the time. I couldn't steer, couldn't make the bike hold its line or pick the throttle back up where I wanted to. We tried everything to fix it, and by the time Sunday morning came around we were desperate. I had qualified in a dismal thirteenth and told the team there was no point me riding if we couldn't find some kind of fix.

As a last resort, my crew chief Chris Pike cut a 12 mm section out of the bottom triple clamp – the yoke that holds the suspension forks in place – and removed some internal bracing. I suddenly went a second quicker in the warm-up than I had in qualifying but the changes affected the overall balance of the bike and now we were heading into race one with no time to rectify it. For example, the gearing we had in the sections I'd been struggling with was no longer right, and now that I could brake much later into the corner, it meant the suspension setting was all wrong. Where I'd been so gentle getting on the gas all weekend, now the rear shock was too soft. A Superbike is a great thing to ride at the speed it is designed to go at, but if you are just two seconds off that pace it will feel like a piece of crap. In the end we had to gamble on a set-up for race one, finishing fifth, and then rolled the dice again in the second one with the exact same result. With Hill and Hopkins on the podium in both races, my hopes of winning the title were effectively gone.

We sorted the bike out for the final round at Brands Hatch and I managed to win two out of three races, but it was too little too late. Tommy took the title in one of the closest ever finishes in BSB, crossing the line over four seconds behind me in second place, but just 0.006 seconds ahead of Hopper in third. The organizers had the dramatic finish they wanted, but it niggled at me that over the course of the season I had scored more points than anybody in the championship, yet I had ended up third – just because we ran into virtually the only problem we had with the bike all season in a Showdown round.

Now who was back on the phone to me but my old mate Paul Bird. 'I'm not doing the factory Kawasaki World Superbike thing any more, driver,' he said, in his usual flippant way. 'I'm coming back to BSB and I want you. It's obvious you're the best rider, I'll pay you whatever.'

It was tempting, because even though I was happy at Honda and had the option of staying there, I was worried about some rule changes that were coming in for 2012, which I felt were really going to affect the Fireblade. In yet another attempt to make BSB a more level playing field, the organizers had announced that they were going to introduce a control ECU – effectively removing traction and wheelie control from the electronics – which I knew would be an issue for Honda.

One of the biggest problems with the Fireblade in full Superbike race spec was that the crankshafts and the flywheel were really light, so the engine picked up really quickly. It wheelied everywhere, and putting the power down to the ground was a massive issue, even with full electronics. Taking them away would almost certainly make the bike virtually unrideable. The Kawasaki, on the other hand, had a really heavy crankshaft, and even though it was a more sluggish bike in full spec, I reckoned it would be the machine to be on in 2012.

Birdy had built a good relationship with Kawasaki by now, and he was convinced he was going to get factory parts and could even swing the same rider performance bonus package that they were paying Tom Sykes in World Superbikes. It would have been worth something like €20,000 a win, which would have been nice if it turned out to be true, though – as always – my priority was not the money but the bike.

To be fair to Tuxworth, he put a good deal on the table for me to stay with Honda, for more money than Birdy was offering, and I thought long and hard about it. Despite the chatter issues we'd had at the end of the season, I loved the Honda, I was fast on it and – other than my differences with Tuxworth – I liked the team, it was a nice place to be. Plus, I really liked Havier Beltran. He had become a close friend and I desperately wanted to win him a championship, but I was struggling to get over my fears about the bike being competitive in the first year of the new rules.

I had the two offers on the table and I told them both that I needed another week or so while I was contemplating which way to go. Tuxworth fired me a text saying, 'Your contract is up at midnight on Monday. If you haven't confirmed before then, you've lost your ride.' I was straight with him and said that I wasn't ready to make that decision. I told him, 'If you want to keep me, give me the week I need.'

Literally, at 11.45 p.m. on the night before my contract expired with Honda, I got another text from Tuxworth along the lines of, 'Please drop your vehicles back – your contract is terminated.' I was so angry, but I knew nothing good would come out of me speaking to the guy, so I phoned Havier and went nuts with him instead. 'Mate, I totally get where you're coming from,' he said. 'I understand that you need time, but this is Neil – he's an accountant and accountants don't deal with human emotions, they deal with numbers.'

'Hav, I don't care what he is – he is your mate and he is bang out of order in my opinion. I'm sorry, but I just don't want anything to do with it any more.' I hung up and called Birdy back to accept his offer.

PBM were also running a MotoGP team by now, entering the new 'CRT' class for bikes that were essentially production-prototype hybrids, with James Ellison as the rider. So my first test on the Kawasaki with the control ECU ended up being at the MotorLand Aragón circuit in Spain, alongside James and a bunch of other CRT guys like Aleix Espargaró and Randy de Puniet. Turns two and three at Aragón are really fast – big balls, side of the tyre, full gas corners – and the track was freezing cold. The first time I went out on the bike with no traction control, I thought, 'What sort of a stupid decision is this? If this thing lets go at full gas in third or fourth gear, we're off to the moon.' I was angry with the organizers because I felt that the new rules were playing with people's lives.

For my own reasons at the time, it was a subject I was particularly sensitive about.

21

What Doesn't Kill Us

I have a tattoo on the inside of my left forearm that says, 'What doesn't kill us makes us stronger.' It's a famous old saying, which has its origins in a quote by the German philosopher Friedrich Nietzsche, and it is something I truly believe in. If you race motorcycles for a living, you don't really have a choice.

However, there have been a couple of situations that have taken place a long way from the racetrack that have made me fall back on this philosophy more than ever. The moment that actually inspired the tattoo happened on 7 January 2012, during my preparations for that season on the Kawasaki, when I was driving the family back to England from our house in Spain.

The previous September, Petra and I had been so happy to be blessed with a precious little girl Lilly – the perfect addition to our brood. I had my little boy Zack and now a daughter too: my dream family. We'd spent our first Christmas and New Year as a foursome down in Spain, and when we set off on the long drive back to the UK we made sure to schedule an extra-early start, to allow time for the additional nappy changes and feeds for Lilly.

It was a particularly dark morning, travelling along motorways as we made our way through the Spanish–French border at La Jonquera. When we got to the toll road at Perpignan it was still pitch black, and a gendarme came over and shone his torch into the van, lighting up the two tired little faces in the back and almost blinding me and Petra in the front, before waving us on. 'That's great, isn't it?' I muttered to Petra. 'Pitch fucking black and some dickhead goes and shines his flashlight straight in your eyes.'

I cracked on into the darkness and put the van back on cruise control until we came to some roadworks, which reduced the motorway to two lanes. There were metal barriers reducing the width of the lanes on either side and, even though we'd hardly seen any traffic so far on the roads, I soon started to catch up with a truck, travelling at its limited speed. I knocked off the cruise control on the approach to the truck and focused on squeezing past, concentrating hard on the obstacles either side of the van: metal barrier on the left, truck on the right.

No sooner had I got alongside this truck than I looked up ahead; emerging right in front of me in the glow of my headlights was a crashed car, which had spun sideways and was stranded across my lane. It was a dark burgundy Peugeot estate – if you didn't know it was there, you would never have seen it – and the truck alongside me never even broke stride. I had absolutely nowhere to go, and as I hit the brakes I ploughed straight into the side of this Peugeot at about 60 mph.

It is hard to describe accurately what it is like to experience a car crash at that speed, because everything happens literally all at once. All I can remember now is the crunching of metal and the smashing of glass, seeing Petra being thrown forward against the airbag and slumping back into her seat, and the sound of Zack screaming from behind me.

When it all came to a stop, I didn't know what to do. Zack was still crying but Lilly was completely still, like a doll, sleeping soundly in her baby seat. I unclipped my seatbelt, leaned over and checked on her and then turned to Petra, who had been knocked out but was coming around. I realized that I had to get them all out of there straight away. At any moment, another car or a truck could come steaming in behind us and do exactly the same thing I'd just done. I *had* to get everybody out of the van and clear of the road.

I jumped out of the driver's door and looked around for a safe place where I could put the kids out of the way of danger. As I stood there, desperately trying to make a plan, my attention turned to the vehicle I'd just hit. 'Fuck,' I thought. 'What if there are people in there? What if I've hurt or killed someone?' At that very moment of extra panic, I heard a screeching noise behind me. I knew exactly what it was and I knew I had to do something, but my brain just wouldn't work quickly enough.

At this point I was standing level with Zack's window, my little boy looking out of the window straight at me as the sound of squealing tyres came skidding towards the van. I looked up and waved frantically in the approaching head-lights as they swerved to avoid the debris that had been left from my own collision. The oncoming car glanced off the rear corner of my stricken van and veered straight towards me. As I tried to jump out of the way the front end of the car swept my legs away and the impact as I hit the wind-screen threw me straight up into the air. I came back down on my head and blacked out.

What Zack saw that night would give him nightmares for months afterwards. So many times, he would say things to Petra like, 'Mummy, I don't want Daddy to get crashed into again,' or 'Mummy, it made me cry when Daddy got knocked down.' The poor kid was only three years old. That was something he should never have had to see.

When I came around on the roadside I was surrounded by paramedics. To my relief, Petra was there too, and the kids. They loaded us all into separate ambulances and took us to a local hospital near Perpignan, where they told me I was lucky to escape with just bruising. They never even checked Petra or the kids before discharging us, at which point we hired a replacement van and headed back down to Spain, to book some flights home and organize for another vehicle to come down and collect our stuff.

After a couple of days at the house in Spain, my legs were still in agony. I said to Petra, 'This ain't cutting it. I know I've done something.' We went down to the local hospital like the walking wounded, me limping heavily and Petra's face still all bruised and swollen, where an X-ray confirmed I'd broken my ankle and leg. They put it in a cast and I got straight on the phone to my bone fixer – the famous Brian Simpson in Ipswich, whose number has been on speed dial for pretty much my whole career – to organize some laser therapy for me as soon as I got home. I called Birdy, who I had just re-signed for, and he was brilliant. 'Bloody hell, driver!' was pretty much all he said.

*

The injuries healed quickly, but when the time came to test the Kawasaki, with no traction control, on a cold March day at Aragón, you can understand why I felt a little apprehensive. As it turned out, the bike was so slow that I would have had to slip the clutch in first gear on the side of the tyre to get the rear wheel to even spin up.

The PBM link with Kawasaki meant that we had our engines built by Akira, who tuned the World Superbike motors, but at the spec they built them to for us, the bike didn't even feel like a 600, let alone a 1000. Looking back, you'd have to say my fears about the safety implications of the new rules were unfounded, because the bikes were made to be as rideable as possible and we never had the crash rate I was expecting. Birdy did what Birdy does and threw a bit of money at the engines, getting a legendary engine tuner called Frank Wrathall to rebuild the motors, and eventually we got our 1000cc engine.

Tommy Hill was the defending champion and the man to beat in 2012, but we were right up there from the start, trading wins with him, Josh Brookes and Michael Laverty again, and after I took a double win at Brands GP in the seventh round of the season, I was trailing Tommy by eleven points at the top.

That's when I went and screwed my collarbone in

practice at Cadwell Park, when I crashed through the tricky Hall Bends section straight after the famous 'Mountain'. You go right, left, through a right kink, left, crest a small hill and grab the brakes hard for the first-gear right-hand hairpin. I grabbed the brakes all right, then just as I leaned right I locked the front wheel and tucked the front tyre, but quickly released the brake and saved the crash. I immediately wished I hadn't, though, as by releasing the brake the bike shot off to the left and with zero run-off through that section I hit the tyre wall and threw myself straight over the bars, landing heavily on my right shoulder.

Surgery was performed the very next day by, in my opinion, the best shoulder doctor in the country, and the man with also the coolest name in the world – Professor Lennard Funk – on a collarbone that hadn't actually broken, but had the ligaments and tendons shorn clean off it. Instead of going from my neck to my shoulder, the collarbone had spun ninety degrees and was pointing front to back. Once Professor Funk had fitted me with artificial ligaments stapled to the bone, I set about multiple trips to Ipswich again and more physio and hyperbaric chamber sessions than you could shake a stick at, to get myself fixed up before the Showdown started in three weeks' time. This year it would start at Assen, followed by Silverstone and then the season decider at Brands Hatch.

There was still one round to go before then – at Donington – but with my place already secured in the top six, it meant I could afford to skip it and make sure I was fit for when it really mattered. I finished the regular season eighty-one points behind Tommy and forty-six behind

Brookes, but this time the Showdown format worked in my favour and when the points were reset and podium credits added, I was just eleven behind Tommy and a point ahead of Brookes.

In a complete reversal of our fortunes the previous year, Tommy's season had started to slowly fall apart, with some not-so-good results on the run-up to the Showdown. He had a change of chassis at Donington Park, which didn't go well for him, and then suffered some terrible luck when a mechanic stepped out in front of him approaching the grid at Assen and poor Tommy had to jam his front brake lever on, flipping him over the bars.

Meanwhile, I felt I was getting stronger and stronger. My shoulder was much better, and I knew my bike's strengths and weaknesses and how to apply them accordingly. After sharing a win and a second place apiece with Brookes at Assen, I knew all I had to do was keep him behind me for two more rounds. We managed that with two second places at Silverstone, where an impressive youngster by the name of Alex Lowes took his first wins, and then wrapped up the title in perfect style with three wins from three races at the final round at Brands just for badness!

Having come so close to doing it the previous season, it felt good to take a title on a four-cylinder bike, and especially satisfying to put PBM Motorsport back up where they belonged. Birdy had gone a long time without getting the just rewards for his investment in the sport, and that season would be a happy start to a long and successful final chapter in our relationship together.

22

Friend or Foe?

I have heard Carl Fogarty say that he never really enjoyed racing, he only enjoyed winning. I can only think that those are the words of somebody who came from a completely different background to me. Carl's father was a racer, Carl followed in his dad's footsteps, and maybe the demands on him were always to win and not necessarily to enjoy the journey. I have never enjoyed losing, that's for sure, but for me, racing motorcycles was my own personal dream from such a young age and I wanted it so badly that I just had to make it happen.

Of course, it's not always fun. It's not fun when you're upside down in a gravel trap with your legs around your ears. It's not fun when you've given everything you have to win a race and you have to settle for tenth place. No racer enjoys that. But it's not like I dreamed of being an airline pilot and the opportunity came up to race bikes instead, or

I could have been a footballer but I chose bikes because it seemed like a cool thing to do. This was all I ever wanted, so how can I complain? How could I be lucky enough to live my dream, and then turn around and say I didn't enjoy it?

A great example of a fun year was 2013, when I ended up missing out on the BSB title to a brilliant young rival called Alex Lowes – a smiley, carefree kid from Lincolnshire with spiky blonde hair and a real glint in his eye. Towards the end of the 2012 season, Alex had shown a glimpse of his talent when he won those two Showdown races at Assen on a privateer WFR Honda, earning himself a chance with Havier Beltran's factory Honda team. To be honest, I felt like I had the beating of all the other guys out there at the time, but Alex presented a fresh challenge and, much like the talent I had seen in Jonathan Rea six or seven years before, I really felt he was going to go places.

Throughout the season Alex rejuvenated my enthusiasm and my motivation for racing. There was plenty of respect there, but I think it would be fair to describe some of his moves as ambitious. I'd think, 'You little bastard, how did you get yourself up the inside of there?' And truthfully, if you asked Alex, I don't think he would have known the answer most of the time. But I loved it, because it was exciting, it was challenging. I guess he was teaching an old dog new tricks.

Just like his identical twin brother Sam, the kid was motivated, focused, with huge self-belief. He also trained extremely hard. He was physically and mentally very strong, a dedicated professional, but he was a great laugh too and we clicked from the word go. I was almost old enough to be his dad but it didn't matter. I knew he looked up to me for what I had achieved in the sport and I showed him an equal amount of respect for what he was doing and what I felt he was capable of.

Over the course of the season, Alex went from being a super-fast, super-aggressive kid with a tendency to crash a lot, to the rounded professional that the factory Honda team required. Our friendship stood up to the test when he knocked me off with a typically brave and optimistic move in the first round of the Showdown at Assen. Obviously I wasn't made up about rolling through the gravel trap at 130 mph because it hurt, but I couldn't be angry with him.

There are two sides to every story – his side was that I was a bit tighter in that corner than I had been on previous laps; my side was that I was in the right place and he rode into the side of me. But it didn't matter who was right, accidents happen. It was a bit like the crashes with Michael Laverty in 2006 and again in 2011 – you accept these things can happen, nobody wants them to happen, so you move on. We've all made mistakes. Plus, it was the Showdown, there was no time to dwell; I had to pick myself up, dust myself down and get ready to go again.

The amount of respect Alex and I had for each other and the amount of fun we were having out there was typified by an incredible battle to the line in both races of the penultimate round of the season at Silverstone. Both races were epic, Alex using all of his and the Honda's ability to run tight into turns and still make the bike hold a line; my wider, sweeping lines on the Kawasaki leaving me vulnerable to his constant attacks but opening up lots of opportunities for me to pass him straight back. It was so much fun that I was actually laughing inside my helmet. We came flat out together through Woodcote – the famous fifth-gear final corner – in both races, Alex beating me by 0.094 seconds in the first one and me returning the favour by 0.012 seconds in the second. They were two of the closest finishes in BSB history and two of the most enjoyable races of my entire career.

It was only right that the championship went down to the final round at Brands Hatch. Alex and I were still getting on really well as friends, and I don't think either of us wanted to jeopardize that, so we had a chat and from my side I told him what I thought. 'Listen, mate, whichever way this goes, you have reinvigorated my love of racing motorbikes and I thank you for that. If you beat me to the championship then fair play, but I want you to know that this year has been amazing and I have really enjoyed it.'

We ended up having that half-wet, half-dry kind of day that you always seem to get at Brands in October. Alex fell off in race two and almost handed me the championship, but then a few laps later I fell off too and I gave it back to him. He beat me in the decisive third race, we shook hands and that was that – Alex moved up to the World Superbike Championship and I sincerely wished him well. I have a lot of time for that kid, and I still absolutely believe that – given the right package – he has the potential to be World Superbike champion.

*

If 2013 reinvigorated me, 2014 took it to the next level with an epic battle throughout the season with my old teammate from my HM Plant Honda days, Ryuichi Kiyonari. If racing Alex Lowes had been a case of an old dog learning new tricks, with Kiyo it was just two old dogs going at it.

After so many years with Honda, they had finally given Kiyo the flick and everybody thought that was him done. Because his career had been so hit and miss, Kiyo had a reputation for being a little mentally fragile, but he rocked up for the new season on a BMW with the Hawk Racing team – a small, family-run outfit led by the sage old Stuart Hicken and run by his son Steve – and nobody really knew what to expect. In my opinion, the Kiyo of 2014 turned out to be arguably his best ever version.

The pair of us had some monumental battles, duking it out from weekend to weekend, track to track. I hate losing but, even when finishing second to Kiyo that season, I'd be laughing to myself on the cool-down lap because I had just had so much fun. It is hard to describe the enjoyment you can get from battling with a rival you have so much respect for, finding his strengths and weaknesses and putting moves on him with just millimetres to spare. We were both on the limit but so safe at the same time, the racing was unbelievable. If I beat Kiyo he always had a big smile and a hug for me at the end, and if he beat me it was the same the other way around.

As always, the championship went down to the six-rider Showdown, but in reality there was nobody close to me and Kiyo that season and it was only right that it came down to the two of us in the final round. I was twelve points in the lead when we got to Brands for three races to decide the title, but Kiyo crashed in a damp warm-up session on the final day of the season and broke his collarbone. I was gutted, genuinely devastated.

Out of respect for Kiyo, I never discounted him from rocking up on the grid for race one because he was a tough little so-and-so, so when he didn't appear I was really sad that he couldn't make it out there and fight me to the end. Of course, you always want to win a championship by beating your biggest rival, but my disappointment was more for Kiyo. I believe that I would have beaten him anyway – I have to – but it would have been a lot of fun to sort it out in the proper manner.

I crashed myself in a wet first race but the weather cleared for Sunday and I took the win in the second race to wrap up my fourth championship. As had happened with every previous title, I went through Paddock Hill Bend, Druids and Graham Hill Bend feeling on top of the world, but by the time I got to Surtees my attention had already turned to the next challenge.

I wondered if Kiyo could come back and do it again, but in 2015 it turned out to be another of my biggest ever BSB rivals – a guy I felt could never be friends with – who came out and produced the season of his life.

*

After Alex Lowes and Ryuichi Kiyonari, the third big rivalry that defined my BSB career was with Josh Brookes, which reached its peak in 2015. I don't recall too much about what started the animosity between me and Josh. I don't think I'm a difficult person to get on with, and I honestly think most of the people in the paddock would agree, so I don't get why Josh and I clashed so much. We went through a load of time racing together in BSB and I have always really enjoyed competing against the guy because he is really fast and really fair. He'll put a hard move on you but you can give him one back and there are no complaints. I admire his work ethic too. He is out first in every session, he digs in and then he goes and does his job, but we just don't get on. Why? Honestly, I have no idea, but I can assure you that I have never lost a moment's sleep over it and I doubt he has either.

Our personal relationship is of no relevance to what happened in 2015, when Josh went on to win the championship, and that is something I still cannot come to terms with. We started the year well, winning five of the first ten races while Josh didn't win any, and then all of a sudden halfway through the season the guy turned into Josh fucking Rossi!

It all started in round seven in July, when I had a massive crash at Brands and was absolutely certain I had bent the chassis, even though the team disagreed. I struggled badly in the next round at Thruxton, then went even worse at Cadwell Park. Meanwhile Josh won all six races during that time and I lost my head with the team, booting equipment everywhere across the tiny garages we have at Cadwell. I got the better of Josh just twice after that, at Oulton Park, but otherwise he won thirteen out of fifteen races between doing the double in the July round at Brands and going back there to win the title at the final round in October.

I couldn't get my head around it. As far as I was concerned, Josh was still the same guy that I'd spent so many years racing against and beating, but suddenly I couldn't get near him. I felt I was riding at 110 per cent, as well as I've ever ridden, and yet I couldn't touch a guy I'd beaten for the championship for the past few seasons. When I tell you I would rather have died than get beaten by Josh Brookes, that's how hard I tried. I gave everything I had, put my body on the line, worked the team like dogs to make the bike the best it could be, and then went out and rode the wheels off the thing. It still wasn't enough.

When you look back now at the stats, they don't add up. This was a guy who had won a total of twenty-one races in his entire BSB career before 2015, after which he went and had a disastrous year on a BMW in World Superbikes, then got back on the R1 in BSB in 2017 and took a grand total of three wins, a number he repeated in 2018. So why was he so unbeatable on the thing in 2015? Did he develop this incredible talent overnight and then lose it again six months later?

23

Seeing Red

Just as I felt I'd hit a dip in my racing career, I also faced a major stress in my personal life: I was told I had skin cancer.

I'd had a couple of spots on my face since at least 2003, when I can distinctly remember noticing them for the first time at a winter test in Spain. I was putting on a new crash helmet, and as I pulled it on I felt a sharp scratch on the side of my face. I thought I must have left a tag or a sticker inside the helmet, but when I pulled it off again there was nothing inside – just two marks that had suddenly appeared, along with a little trickle of blood on the side of my face.

The spots had remained there ever since, sometimes increasing in size – when Petra would bug me to get them looked at – and then they'd go down again and I would forget all about them. Other times, I'd get out of the shower, dry myself with a towel and they would both start to bleed. In 2016 my skin went completely to shit – I had a rash on my cheeks and nose, I was getting acne and it was all really uncomfortable, and bloody annoying too.

Eventually, that summer, I went in to the local doctor with it. 'Doc, I'm forty years old,' I said. 'I never had acne when I was a kid – I don't need it now. What's wrong with me?' The doctor started examining my face with his pen torch, going, 'Yeah, that's acne, we can give you something for that . . . that's the same thing, nothing to worry about there . . . oh, and that's cancer.' He might as well have punched me straight in the stomach.

Just like that, a million thoughts went through my head at a million miles an hour. 'I haven't paid the mortgage off, what am I going to do? How am I going to tell the kids they're not going to have a dad?' I was in a blind panic. I actually had a pop at the doctor for being so blasé about it. I know it's what they do, but after what happened to my own dad, I guess I just hoped never to hear that fucking C word ever again. He could have told me he wanted to do a biopsy, or take a closer look at it, or tell me gently what his worry was, but no. 'That's cancer' – the two words nobody wants to hear.

I was confused and upset and I pretty much stormed out of the surgery and booked myself straight into a private clinic in Canterbury for a second opinion the following week. For those few days I was all over the place, but I quickly had to pull myself together to go and race at Brands Hatch. I actually ended up winning the double that weekend, but I wasn't in a good place. Wag said to me on the Sunday night, 'Mate, what's up? You ain't yourself, we've just won two races but something ain't right, is it?'

'Listen, mate,' I said. 'Don't tell anybody but I think I've got cancer. I've been told by this doctor that these things on my face are fucking tumours.'

'I knew it,' Wag said. 'I knew there was something wrong with you. What we gonna do?'

That was typical of Wag. Any problem I had instantly became his problem too. Since he had first started travelling to the races with me back in 2004, he had become my wingman. We won races together and we tackled problems together too. Wag can be the loudest, most obnoxious man in the room, but there is only one part of him that's bigger than his gob and that's his heart. 'I've already been to see the doctor,' I told him. 'I've got an appointment with a specialist next week.'

I'd booked myself in to see a skin and laser specialist in Canterbury called Dr Mark Hudson-Peacock, who it turned out was into his bikes and recognized me from racing. He confirmed that the spots were tumours, but that they were benign, carefully explaining that everybody has cancer in their body, it's just whether or not it manages to manifest itself.

'I can remove them and get them tested and you'll be fine,' he assured me. 'If you've had them since 2003 and they've only got that big, then it's nothing to worry about. If you left them for thirty or forty years they would probably kill you, but they are literally so slow at growing, you can come back in November or December when your season has finished and I'll take them out then.' That put my mind at ease a bit.

When I went back to get them taken out, they were like two Smarties. The doctors closed me back up and the tests came back clear – job done. I was one of the lucky ones, but with the stress and the worry that I went through at the time, I can only imagine what it must be like for people who have to deal with the worst-case scenario.

Meanwhile, whatever my feelings about my racing results were in 2015, I'd decided that I needed to make a big change for 2016. Birdy's relationship with Kawasaki had probably been in a slow decline ever since he'd lost the factory World Superbike contract at the end of 2011, which I think he felt was unfair. There had been this whole drama about one of the team trucks getting caught at Dover with a load of drugs and a gun on board, which was later proved to be nothing to do with Paul, as he'd maintained all along. The guy who was responsible for it got locked up and that should have been the end of it, but I don't think it did his relationship with Kawasaki any good.

The title we had won for them in 2012 had been Kawasaki's first in BSB since 1992, yet we got nothing for it. I pushed them for a move back to World Superbikes, which I felt I'd earned, but they were adamant they weren't going to support it. I felt pissed off because I'd missed the chance to ride a factory Kawasaki in WSB when Birdy pulled the plug in 2011 and gave the chance to Tom Sykes, who went on to become World Superbike Champion in 2013. Fair play to Tom, but I always saw that factory Kawasaki as 'my' ride.

Ironically, Paul and I were now back on the same side again, and whether it was going to be World or British Superbikes, he was my best option. I spoke to him before the end of the season and I said, 'Look, mate, I'm over the whole Kawasaki thing. I am being beaten to the title by somebody I don't think is better than me, riding a bike that the team are telling me isn't going to improve by much next season. I need some fresh motivation.' For probably the first time ever, his initial reaction was to try and keep me happy. 'You want to leave?' he said. 'You can't do that. What do you want? I'll try to sort it.'

'I think we need to talk to another factory,' I said.

There were all sorts of potentials there at that point in time. The SMR team that Brookes rode for in 2015 were taking him to World Superbikes and switching to BMW, so there was some possible Yamaha support available with the bike that had essentially just won the title. Suzuki were also rumoured to be firing some development at a new GSX-R1000, while BMW were putting together a budget for the right team to run the new S1000RR. 'What about running Ducati's again?' I suggested.

John Hopkins was riding an 1199R Panigale in 2015, but he was struggling for results, and at that point he was yet to score a podium, so Birdy wasn't too keen on the idea at first. Meanwhile, I got on to Ducati UK and got hold of a road version of the 1199R for myself, and conducted a bit of 'research' on a quiet road near the Isle of Sheppey bridge. I fell in love with the bike from the moment I opened the throttle – it wheelied in every gear as I went up through the box with the quickshifter, flicked it into a fast right-hand bend and rode it to the rev limiter in top gear. I looked down at the speedo and I was doing 185 mph, and I thought, 'This thing's absolutely bonkers!' It was exciting, exotic – everything that a Ducati should be – and, with the right support, I felt sure we could turn it into a race winner.

By this time, Birdy was already quite a long way down the road with BMW, and I actually think he thought he had the thing wrapped up, but the TAS Racing team had put a better proposal together and ended up getting the contract. In any case, I was adamant that I needed to be on a Ducati.

I love Ducatis to the point that I have a tattoo on my arm of a skeleton riding a Desmosedici – their most exotic and expensive road bike – just because it is a dream of mine to own one and I want to make sure I tick that box before it's too late. I had always had a good relationship with the Italians since I first rode one of their bikes in 2002, and I'd won a lot of races for them in the past. If we could bring them some success with their Panigale in BSB, I knew they would treat us like heroes.

Paul had already spoken tentatively to the Ducati bosses at the British MotoGP in the summer of 2015, and they were immediately interested, just because of the success we'd had the last time we all worked together, albeit more than a decade ago. After the BMW deal fell through, Paul went back to Italy and got the contract signed with Ducati, and on the Wednesday after Josh had beaten me to the championship at Brands Hatch, I went straight down to Valencia to test the Ducati factory development team's WSB spec machine.

My old data technician Giovanni Crupi was there as my crew chief, and we ended up going almost as fast on the Superbike as their factory test rider Michele Pirro was going on the MotoGP bike. All of the Panigale's strengths were completely opposite to the Kawasaki – once it was in a corner you could get on the gas so hard and it just railed the turns, it was almost like riding a motocross bike in a rut, it simply didn't move. For everything I had been struggling with on the Kawasaki, this bike had the answer. The only thing I didn't like about it was the steering, but I knew that we'd be able to fix that with a bit more time. After all, this was a Ducati – a proper race bike!

The first test of 2016 was at Portimão. The team got the bikes really late from Ducati, but I'd asked for Giovanni as my crew chief for the year, and that had been confirmed. I'd been working with Johnny Mowatt, a great guy with whom I'd won a couple of championships, but Johnny could be reluctant to try new ideas and I felt it was the right time for a change. Besides, Ducati were going to make one factory technician available to us, so it made sense to take them up on it. I told Johnny my reasons and he moved to the other side of the garage with my new rookie teammate Glenn Irwin.

The one thing I said to Giovanni after the Valencia test was, 'You have to sort out the steering on that bike because I feel like I'm riding with one arm behind my back.' He told me not to worry. On my first exit at Portimão, boy had he fixed the steering! As soon as I even thought about leaning into the corner, the thing was riding up the inside of the kerb. We ended the test faster than Davide Giuliano on the WSB spec machine, so considering we were running the BSB control ECU on the bike for the first time, I was absolutely made up.

We went to Cartagena afterwards for a BSB test, and I was super-pumped because I thought I was going to smoke everybody, but the bike was a bucking bronco and I was struggling to get up to the pace I'd done there on the Kawasaki. I threw it in the gravel a couple of times, crashed at turn one, and I was on the verge of a meltdown because I couldn't understand why I couldn't get the thing to work. I read a headline in *MCN* the week after the test, saying 'Shakey's rattled'.

'Cheeky fuckers,' I thought. 'I'll show you rattled!'

The bike was still a bucking bronco for the first round of the season at Silverstone, but I managed to fight for the win in both races, finishing half a second behind Michael Laverty in the first one and then losing to Peter Hickman by 0.099 seconds in race two. Ducati were peaking but second place was nowhere near good enough for me. The bike still hadn't won a BSB race and I wanted to be the one that went, 'Bang, have a bit of me.' It took until race two of the third round at Brands Indy for that to happen.

Birdy made me laugh. A few months earlier he had been questioning my sanity when I had said I wanted the Panigale, now he was telling me I was winning because he'd given me the best package out there. In his heart and in his head, the guy truly believes that whatever bike he puts out is the best on the grid and anybody can win on it. If you lose on Birdy's bike he'll tell you that you're a shit rider, but if you win it's because you're on his bike. You have to take it *all* with a pinch of salt. At the end of the day, if you agree to ride for Paul Bird you are in a lose-lose situation, unless you can win-win-win.

Luckily, that's what we did for most of our time together, and once that first win had come on the Panigale, the momentum came with it. We took another win at

Knockhill in round four and then another at Snetterton in round five, where we made a real breakthrough with the bike's manners. She had started the year as a feisty old girl that was happy to try to fire me into orbit at any given throttle application, and at Snetterton we found that the rear tyre just couldn't cope with more than ten laps on the limit. Ducatis tend to be a touch more rigid, in terms of the chassis, than some Japanese bikes, and a stiff chassis and aggressive power delivery do not go that well together. We chipped away at making the engine more user-friendly, and step by step we were getting there.

Our hard work paid off at Thruxton, where I was sent out for first free practice on the Friday morning with some unusual advice from Giovanni. 'Please, please just don't get on the gas,' he said. 'Use your and the bike's ability to run through the turns fast and be patient with the throttle.' I was a bit concerned about what he meant, but Gio was still a full-time employee of Ducati and he'd been heavily involved in developing the V4 Panigale. I trusted him implicitly and I thought, 'Hey, he knows this bike a hundred times better than I do.'

With new tyres and new brake pads in, I did a lap to bed them in, and spent my first semi-flying lap doing just what Gio had said – going easy on the brakes and throttle – only to look down as I crossed the line and see a lap time that was already a full second quicker than my best effort the previous season on the Kawasaki. I couldn't believe what I was seeing!

Much like when I rode the 1098 there back in 2008, the Panigale and Thruxton were made for each other. I was able to make up so much time in the 'big balls' sections of the track, places like Church – the fastest corner in the UK, which you approach flat out in fifth gear before braking, grabbing fourth and throwing the bike towards the apex at around 120 mph. Maintaining a super-high corner speed, you get the rear tyre hooked up gently with the throttle and then stand the bike up, firing it off the corner right the way to the outside of the white perimeter line of the track, to within an inch of the aggressive red, white and blue kerbs on the outside.

If you exit that corner inside the white line, then you haven't got on the gas well enough, but pick up the throttle a split second too early at the apex and you'll be out onto the kerbs, enjoying a 150 mph tank-slapper that will rattle your fillings out and wash off all your drive for the Brooklands straight. In the second qualifying session that weekend, I went so fast through Church that my average speed over the lap was faster than the average speed record for any of the circuits in MotoGP at the time, although Jorge Lorenzo subsequently changed that later in the year at Phillip Island.

My confidence was sky-high on Sunday morning, and the first race turned out to be one of my most enjoyable, most comfortable wins ever. Thruxton is known for being tricky to escape at, because riders tend to benefit from each other's slipstream and form big groups, but I got away cleanly at the start and was leading by more than five seconds when the race was red-flagged on the tenth of twenty laps because of oil on the track. When it was restarted, Michael Laverty got the jump on me at the start, but I passed him on the second-lap and got straight back into my groove to win by more than three seconds.

The second race was looking likely to be exactly the same, but as I led the way onto the back straight on the second lap, I went to change gear and the bike wouldn't shift up or down. I had to pull out and I was devastated because I knew I was giving up a certain double. It was only that a little rod which goes between the gearshift lever and the engine had broken. Still, we put together a run of seven wins from ten races, including a double in the first of the Showdown rounds at Donington, and I went on to win the championship with a race to spare at Brands Hatch.

That was one of my proudest moments because we had taken a bike that couldn't get on the podium, worked so hard to make it a winner and not cut a single corner along the way. We did everything we had to do and we did it once, properly, so that there would be no looking back once the Showdown came around, thinking, 'Maybe we should have done it this way.' We'd done our job and we reaped the rewards, a lot of which I put down to Giovanni and my electronics technician Chris Adams – both absolute gentlemen and both top-notch at their respective jobs. Together we turned the Panigale into a championship winner, and nobody could take that away from us.

*

By now I was enjoying another big rivalry in the familiar, stocky little shape of Leon Haslam, who had come back from winning the final round of the World Superbike season on an Aprilia in 2015 and pushed me all the way for that BSB title in 2016 on a Kawasaki. Leon had returned for nothing less than the championship, so it had been really satisfying to hold him off and I knew that the 'Pocket Rocket' would be ready to light the fuse again in 2017.

Leon is a hard rider, the most tenacious little bastard you could ever race against, and even when you think you've got him beat, he'll come back. Unlike Kiyo or Brookes, Leon will not think twice about launching a lunge from fifty metres back – just because it's his last chance and there's a slim possibility it might work. This guy will find any possible way he can to beat you, and one of his biggest strengths is just how creative he can be; he will produce a move where you least expect it. Over a lap, when everything is perfect, the guy can be incredibly fast, but his biggest weakness is that he can make mistakes under pressure. Sometimes Leon could have a two-second lead but he'd still be pushing so hard that he'd run off track and lose the race. It is like he wants it so badly, he rides at 110 per cent for the whole race – but that is only going to work if you have a lucky day. When he is not under pressure and he backs off slightly, he actually rides much better.

Even though Leon and I are good friends now and have a huge amount of respect for each other, we actually never got on that well in the beginning. We had raced each other since 2002 and, particularly in the early days, his determination to get one over you occasionally spilled over off the track. Even later on he could be sneaky, like putting a rumour out there in the paddock that I'd been caught cheating and Petra was going to leave me. It was all just mind games, something to upset the apple cart, and he probably didn't see anything wrong with doing it, but it didn't help my relationship with him.

More significantly, in 2007 we had an incident on the

track at Brands, when he put me on the grass going down to Hawthorns, the fastest corner on the circuit, at around 175 mph. I went across the gravel and got back into the race, but I was absolutely fuming, and when it was over I pulled into the collecting area, where he was already waiting, debriefing with a couple of his team members, his feet only just touching the floor on his GSE Ducati 999. I threw my bike at my mechanic, took my helmet off and went steaming over to Leon, and shoved him really hard from behind. He turned around and said, 'What the fuck are you doing?'

'You are fucking out of order,' I shouted back at him. 'What the *fuck* were you fucking playing at?'

He looked at me as if he didn't have a clue what I was talking about. Maybe he didn't, but the more he tried to make me look stupid by denying it, the angrier I got. Eventually I totally lost control and I just backhanded him straight across his face. It is not something I'm proud of, but for him to have done something so unnecessary and so dangerous and not take responsibility for it, I just lost my shit.

Many years later, at the end of 2015, I broke my leg in a motocross training accident in Barcelona, and when I went into the hospital for surgery, who was sitting in the waiting room but Leon, who was there to have an operation for arm pump. We ended up meeting up afterwards and sitting down on the beach together and having a long chat. We talked about lots of things, including how good it would be if he came back to British Superbikes, that there was no point in him staying in World Superbikes on an un-competitive bike. It cleared the air between us and ever since then we have got on great.

Still, there had been a few occasions during 2016 when I felt he'd pushed it too far. He'd had a few issues with the engine braking on his Kawasaki, and run me wide so many times in the early part of the season that it was getting beyond a joke. I knew it wasn't personal, because in that situation Leon just does not care and would do it to anybody. Anyway, midway through the season, somebody from their team got the sack and this problem with the engine braking suddenly seemed to get fixed. From that point on Leon rode a lot cleaner and the respect between us on track was maintained.

With Leon staying at Kawasaki for another crack at BSB in 2017, it had been an easy call for me to stay with PBM and defend the title on the Panigale, especially because Ducati had announced that they were going to bring out a brand-new V4 model in 2018. The details that had been released about the V4 suggested it was going to be another very special motorcycle indeed, so Birdy and I agreed over the phone to make it a two-year deal, running the V4 in the second season.

I was made up with life and looking forward to going at it again with Leon and Josh Brookes, who was also back from his nightmare in WSB, but the season turned out to be a much harder one than we'd envisaged. It took us a while to get going. I knocked myself out in the first round at Donington Park and missed both races, and after a fourth place and another crash in round two at Brands Indy, I was fourteenth in the championship on thirteen points. If there was one thing I learned that year it was that you can't win the title in the first round but you can damn near lose it.

By the time the Showdown came around, we'd had some good battles with the boys, scored a few wins, and when they reset the points with the podium credits, I actually had a small margin over Leon. Then we went to Oulton Park and fell apart like a cheap suit. After an average weekend at Assen, I went to Brands Hatch for the final round trailing Leon by thirty-three points. Things just weren't going my way, and when your whole life is about winning races and it doesn't happen, let's just say I was not enjoying myself.

The last round of the season is always a funny one, because you know it is your last chance to do what you love for at least a couple of months. We got to Brands and I thought, 'You know what? Being a motorbike racer is all you ever wanted from being five years old. Get your shit together and enjoy being what you always dreamed of being.' I figured that if I could just get my mojo back that weekend, it would at least set me up in a more positive frame of mind for 2018.

I went out onto the track with a smile on my face, went quickly from the first lap and put the bike on pole on the Saturday. Race one was later that afternoon and I won it convincingly, while Leon really struggled for a fourth place. Suddenly I was only twenty-one points behind him, with two more races and fifty points still to play for on Sunday. That night, lying in bed on my own in my motorhome, something clicked in my mind. I closed my eyes, feeling convinced that this championship was mine.

The next day, I won again in race two, while Leon had a dreadful race and finished tenth – his worst finish of the season. Now there were two points in it with one race to go, and pretty much whoever crossed the line ahead of the other would win the title. The pressure and the tension on the line for that race was probably the most intense I have ever felt, so God only knows how Leon was feeling. I was starting on the front row and he was back on the fourth. I wasn't sure whether to go balls out and try to disappear at the front, or let Leon try to work his way through, and keep an eye on my pit board to see where he was, relax and see how it panned out.

I didn't get the best start but I was there or thereabouts, in the front group and trying to keep out of the way and let all the usual first-lap argy-bargy settle down. Meanwhile, Leon was getting typically creative and, in the second turn, Druids Bend, I got a bit blocked on the inside, while he came all the way around the outside to move up to fifth. I followed him into Bottom Bend, nobody stuffed me up the inside, followed him to Surtees and again nobody attacked. I thought, 'This is perfect.'

All I had to do was stay behind Leon, keep him in sight, and then with a few laps to go try to pull out the extra half-second that I had in my pocket. Every lap we came around I looked at his pit board, which read: SHAKEY +0.0. I checked my own lap times and we were lapping over half a second slower than I had gone in the previous two races, yet Leon looked as though he was already on the limit, starting to make the odd mistake here and there. I knew that the longer I sat behind him, the more likely it was that his head was going to pop under the pressure. I wasn't even looking at my own pit board, just making sure that his said SHAKEY +0.0 on it every time we came past.

Leon started making more and more mistakes, running deep into almost every corner, getting early on the gas, with the bike squirming around underneath him. I felt so confident and comfortable, everything felt as if it was happening in slow motion. Then, all of a sudden, on the sixth lap, we peeled into Hawthorns and he jumped off right in front of me at about 150 mph.

It was a *big* crash, like, worryingly big, and it absolutely popped my head. I was like, 'Fuck, what do I do now?' I made mistake after mistake for the next few laps, because my only focus in the race – to beat Leon Haslam – had gone. Maybe it was selfish, but I wasn't necessarily worried about his well-being at that moment. If I am honest, I wanted the glorious comeback. I wanted to cross the line in first place and win the championship. I didn't care if he finished second or if he was fifth, I just wanted him to be there at the end. If it was a boxing match I wouldn't have wanted to win it on a technical decision. I wanted a knockout.

It is weird how these things play tricks on your mind. Suddenly, simply making it to the finish line seemed like a bigger task than beating my main rival in a straight battle on the track. I started hearing odd sounds from the bike, making me think it was going to break down. I was getting into the corners too hot, running wide, and I was out of my seat in a couple of places. I kept telling myself to calm down but I had this overwhelming desire to just pull over and stop.

Meanwhile, Josh Brookes was making his way to the front of the race. I had enough on my mind to be thinking about him, but the fact was that if he won and I didn't finish, it would be Josh who took the championship. The team were careful not to add that extra pressure, so my pit board simply read 'OK'. As far as I knew, it didn't matter where I finished so I just kept going, and when Dan Linfoot came past me for seventh place, I decided to focus on riding with him and nothing else. I almost ran into the back of him a couple of times but, in the end, Dan got me through the last few laps of that race.

After the chequered flag had finally waved, I rode past the pit-lane entrance and continued down the start-finish straight for the celebrations, but as the fireworks went off and the cannons fired confetti over the finish line, something didn't feel right. I was happy to have won the championship, but it dawned on me that my great rival and friend had been left in the gravel. I gave Petra and the kids a kiss and the team crowded round, slapping me on the back, hugging me and giving out the high-fives as the television crew came in for the interview.

Just then, the crowd parted slightly and Leon appeared, being carried by his dad, the legendary Ron. Leon's ankle and wrist had both been broken in the crash, but the tough little bastard refused to go to the medical centre until he had been up to congratulate me. It was hugely emotional, a great show of sportsmanship and respect between two guys who had put it all on the line. The Haslams are a very special family in racing, and for everything Leon and I had been through over the years, to have them congratulate me like that was a significant moment for me. I truly hope it meant something to them, too.

It also signalled my first ever back-to-back British Superbike titles, achieved on a bike that some people had told me wouldn't even be able to win a race. I can't tell you how satisfying that was; but by the time I had embraced Leon under the setting sun of that autumn afternoon at Brands Hatch, my thoughts had already turned to next spring – and trying to do it all again.

24

May Day Mayday

Leathers have come a long way since my first set – those hideous, ill-fitting, purple, white and black Frank Thomas ones from Paul Smart's motorbike shop in Paddock Wood, which had ended up being held together with duct tape. I can rip a suit to shreds in a crash now and Alpinestars will have them repaired or a replacement suit ready within a matter of days. Every suit is made to measure, and they are so well fitting and comfortable that I could wear them to bed.

Modern leathers are awkward to put on because the back protector is built in. The development of the suit over the years has become so perfectly tailored to when you're on the bike that it's difficult to walk – or even stand up straight – in them. They're made of kangaroo leather – the lightest and toughest leather there is – with highly evolved protective plastic and titanium pads on the shoulders, elbows and knees, an aerodynamic hump on the back that can even be used to store a drinks pack, and a built-in airbag that activates at the first sign of a crash.

I can easily slide my legs into my leathers on my own, but usually need a hand hauling the rest of the suit into position, so that I can work my arms into the sleeves. Then in goes my chest protector. I zip it up, Velcro the top, and seal the magnets together that activate the airbag. Then it's left boot, right boot, ride over to the garage from the motorhome on the scooter, left earplug, right earplug, helmet on, left glove, right glove, and we're good to go.

Keeping that whole rigmarole the same is partly superstition, partly procedure, because the equipment is so well thought out that each item kind of locks into the next, so it needs to be put on in a certain order; the inner boot works with the design of the leathers, which slot inside the outer boot, and so on. After more than two decades your habits and routines change, but I'm lucky to have such a great sponsor, as well as a nice motorhome, so this particular procedure has remained the same for a long time.

However, most of that had gone out of the window when I turned up to Snetterton for a one-day test on 17 May 2018. The PBM team truck, which is an ultra-modern, shiny, moving office block with a built-in workshop and storage space, was in Northern Ireland, where my teammate Glenn Irwin was competing at the North West 200 road race, and the guys had driven down to Norfolk in a Mercedes Sprinter, with my kit thrown in the back along with the spare parts for the bike. Even my trusted 'right hand man' Dan Duguid – a really close cycling friend who had started coming to the races with me in the last couple of years, taking care of my kit and generally keeping everything outside of my riding under control – wasn't with me. So, here I was – probably for the first time since the days I used to throw my own bike and kit into my trusty old Mercedes 508 camper – on my own at a race-track and getting changed in the back of a van.

Three rounds in to the season and I had got off to a pretty decent start. Unfortunately, even though the V4 Panigale was already in the showrooms and on the roads, develop-ment of the race-going Superbike had been delayed by a year, so we faced another season on the V-twin. There would be no more development of that bike, and I was worried about that, because there had been times towards the end of 2017 when it had been really difficult for me to win races. I knew we were going to be up against it, trying to squeeze another title out of what was now a six-year-old bike, but this was the challenge we faced if we wanted to match another Niall Mackenzie record and win the title in three successive seasons. That would be my seventh in total.

Alongside Niall, the only other guys with three titles to their name were Ryuichi Kiyonari and John Reynolds, and I knew that if I could make it seven, and then hopefully eight, it would be a long time before anybody could touch my record. I don't want that to sound rude or disrespectful to those three guys, or any of my competitors, it is just the way a racer thinks. Things might not have gone my way on the world stage, but I had since made it my mission to obliterate every record at national level. And if the chance ever came my way again in World Superbikes, I would be ready.

In the first round at Donington, I went backwards after a terrible start and ended up down in twelfth. I got myself back to within striking distance of the win on the last lap, and maybe another time round I could have done it, but 'could haves' and 'should haves' count for nothing in racing. I'd worked hard to get on the back of Bradley Ray, the surprise package of the weekend, and I was happy enough to take second in that race, which took place in freezing temperatures and mixed conditions, with the track wet in some places and dry in others.

In the second race Brad showed guts, not to mention talent, to push on despite the conditions to make it a double win, his first in BSB, despite being just twenty years old – less than half my age. I'd liked Brad for a while, he was an exciting prospect, and I knew that he was the short-term answer to BSB's long-term problem, which was a forty-two-year-old guy going out and beating everybody week in week out. It becomes an issue for any racing series when one guy dominates, like Mick Doohan did in MotoGP in the Nineties or, more recently, as Jonathan Rea has in World Superbikes. Suddenly, just because one guy is doing a better job, the championship is criticized for being boring or predictable, and from experience I knew the measures they were prepared to take to stop that happening.

There was no suggestion of anything untoward going on at the start of 2018, though. Bradley Ray could ride a bike, and his arrival on the BSB scene reminded me of myself some fifteen years before, when Birdy had sacked Steve Hislop and handed me the ride. Back then there was no such thing as social media, and I knew the pressure and expectation would start mounting on Brad in the same way it had when I got Hizzy's ride. So, before the second round at Brands Hatch, I took him to one side and said, 'Listen, mate, you just keep enjoying riding your motorbike. People will build you up to be the next big thing and you don't need it. Keep riding your bike as good as you are doing and try not to get caught up in the hype.'

Brad rode well again at Brands, but I managed to take my first win of the season in race one, and after three rounds of the championship I was there or thereabouts – third overall and seventeen points behind Leon, who had made a consistent start and would probably be my main rival for the title again. The tracks I always struggled at with the Panigale were the tight, scratchers' tracks like Knockhill in Scotland or the short Brands Hatch Indy layout. On bigger, more open and fast tracks, the Ducati flatters my style, so I was really looking forward to round four of the season at Snetterton. I'd won eight of the last ten BSB races to be held there, and I was keen to make it ten out of twelve this time around.

The chance to test there a month beforehand would be an opportunity to keep ticking over and try a few things with the set-up of the bike. Even at my age and with my experience, a one-day test was an exciting prospect; the weather forecast was good, and I could think of few better ways to spend a day than riding a Ducati in the sunshine.

If there was one thing that could have made the prospect of going up to Snetterton any more enticing, it was flying a helicopter up there and – having renewed my pilot's licence just a week beforehand – I booked to loan one for the day. I had done the medical, filed all the paperwork and submitted it all to the Civil Aviation Authority, and was just waiting for the paper licence to come back through the post so that I could fly myself up from Manston. The plan was to take off first thing in the morning, ride my Ducati all day and then fly home: the perfect day.

It started badly when my licence failed to appear in the morning's post the day before the test, so instead of taking a quick forty-minute flight, I had to drive the couple of hours up to Norwich the night before and stay in a hotel. It was annoying but it wasn't a big drama – I got up there in good time, had a bit of dinner with the boys and everything was cool.

Now here I was getting changed in the back of a Mercedes van again, all these years after doing it on a weekly basis. With no windows in the back of a van you need to have the door open to see what you're doing, which was never a problem back in those early days in the 508, but now there were a bunch of fans hanging around by the back doors of the Sprinter, waiting for an autograph or a selfie. Not a good time to be stripping down naked!

Eventually I managed to squeeze into my leathers without embarrassing myself or anybody else too much, sent Petra a quick text and went to throw my leg over my beloved motorcycle. Deep down, a racer knows that each time he does so it could easily be his last, but you genuinely don't take the time to think about it much. That day at Snetterton, it was the last thing on my mind.

'You've got new brake pads in – front and rear,' Giovanni told me before I headed out. 'Just spend a couple of laps bedding them in.'

It was the usual drill for me: a final word from my main chassis mechanic Kev once I'd swung my leg over the bike, a few steady laps to get a feel for it and then, as we got going, I would come back in and we could start to work on other aspects like the new swing-arm. The new exhaust we were waiting for from Termignoni hadn't arrived, so that would have to wait until later in the season, but I was cool with that as I figured a few little performance-enhancing parts towards the Showdown would be perfect. Even though the bike itself was six years old, these small, incremental upgrades to it could make the crucial few hundredths of a second difference to the lap times that could mean winning the title or not. Every little advantage counts, and that's why we were there to test.

As I always liked to do, I was the last rider out onto the track. I have always been able to get up to speed within a lap or two, even if I've had a few weeks off the bike, so I would let everybody else go out first and have a couple of laps before I joined them. Otherwise you can easily get caught up in somebody else's mistake. The weather was perfect and the track temperature was good – everything was looking promising as I set off up pit lane and performed my last stretches on the bike.

I rode nice and steady for my first lap, just playing around a little with the brakes, using both levers to scrub the new pads in. I completed the first lap no problems, came up the start-finish straight and got on the brakes for turn one nice and early. I did the same for turn two – another tight, second-gear right-hander – and on my way out I picked the bike up off the right-hand edge of the tyre as I twisted the throttle and accelerated hard. Two gear shifts up and five seconds later and I was off the throttle again, braking hard into the first left-hander on the circuit at turn three.

The sequence for a track-day rider will generally be to get towards a corner, shut the throttle, hit the brakes, select the right gear, shift their bodyweight and then pick their line through the turn. A professional rider does all of that in one movement, so as I lifted the bike up and transitioned over to the left-hand side of the tyre for turn three, I chopped the throttle shut, not using too much brake, but the engine braking was really tight. As a result, the rear of the bike locked and came around on me as if it was going to high-side me, off the throttle, and throw me over the top. I managed to control it and catch the high-side, but the bike pinged back so violently that it practically turned right, rather than left.

The problem was that I was now going at 130 mph in completely the wrong direction. Usually there would be air fencing in a corner like that, and you would pretty much just aim for whichever part of it you wanted to hit. But ahead of me, looming large, all I could see was the vast, dense blackness of the tyre wall.

I had just a few metres of tarmac to get on the brakes as hard as I could and scrub off speed before running onto the grass. With no gravel trap there to slow me down, I tried everything to get the bike to change direction again as it skidded across the grass. I grabbed the brakes but the front wheel locked and almost made me crash, so I let go and tried again, and again, and again . . . battling to wash off speed and get the bike to change its course without locking the front.

Those couple of seconds felt like minutes before I finally thought, 'Fuck it, this ain't gonna happen. I'm going to have to jump.' The last thing I remember seeing is the bike veering off away from me as I slid head first into the crash barrier.

*

When I came around it was as if I was looking at the world through a virtual-reality mask. My field of vision was like a letterbox, surrounded in darkness, and through it I could see what looked like the dashboard of my bike. There were numbers and dials and dashes and bars going up and down, accompanied by a weird throbbing noise: *wow-wow-wow-wow* and then *ding-ding-ding-beep-beep*. I couldn't work out what was going on, and even though I couldn't hear it over the noise of the 'dashboard', I could feel that I was screaming. I felt locked inside this virtual reality and couldn't hear or feel anything outside of it. I knew that it must be bad, but I couldn't feel any pain.

Just like that, the mask came off and I was back in the real world. I heard a voice. 'Shane, I'm Dr Cook.' I blinked hard and looked around. Petra was there, Giovanni and Waggy too. 'I'm going to be looking after you while you're here at the Norfolk and Norwich University Hospital.'

Norfolk and Norwich Hospital? Oh yeah, I was at Snetterton, wasn't I? I couldn't remember being in the circuit medical centre, but I could vaguely recall distant talk of an ambulance. 'Can you move your arms for me?' he said. 'And now your legs?' I obliged. 'I am astounded,' he said. 'How are you doing that?'

'You're the doctor, mate,' I groaned. 'You tell me.'

It was the first thing I'd said since I left the garage to bed those new brakes in.

'Well, frankly, Shane, the fact you are not paralysed – or even dead – is a bit of a mystery to me.'

Petra Byrne, June 2018
Isle of Sheppey, Kent, UK

Some days I see two different people in the same house. It's almost like I am married to Shane, but having an affair with Shakey. Maybe that's why it works! From Monday to Wednesday of a race week he is Shane – a loving, funny and caring family man. On a Thursday he starts changing into Shakey. Sometimes I'll say, 'Oh, I see Shakey has woken up today, what an arsehole!'

Shakey can be arrogant, full of himself. I tell him he's a proper little prima donna. He doesn't believe it, but it's true. Even his team, they know how to deal with him when he is angry. Nobody speaks to him, but eventually he comes round. It's hard work but it goes with what he does. Some people never even get to meet Shane, they only ever know Shakey. When he races, he is a completely different person to when he's at home. Not even a tiny bit of him is the same.

I suppose the ironic thing is that I was a fan of Shakey before I met Shane. I followed motorbike racing my whole life, so the modelling work seemed a good way to get close to it. I wasn't really interested in the £150 they put in your hand after the race, but I was fascinated with the racing. I would be standing on the grid holding an umbrella, but I was staring at the bikes. My favourite riders were Shakey, Valentino Rossi and Michael Rutter – what a combination!

I saw him in the paddock at Valencia and the girl I was working with said, 'Hey, that's the rider you like!' He was walking along, chatting with James Ellison. I introduced myself to Shakey, and then I fell in love with Shane. I guess when you meet somebody you just know. Only a couple of hours after asking him for a photograph, I was pretty sure I was going to marry this guy.

The first time I saw him lying there in his hospital bed, it made me feel physically sick. He looked crushed. Well, he *was* crushed. The doctor had explained that the worst damage was to the C1 and C2 vertebrae at the top of his neck. 'Imagine you put a CD on a table and hit it with a hammer.' That's how he'd described it. Shane needed operations to fix his shattered bones, but he was too poorly for surgery. That was on the Thursday, and they set Monday as the day of the operation.

Before they took him to theatre, the surgeon came to me for a final word as his next of kin. 'Do you want me to fix him for life or for racing?' he asked. It was a strange question, and at first I wasn't sure what he meant. He explained that the quicker, safer way to operate was to fuse the broken vertebrae in his neck together, so that there would be no danger of snapping the spinal cord. This would mean that he wouldn't be able to turn his head any more and so there would be no way he could ever ride a motorcycle again – not even to the shops to buy a pint of milk.

However, the recovery would be much more straightforward and much quicker than the alternative, which was to try and piece everything back together. That would require a slower, more dangerous, operation and the outcome was not so clear. If it worked, he might recover full movement in his neck and, possibly, have a chance to race again. If it didn't, there was the risk of paralysis – or worse.

I felt as though the doctor was asking me to choose between the two men I loved. I could save Shane, but it meant that Shakey would have to die. What was I going to say? I couldn't kill Shakey. That's not my call. I can't just have a man who wanted nothing in his life since he was five years old but to be a motorcycle racer, and take that away from him. It would devastate him and it could ruin us. Because one day in the future, he might resent me. 'Why did you take that away from me?' I can almost hear his voice now. I couldn't bear that. Instead, I knew we would just have to go through hell to try and fix him again.

Dr Cook said, 'I will do whatever I can, but I have to tell you that the risk of your husband being paralysed from the neck down is really very high.'

Shane wasn't really speaking, he was pretty much out of it on drugs, but as they wheeled him off to the operating theatre he seemed agitated, and I saw him wiggling his legs.

'What's wrong?' I said.

'Nothing,' he replied. 'It's just, I figured I'd better do it now as I don't know if I will ever be able to do this again.'

That absolutely did me in. I couldn't help but wonder if he would even want to come through the operation at all if that was the case.

When he came out of the operating theatre, they had fitted him with a neck brace and a halo, which was screwed directly into his skull, to hold all the plates and rods and everything they had put in his neck in place. They didn't let me stay over in critical care so, on occasion, Shane's mum would come to the house to look after the kids and I'd book myself into a hotel in Norwich for the night. I'd put a brave face on all day, smile at the visitors, chat to Shane and try to put a smile on his face too. At the end of the day I'd say, 'Bye, see you tomorrow!' and then the minute I walked into my hotel room, I would completely break down. I cried myself to sleep every night for two weeks straight.

All the while I had to see announcements coming from the organizers or the team, like a tweet from the team the day after his crash that said he 'will make a full recovery' or a later statement on behalf of our family that said he was 'alert and in good spirits'. I never agreed to any of this and I knew Shane would be furious if he heard about it. I even hid his phone from him, kept telling him I'd left it at home by accident as I'd been so stressed travelling back and forwards. For some reason it seemed like everyone else was trying to cover up the severity of the whole accident and his injuries. I started to get messages from well-wishers. I remember I got one from Charley Boorman, who meant well, of course. It said something like: 'I'm so relieved to hear he's just got a couple of bruises.' I couldn't get my head around who was giving people this misinformation. When I told Charley how Shane really was, he was pretty shocked.

When people started coming to the hospital to visit, Shane would make this huge effort.

'How are you, Shakey?'

'Yeah, I'm all good, brand new!'

I found myself going along with it. The other parents at school would say: 'Oh my god, we read about your husband in the paper! Is he OK?'

And I'd be like, 'Yeah, all good!'

'And how are you? You must have been so worried.'

'Ah, I'm used to it.'

It's funny really, but I'm not going to lie, there were times when I was heading home from that hospital and I felt like driving into a wall myself.

25

Braced for the Worst

The medication they were giving me just after my operation must have been really strong because I had these incredibly vivid hallucinations that I can still remember now. At one point, when they moved me from critical care to the intensive care ward, I had it in my head that they had transported me in the back of this Luton-type box van. I can clearly remember being pushed into this big day room, which had a bar and big chesterfield sofas and stuff to chill out and watch TV. Petra was there with my friends Ian and Wag, and for some reason, a load of kids were running about the place.

Apparently, I said to the nurses when I got to intensive care, 'When we get done here can I get back to that day room where the bar is, please?' Of course, they didn't have a clue what I was on about. 'Oh, and I hope all those kids are going to keep the noise down if I'm going to get any sleep.' I drifted off and the next thing I knew I was back in the Luton van and then, bizarrely, getting wheeled out into the car park of Frank Bird Poultry.

Before the accident I'd been seriously thinking about finally buying myself a Ferrari – I even went to London to test-drive one and was made up with it. I still really wanted a 488, but it would not exactly be practical for a family of four, so another option I'd been checking out was an Audi RS4 – still pretty quick but much more suitable for whenever I needed to throw my pushbike or a load of bags into the back. Now, for some reason, every car in the car park at Frank Bird Poultry was a brand-new Audi. Big Frank – Paul's dad, who owns everything – had got himself an S8 and Birdy had some super-special thing with a thousand horsepower that he'd had designed and built just for himself.

Petra came to see me in the morning. 'You're not going to believe this,' I said.

'What?' she replied, pulling up a chair next to the bed.

'They made me sleep in the back of a van last night.' She looked at me all confused. 'Honestly! And I'll tell you something else, that fucking Birdman has only gone and bought every staff member at Frank Bird Poultry a new Audi each! I swear, the whole place has a new Audi – from the cleaners to the boss!' She just went along with it, bless her, but when I tried to ask the nurses why they made me sleep in a van, they put me straight. 'Shane, you slept here last night. Right where you are now, in this bed.'

It sounds so ridiculous now, but at the time I honestly couldn't figure out what was real and what was not. If anything, my hallucinations and dreams felt far more lucid than reality.

One particular night, I got extremely agitated. To some people, the opportunity to knock a load of drugs down and kick back in bed for a week might sound like their idea of heaven. But when you've broken virtually every bone in your upper body, being stuck in one position is pure hell. To relieve it, the nursing staff do what they call a 'log roll', where three or four people roll you onto your side and give your body a bit of a rub down with a cloth, just to try and stimulate your body and skin and relieve the pressure sores before rolling you back over on your back again.

At this point I was having a lot of issues with the nerves in my chest. If you touched my skin as gently as you could with your little finger, it genuinely felt as if you were holding a cigarette lighter to it. I couldn't even have the bed sheet up above my waist, otherwise it felt as though my whole chest was on fire, and even a little graze from the cable from my finger pulse monitor would have me screaming in agony. The first couple of times they tried this 'log roll' thing, a couple of them put their hands on the right side of my chest and I absolutely lost it – swearing and shouting at them to leave me the fuck alone.

After a few days I started being able to help with the log roll a little, by holding my own weight on the frame of the bed. One night, I had got so frustrated of being stuck on my back, I thought, 'You know what, I'm gonna roll all the way onto my front.' The halo that was screwed into my head was ready to be attached to a chest brace, but for now it was all still held in place by a neck brace.

When you are that broken, you have to plan every move you make. Even if you want a drink from the bedside table, you have to plot every little detail – from operating the electric bed to lift you to the right point without squashing your ribs, to making sure you are always within reach of your glass. I had my manoeuvre all worked out: I just had to get onto my left side with my arm under my body, which I could then use as a lever to initiate the roll. I had a broken collarbone on that side, so that was sore, but I managed it and with a big groan I pushed myself with my legs and – after a bit of to-ing and fro-ing – I rolled over onto my front. Hooray!

The only problem was that I was now face down on the pillow and could no longer see, or breathe. It was at this point, as the saying goes, Shane realized he had fucked up. It is quite comical now, but at the time I was shouting a muffled '*Fuuuuck!*' into the pillow. I scrabbled around with my hand for the alarm but I couldn't reach it. I went straight into this fast-forward action, this time with no plan, to get myself back over. It must have taken me twenty minutes to fully wriggle myself onto my back again, by which time I had almost suffocated myself and was in even more pain and discomfort than ever before.

A few days after that, the physio came and sat me up on the side of the bed. It hurt, a lot, to get up, but when I first sat upright it felt as if the middle of my spine wasn't connected to either the top or the bottom of it. It was as if my neck and the top of my back were in one piece, and the bottom of my spine was intact, but there was a big section completely missing in the middle. It was the first time since the crash that I had taken the strain of my upper body, and with the halo on top it felt like the weight of the world was pushing down on my mushy insides. My head was spinning.

'I can't do this,' I said to the physio. 'You're going to have to lay me back down.'

'It's fine, it's fine,' she said. 'You got up. That's a good start.'

By now I was starting to be a little more 'with it'. I was on some pretty serious painkillers still, and would be for some time, but I got around to wanting my phone. Petra had it in her bag, so we plugged it in and turned it on.

I had so many messages from people saying they were glad I was OK, that they'd see me in a couple of weeks at Snetterton. I was grateful for every single message, but seriously? See me in a couple of weeks? It was doubtful I'd even be out of hospital by then. Straight away, I put maximum concentration into posting a tweet and an Instagram update, revealing the full extent of my injuries. This was no bruising and I certainly wasn't 'alert and with it', as had been reported. I explained what had really happened and, bloody hell, if the phone was beeping and buzzing when we first turned it on, it went absolutely cuckoo within ten seconds of me hitting send. At least the truth was out there now.

It dawned on me that I had a lot of hard work to do to get fixed up but, little by little, I found I could sit up on my own and soon started to feel as though I was making progress. Dr Cook came in on the Sunday morning, six days after the operation, to put the body brace part of the halo on. He warned me that once it was on, everything would feel really different, and that all of my natural movements would come from different places to normal.

It was a big physical effort to get it on and, bearing in mind that this was only a week or so after the crash, virtually every bone under the brace was still broken; it felt as if they would give way as he ratcheted the brace up tighter. My chest was on fire, but there was no relief as he tightened it even more. When he was done, he gave me his arm and pulled me upright. I can't tell you how much that hurt – I didn't know if I was going to piss myself, shit myself or both. It felt as if we'd snapped my spine in half again and I screamed in pain.

'I can't take this,' I pleaded with Dr Cook. 'You can't leave this thing on me. Please, take it off.' To my huge relief, it was agreed that before they could proceed any further with the body brace, they would have to address the nerve damage that was causing the issues in my chest. Essentially, I was so badly hurt in so many places that my brain had scrambled, and it couldn't process all the signals that were coming from my nervous system, which is why the pain of my shattered vertebrae was manifesting itself like boiling water on my chest. I would need specific medication that would take five days to kick in, and that meant another five days in the neck brace.

Petra brought the kids up to see me later that afternoon, but the procedure had taken so much out of me that I slept through their whole visit. I remember seeing them briefly, for as long as it took me to say, 'Hi darling, how are you? All right, kids?' and then I was gone again. I couldn't keep my eyes open – it was as though somebody had stapled them shut. When I woke, I was on my own. I was devastated because I knew they'd driven three hours to see me, and then three hours home again after watching me do nothing but sleep.

When eleven o'clock that night came around and the

nurses came to give me my tablets to put me to sleep for the night, I was wide awake. They left the room and for the first time I could remember, I started to cry. It was out-and-out pain, depression and anxiety. It all came at once, all at its worst.

26

The Devil Wears a Halo

The next morning was Sunday. I knew that they were preparing to try the body brace again on Friday, so I had five days to get well enough and I put all my focus into that. My first target was a shave – I hadn't had one since I'd been in the hospital and I felt as if I'd really let myself go. It's not like I could do anything about it, as such, but when Petra brought my trimmer up and I got to have a tidy-up, I felt so much more presentable and happy.

My next little target, and a far more pressing one, was to have a shower. I'd been having bed baths for a week and a half and I'd been pretty paranoid about it because the last thing I was doing before I was taken into hospital was riding my motorbike. I'd only done a lap and a half before I fell off, but I had it in my head that I needed a shower before the body brace went on. Once it was on, it would be on for three months, and there would be no chance to have a shower then.

I was sitting up a lot more in the bed by this point, trying to be more alert and really making an effort to get going. The physios came in one day to stand me up, which lasted about five seconds before I went dizzy. From that point I worked myself, whenever I felt I had the strength, to sit on the edge of the bed, stand up for as long as I could manage and then sit back down and go to sleep for a bit. Each time that I was able to stand up for a few seconds longer was a little victory.

I was trying so hard but the problem wasn't so much the dizziness, it was the fact that my body felt as if it was in three parts. The middle bit didn't feel connected and the coordination required to get my legs working in sync with everything else was exhausting. Eventually I got to the point where I could take a couple of steps and make it to the open window. I stood there for a few seconds, filled my aching lungs with fresh air, and looked out at the big entrance to the hospital car park. I tried standing there long enough to be able to picture how nice it would be to drive out through that barrier and go home.

It had been a couple of days since Petra had been with the kids and seen me sleeping all day, but they were due back in again that afternoon and I was determined to show them how much progress I was making. As soon as they came in I sat up and spun my legs to the edge of the bed. They immediately panicked.

'Dad, what are you doing?'

'No, no, don't worry, kids. Watch, I can do this, Daddy's getting better.'

I hauled myself up by the window, looked out at the car park again and smiled to myself. Now, it turned out that for some reason that day I had really low blood pressure, which could have been a reaction to the medication, so as I turned back towards the bed I felt myself go all wobbly. That was it, I just went. I dropped to my knees and Petra lunged in and half caught me by my left arm, the one with the broken collarbone, and half by my halo. She managed to haul me back onto the bed and then yelled at me, which was understandable. Lilly had got trapped underneath me, so both she and Zack were pretty shocked and started crying. They hung around for a while and I managed to talk to them a little before they left to get home for tea and ready for school the next morning.

It felt like weeks, but that Friday eventually came around. 'Morning, Shane!' said the nurse as she breezed into my room.

'Morning, Nurse!'

'If you've had your tablets and your breakfast, it's time to do your bed bath,' she said.

'Ah, can't I just have a shower today?'

'A shower? I don't know about that, let me have a look at your notes.' While she was flicking through the paper-work I stood up at the side of the bed. 'Hey, be careful, you're only supposed to do that with the physios.'

'Nah . . . look! I can do it, honestly. If you walk with me, we'll do it together.'

'Are you sure?'

'Yeah, yeah, I've done it before, I walked to the toilet yesterday and I've been this morning too,' I lied.

For the first time since I'd been in there, I started my

journey to the bathroom. It was about three and a half metres from the side of the bed, past the toilet to a chair underneath the shower and, with the help of the nurse, I just about made it. You know when you're just about to pass out but you're not quite there? Well, that was me at this point. 'Whoa, baby, play it cool!' I said to myself.

'Nurse, this might have to be a dry run,' I eventually conceded. I sat down on the chair in the shower and my senses started to flood back. 'In fact, do you know what? No, let's do it now.' I stood back up and leaned to one side to get my halo out of the way while the nurse switched the taps on. That sensation of warm water running down my skin – especially on my back, where I'd been laid for so long – was a relief like nothing I had ever felt before. It was *so* nice! I was holding on to this rail, thinking, 'I'm going to pass out any second but I just don't want this to end!' Never mind a small victory – by the time I got back to my bed, all clean and dried off, I felt as though I'd won another championship.

Later that afternoon, Dr Cook came back to have another go at fitting the body brace. The drugs he had put me on since the last time had eased the problem with the nerves in my chest, but they also made me feel relaxed. I'd had a couple of really good nights' sleep, the best since I'd been in there, and this time he had no problems ratcheting the brace on. It was tight and solid but after a few days of starting to feel mobile, I immediately went back to being bed-bound again.

With the brace connected, I couldn't work out how to turn myself sideways, sit up or get my legs out of the bed, and I felt beaten down again. I knew I needed the thing on and knew I was stuck with it for the next three months, but I was devastated to feel as if I had taken a step backwards. Petra was there and I didn't let on to her, but after she went home I started rolling around in the bed, working out which muscles I needed to use to get myself upright again. Eventually I found myself perched on the edge of the bed and then back up on to my feet. I stood at the window and took another selfie to upload to Instagram.

I figured Dr Cook would probably want to see how I managed with the brace over the weekend before maybe setting me free on Monday. Being at home when the kids came in from school was my new target. It was a steady weekend, progressing as much as I could with the physio and improving my movement. When Dr Cook came in on the Monday morning, I was excited to see him.

'How are you feeling, Shane? Are you moving around OK?'

'Yeah, yeah. All good.'

'OK, good. Well, we'll give it another couple of days and maybe we can think about sending you home.'

It was another blow and I was devastated again – partly because I just wanted to go home and see my kids, but mainly because I realized how poorly I must still be for him to not let me go. I had been in hospital for two weeks by now and the thought of even another couple of days felt like a life sentence. Petra came up and I gave her the news. I felt like I'd let myself and my family down. 'Shane, you're staying here because you're poorly,' she assured me. 'It's not because you're doing badly and the doctors want to punish you. They just want to make sure you're OK with this thing on.' She was right, I knew it, and after another week of watching the seconds and the minutes drag by, my time finally came on Tuesday 5 June 2018.

A sponsor and by now a good friend of mine called Ian Fern had kindly offered to pick me up in his helicopter on the day I was to be let home. I rang Ian straight away, but he had a meeting that he couldn't get out of. 'Don't worry, Shane,' he said. 'I'll send a pilot to pick Petra up and we'll get you out of there.'

Petra was petrified of going up to the hospital in a heli-copter. I'm not too sure why, but she's never been massively keen on them. 'You've flown under the Golden Gate Bridge and landed in the Grand Canyon in one before now,' I told her. 'Surely you can manage flying over the Thames Estuary!' The pilot was competent and experienced, plus the helicopter was brand new – in fact, I assured her, I'd flown it myself just a few weeks previously and it was abso-lutely lovely. It also had a new version of the safety system that prevented the helicopter from even being started if there was anything wrong with it.

I was right about the last part of that, because when the pilot got to Ian's helicopter to fly it up to the Isle of Sheppey and collect Petra, he discovered that it had a battery issue and wouldn't fire up. I had to text Petra and tell her what was going on, and as far as she was concerned that was it – she wasn't getting in any helicopter.

Ian managed to sort another one out, but the pilot had to get himself to another airfield to collect it and then he got delayed even further by a no-fly zone due to a massive military convoy. Finally, he made it to the helicopter pad at Norfolk and Norwich University Hospital, the porters wheeled me out of the door into the refreshing blast of air being given off by the rotating blades, and thirty-five minutes later we were touching down at a small airfield just a few hundred yards from my house.

When we landed, Petra was already there with the car engine running. She whisked me home and dumped me indoors, ordering me not to move before dashing off to get the kids from school. I sat and waited in the front room, flicking through the hundreds of 'Get Well Soon' cards that well-wishers had sent. Before long I heard that familiar click from the front door latch and then the murmur of Zack and Lilly's voices as they shoved their way into the hallway, pestering Petra to let them play on their Play-Station or watch their iPads.

'Oh kids, I forgot to tell you something,' I heard Petra say.

'What? What?'

'Daddy has had *the* best card *ever* today. You have to go into the front room to see it.'

'The front room?' The kids never really go in the front room; it normally only gets used by Petra and me in the evenings to chill out.

'Yes, the front room.'

The door creaked open and the pair of them came into the room and looked blankly at me, sitting on the sofa.

'Daddy? . . . Daddy! . . . *Daddyyyyyyyy!*' The pair of them came running over. I was like 'Whoa! Don't jump on me!' It was an amazing moment, a feeling that I'll never forget. I'd never felt so happy in my whole life, yet at the same time I felt so sad. Here were my babies, my family, and I could barely reach out to put an arm around them, never mind hold them. I just wanted to squeeze them tight and embrace every second of the moment, but I couldn't. I felt elated and frustrated all at once.

But at least Daddy was home.

*

I immediately tried to get on with living as normal a life as possible, which wasn't easy when I was walking around with a mobile telephone mast on my head! I used to joke that I had the best signal in Medway. I really wanted to get straight back to being a dad, doing the school runs with Petra, even if I couldn't drive the kids there myself. For the first couple of days, the medication was working and I was feeling pretty good.

Dr Cook had told me that the best thing I could do to help stabilize the metal rods he had inserted in the top of my back was to walk. It was so hard for me to do at the time, because my whole body was still so out of sync, but walking literally was the first step on my recovery programme, and I wanted to give it a good go.

Petra has this fancy running machine with a display monitor on it that plays scenes of real-life routes around the world. You can be in your garage in the middle of Kent but running along Fisherman's Wharf in San Francisco, so I set it to a slow walking pace and went off for a ten-minute stroll down the Grand Canyon. I felt so proud of myself. A couple of days before I had been bed-bound in a hospital in Norfolk, and now here I was knocking out a couple of kilometres in the Nevada desert!

I got off the treadmill after ten minutes or so and I felt great. Later that night I went to bed and drifted off to sleep, in discomfort from the halo but free from pain for the first time since the crash. However, the next morning I woke up feeling really rough. Petra was already downstairs, as usual, making up the kids' lunch boxes for school, so I pulled myself out of bed and went to go to the toilet. I didn't feel right at all, I was struggling to breathe and I started to feel nauseous.

I tried to lie back down on the bed but it was too soft. I couldn't get comfortable. I moved myself onto the floor and that was too hard. In the end I curled up into a foetal position, trying to relieve this horrible feeling of general pain and anxiety. Petra came back into the bedroom and found me there, which obviously caused her to panic. I told her to give me ten minutes – to go sort the kids out and come back. I just needed to get myself together. In those ten minutes I went from bad to worse, and started moaning to her for some painkillers. 'I'm calling an ambulance,' she said.

'You don't need to do that,' I replied. 'Just give me a few minutes.'

She called one anyway and before those few minutes had passed, I was begging her not to wait for it and to take me straight to the hospital herself. Before she had time to work out what to do next, the ambulance arrived.

'I'm sorry to say this but I think you might be having a heart attack,' said one of the doctors when I arrived at the hospital. 'You might just have been pushing your recovery too hard.'

'I ain't being big-headed, but I am a professional athlete,' I gasped. 'I don't do a ten-minute walk on a treadmill and have a heart attack!'

'Well, sometimes the human body can't take the amount

of trauma it has been subjected to and this kind of thing can happen,' he explained.

I went into a bit of a state of shock; I was shaking and not in a good place. They were worried about my spine as well as my heart, but after a bunch of tests it turned out it was just a bout of pneumonia. So after another five days laid up in Medway Hospital, I was sent home again.

*

Within a couple of days I was back on my feet, and I knew I had to get back to work in some way. I had been working as a pundit for Eurosport on their World Superbike coverage for a few years by now, and they were good enough to accommodate me as part of their BSB team as soon as I was ready.

Being in the paddock for the first time was hard. It was at Brands Hatch in the July of 2018, just over two months since the crash, and I still had the halo on. I was still in a lot of pain but I was hurting more inside because it was the first time I had seen my bike going around the track without me on it. It is odd when something like that makes you realize how little you mean in the grand scheme of things. I had always assumed that I would be a part of this sport until the day I decided otherwise. I watched a talented young rider called Andrew Irwin – younger brother to my teammate Glenn – ride around my home circuit on my title-winning Ducati Panigale, and a tiny part of me had to concede that I might not be a part of it ever again.

The paddock immediately became a different place to me and, in a way, I enjoyed it. Racing is a bit like boxing, in that you can't really get on too well with the guy whose face you need to smash in five minutes later. But by doing the television job, I was able to walk into different hospitalities and have a coffee with different teams, talk about stuff outside of racing. It was nice not to feel like every person just wanted to beat me.

It was also good to have a focus, to keep going to the circuits as I had always done, although putting myself amongst the public wasn't easy. An easy introduction for people to make when they want to speak to me was always, 'When you going to get back on the bike, Shakey?' They were just doing it for something to say, I knew that, but it was the hardest question they could possibly ask me. They might as well have asked me for my bank details. All I could say was, 'I don't know, hopefully soon.' That killed me.

Brands Hatch is a place that has given me so much in life, but when I went back there for a second time in October, for the final weekend of the 2018 British Superbike Championship, it made me feel like I had nothing. The race-going V4 Panigale Superbike that I was supposed to have been riding that season was finally unveiled for the first time, with the official factory Ducati test rider Michele Pirro coming over from Italy to complete a demonstration lap. Giovanni gave me a sneak preview of the bike on the night before Pirro was due to ride it. He pulled the covers back and I sat on it and I swear I could have cried. I looked around at my boys, at my team, and I thought, 'What am I going to do now?' This moment was meant to signal the start of the next chapter of my career, not the end of the last one.

In the latter years of my career, as I reached my late thirties and early forties, a lot of people made the wrong assumption that other riders must be hungrier than me to win the championship because I've already won it so many times. It is a question I've been asked many times. How do you keep your hunger? How do you match their motivation? To me it was always really simple: those other guys don't know how good it feels to be a champion. How can they possibly understand what it is like, for just one moment, to feel so on top of the world? So how can they possibly want it as much as me? Because I *do* know what it feels like, and I want to feel it again. And then I want to feel it again, and again, and again.

They say winning is like a drug. It only satisfies your need for a short period of time, and then you need another hit. Throughout my recovery, for all the painkillers I took, it was still the drug I needed more than any other, but the truth was I couldn't have it. I looked at the British Superbike Championship in 2018 and I thought, 'I smoked all those guys before, I'll smoke them all again.' And that's not braggadocio. I was looking at the lap times, seeing what they were doing, knowing inside what I could still do if my body would let me.

I knew that weekend at Brands Hatch would be hard; to say goodbye to a season that had ended so early for me. To go there and say 'Well done' to Leon Haslam for winning a championship I always felt was mine. I don't mean that to sound bitter – Leon did the best job and he thoroughly deserved to be a champion. I was the first one there to congratulate him, just as he had been for me twelve months before, but that doesn't mean it was easy. To think that I might never experience that feeling again myself? That was difficult to face up to. So what did I do next? I did what I always do when things feel shit. I went home, looked at my kids and smiled again.

Petra Byrne, November 2018
Isle of Sheppey, Kent, UK

For months he had all these drugs in his system, morphine to make him sleep, and he'd lie there in complete silence with his mouth open like he was dead. Shane has never snored, which has always been a good thing. But suddenly I wished he did. How can you lie on your back with your mouth wide open and not make a sound? I would listen harder but still nothing. I'd nudge him or prod him with my finger to check he was still alive, and if he didn't react I started looking for a pulse. I wanted to listen to his heart but he had a huge harness on his chest so I couldn't put my ear there. Instead, I started shouting, 'Shane! Shane!' He'd open his eyes, 'What? What?'

'Are you alive?'

'Yes, I'm bloody alive, and now I'm awake!'

I was doing that to him for weeks, the poor guy.

I have pictures on my phone from the first time they

tried to fit that body brace. I don't know why I was taking them. I was traumatized and I think I wanted something to compare to during his recovery. I think, through the blur, I knew that one day it would help us to look back and see how far he has come. Even after two weeks I looked at those photographs and I couldn't recognize the man in them.

They had eight people to hold him down that day. He was in so much pain, he was swearing at them all. He would scream and he would shout, then he would calm down, and then start screaming again, pulling his tubes out. At one point he grabbed me and shouted, 'Please let them end it for me.' They were shoving painkillers down him and talking about knocking him out because he couldn't take any more.

Once we were home I became worried about his mental health, so I made a point of calling his childhood friends and making sure he was always occupied. Otherwise I could leave the house to take the kids to school or whatever, and he would sit on this chaise longue we have on the landing and stare at the wall until I came back. He just couldn't be constructive with his time in the way he had always liked to be, and his head was literally trapped in a cage. That must have been so claustrophobic.

Normally, if he breaks an arm or a leg, the plaster cast comes straight off and he has laser treatment and physiotherapy and before you know it he's back on his motorbike. This time he couldn't do that and I knew it was getting to him. It made me feel guilty to exercise myself. Before, I could go and run twenty kilometres and he would sit with me in the kitchen when I got back – comparing notes, asking me about my cadence and my split times. That would be a normal conversation for us. 'How many calories have you burned?' Suddenly he didn't want to hear what I'd done, so I didn't tell him unless he asked, and I only went running when somebody else had taken him out of the house.

People came around to visit; *MCN* came and did a feature with him and he was smiling, having his picture taken. He was uploading grinning selfies to Instagram so that people thought he was all right, but he wasn't – he was still more broken than fixed. I posted things online myself as a distraction, but I never looked at anything from anybody else. I had been living in a bubble from the moment I saw that red flag on the live timing app.

One day I was in the garage, because my running machine is in there, surrounded by all his motorbikes. Shane came in to get something and I said, 'What are you doing in here?' He was getting a little computer thing off his pushbike and I said, 'Don't touch Shakey's things!' It's funny really, I know. I love Shane and I love Shakey, but right now I miss Shakey a lot.

That face in the helmet, I can't imagine not seeing that again. I can't imagine not seeing him win a race again. But if he doesn't, I know we will adjust. I just don't know if Shakey died on that day at Snetterton or if he is still in there. Or am I going crazy? I feel like I don't know the answer to anything.

Epilogue

Over the months and years that followed after the crash at Snetterton, I really had to become a different person. It may sound stupid for a man who was forty-four years old at the time of writing this, but I have had to grow up – a lot. We started working on this book in March 2018, before my crash even happened, and it was supposed to be a different kind of story, but this is what it became. I pictured promotional book tours with another title or two under my belt, maybe a hundred BSB wins to my name – not the situation I find myself in now.

When I read back over the first chapters, I see and hear the words of the person I was when I was a kid and then the person I became as a professional motorcycle racer, and there are things about the latter that I don't particularly like. But I can't change them. That's the thing about your past: there's not much you can do about it now – good, bad or indifferent – so it is better to try and look to the future. For me, that hasn't been easy since the day I went to ride my Ducati in the sunshine at Snetterton.

The first couple of months after the crash were pretty desperate, mainly because of the drug I was forced to take, called Gabapentin, to control the pain from the nerve damage. That stuff kept me awake all night and it was like torture, so when the doctors told me after a couple of weeks that I could start decreasing the dosage, I did what any motorcycle racer does and I just knocked it on the head altogether to accelerate the process. It accelerated the process all right, just not the right one!

Have you ever done an all-nighter and felt like shit the whole of the next day? Well, I went cold turkey on this stuff and never slept a second for six nights straight, so you can imagine how I felt. By the fourth night I thought, 'Bollocks to this,' and I nailed a full bottle of red wine, while still on loads of other types of medication. I literally didn't know what else to do to get myself some sleep. I went to bed, still never closed my eyes for a second all night, and then had to deal with a massive hangover. It was like in the movie *Trainspotting*, when Renton comes off heroin – I can't describe the feeling better than that scene when he's locked in his bedroom, climbing the walls.

Eventually I gave up and called Dr Cook. I couldn't take what this was doing to me any more – I didn't want to be here, didn't want this life I was living. It was a muddled-up version of such a shitty existence that I thought, 'What's the point?' When I had cried for them to end it for me in hospital, I had been on a combination of ketamine and morphine, but I felt as if I still had some clarity to the point that I actually thought some of those crazy dreams had really happened. But this was so confusing. I hated the life I had been forced to live and something had to be done. I needed to talk to somebody.

'Shane, are you crazy?' Dr Cook said when I told him I'd binned the pills. 'Get back on them, immediately. I said wean yourself off them – not stop them altogether!' I went straight back up to twelve tablets a day, dropping one each week, but it took weeks to get back to feeling anything like normal. I had been to a pretty dark place, and it definitely wasn't the insides of my eyelids!

The halo came off on 26 July 2018. For the best part of two months it had been screwed directly into my skull with four bolts – one behind each ear and two through my forehead – which needed to be tightened up with a ratchet twice a day. The human skull has two layers and these screws basically sat between them. If any of them became loose it would cause some dramas, so Petra would have to turn this ratchet on each of them until they clicked. I swear, eight times a day it felt like the inner layer of my skull was being pulled out through the outer layer.

When Dr Cook came to pull the bolts out, it was as if they were held in place by ten-centimetre washers. It was a strange sensation – painful, obviously – and I got myself in such a pickle all I could think of to say was, 'Doc! You are making my armpits sweat!' He pissed himself laughing. It didn't do my mobile phone signal any good, but getting that bastard thing off my head was a massive relief, and the photo I put up on Instagram moments after, with two little plasters over the holes in my forehead, was probably the most liked picture I ever posted.

Over the following months I gradually weaned myself off the drugs, went to hyperbaric chambers and had laser and magnetic-field therapy to try and help the bones heal. With physio sessions in between, there wasn't a day went by that I didn't at least try and take another step back towards full health.

When I went back to see Dr Cook in the February of 2019, I would say I was cautiously optimistic that he might give me the news that my vertebrae had healed, and that I would be good to race a motorcycle again soon. Maybe not right away, but soon. I just needed to hear something positive, a step forward – no matter how small – that would have been great. Instead, he told me that it wasn't really healing at all, and that there wasn't any point even coming back for another six months or so. I thought, 'How on earth can I put my whole life on hold for that length of time?' But that's what I had to do – thinking, dreaming and hoping on a daily basis that another six months would fix everything.

It was during that period, though, that I came to realize I was more broken than I had thought – and the bones at the top of my neck were only part of the problem. It's not nice to have to admit this, but the fact that I haven't been able to go to the toilet properly for the best part of two years kind of sets the alarm bells ringing. The damage to my spine is like having a couple of loose connectors in my circuit board, and because your bladder and your bowel are the furthest thing away from your brain, any problems show themselves up there first.

I have had to retrain my bladder to fill up and empty itself in the way it's supposed to, which is an ongoing process. Sometimes it strikes when it's almost too late. I can be busting for a wee, go to the toilet and the tiniest little dribble comes out. I zip my flies up and I'm busting to go again. If I sit down I can sometimes override the circuit, if you like, and regulate the pressure. And then, just when I think I've worked out the override command, the whole system resets and it all changes again. It's mad how much you can start thinking about it, analysing every little function in your body.

It wakes me up in the night and – because my mind is racing anyway – I know if I get up to go to the toilet, I won't get back to sleep again. But I have to drag myself out of bed because I am bursting, and nothing happens. It is pure mental torture. When I really can't go, I have to self-catheterize, which then makes me prone to water infections. For all the pain and the trauma of a major injury like mine, it can be the little things like this that drag you down the most.

This might be too much information, but sometimes I can go a fortnight without doing a number two and then, when nature calls, I *have* to answer. I was out walking with Lilly near our house in Spain one day and I had to run behind a bush in the street. When I stood up it looked as though somebody had been and chopped a couple of oak trees down! It's not a nice image, I know, but it's what I have to deal with. Excuse the pun, but everything in my life at the moment has to be planned around shit like this!

The specialists I have seen say there is still a lot about the nervous system that we don't understand. They book me in for an appointment for another consultancy, not knowing if I'm going to have made any progress since my last one, or whether it might just have completely fixed itself. It's like asking them to fix my dodgy circuit board without removing the cover. Nobody knows when or if it will heal, and that takes its toll, mentally.

Even the prospect of a small physical task can be the source of a lot of anxiety right now. I might want to shift a piece of furniture in the house, and even though I am confident I can do it, if I try it Petra will do her nut. In a way she's right, because if I pull something in my back it might mean I can't take a shit for a week. It is a constant cycle of problems – mental to physical, physical to mental.

It's a weird kind of analogy, I know, but I would liken my body right now to a speed camera. When you see one of those yellow boxes at the side of the road, you know the speed you're supposed to be going, but you also know there is a percentage of leeway so you keep nicking an extra mile an hour each time you pass it until – *bang!* – the camera flashes. You think, 'Bollocks! That was a bit too much.' My recovery has been like that, and the frustrating thing is that I don't actually know what speed the camera is set at.

This isn't just a broken wrist that I know I'll be able to ride with again in a couple of weeks or a collarbone that will be fine in a week to ten days. It is not even just a broken neck, which might take another year or so. This is a case of constant discomfort in my body and anxiety in my head at a level I've never had to deal with before. How do you cope with that? What is the right and wrong approach? These are the things I have to work out now.

People have kept telling me there is light at the end of the tunnel, but I feel like every time I get there, there is another corner. I can't see the end, can't see the light. I have always been motivated, never struggled to get up and get out on my bicycle even if it's snowing outside. If I need to go to the gym and I have a busy day ahead, I just get up earlier and make sure I get my training done. If I need something to happen, I have always found the drive to make it happen. For the first time ever, no amount of determination can help me fix these problems.

While working back in the BSB paddock doing the television job, I've been lucky to get regular treatment off the medical team there – including one of the physios, Amanda Hughes. One day I opened up to Amanda and told her I was sick of being in pain, and sick of worrying about it all. Amanda's a great woman, I really trust her, so I kind of spilled my heart out a little and she told me she thinks my pain might be related to my anxiety – like a kind of PTSD, which makes some sense.

Even after all this, there is not one bit of regret in me. I don't have an illness, like my dad did or millions of others have. I am not comparing myself to those people and I am not asking for sympathy. This is the destiny I made for myself, but for the first time ever I was not in control of my future in racing. Now it was in the hands of Dr Cook, who would give me his verdict on Tuesday 10 September 2019.

*

Where do you draw the line? Everybody is different. If somebody offered you your dream job but told you it would cost you a broken leg, a broken arm, a few nights in hospital, it would skin you, knock you out and at some point it would probably almost kill you, you wouldn't necessarily look at that and think it was a good idea. Not for any money in the world. But a motorcycle racer doesn't think like that. Getting injured, riding hurt, is just part and parcel of the job, so that's where he draws the line.

Maybe in your job you could get a sick note from your doctor, and the line you are prepared to draw is six months later – the maximum time he says it is OK for you to have off work. It depends on the dedication you have to the life you live, I suppose, and the extremes you are willing to go to. As the big day approached, I knew that my line was about to be drawn for me.

The closer I got to my appointment with Dr Cook, the more my anxiety levels went off the scale. The Friday before, I went to an open evening at a bike shop called Fowlers of Bristol. I rocked up there and the shop was rammed, one of the best open-day events I've ever been to, but by the end of the night I had heard the question 'When will we see you back on a bike, Shakey?' so many times, I felt as if I was slipping into a nightmare. 'I'll find out on Tuesday,' I kept saying, trying to smile, not giving anything away. But each time I said it, it was like another nail driving the fact home in my head: the months of thinking, dreaming and hoping were nearly at an end.

The funny thing is that – just like the day before my crash – I was determined to take the helicopter up to Norfolk. I was so scared of what might be that I figured the only way to take up all my mental capacity for the journey to the hospital would be to fly. There was no need to sit in a car for three hours stewing on what Dr Cook might say, when I could spend forty-five minutes concentrating hard and be there, so that's exactly what I did: I hired a helicopter the day before, landed it in the garden overnight and then flew up to Norwich the next morning after I'd done the school run (in the car, I might add!).

After a CT scan I sat down with Dr Cook, who gave me some good news: the bones in my neck had started to heal. They were never going to be much more than bits of cartilage and co-joined bone but they were coming together and there was even a chance that in 2020 he might be able to remove the rods, screws, plates and God-knows-what-else that is currently holding my lower back together. Taking all that metal out carried its own risks, but going back to racing with it all still in there would be a non-starter.

However, there was still no further clarity on the extent of the nerve damage. For two decades and more I had convinced myself that my body was invincible, but when Dr Cook suggested that another big knock would make paralysis 'a wonderful outcome', it didn't take a genius to figure out what he meant. Every chef will cut his finger, every electrician will get a shock, and every motorcycle racer will crash his bike. My job comes with an occupational hazard that I knew I could no longer afford to assume.

How could I take those words on board and then look at my kids and say, 'Guess what, kids, Daddy's going straight back to race again!'? How, as a husband, could I look Petra in the eyes and say, 'Don't worry, I won't crash for a bit'? How, as a son, could I tell my mum the same thing when she's spent the last twenty years worried sick about me anyway? The selfish person I was eighteen months ago might have taken that decision. But not the person I am right now. Not after all this.

For twenty-two years I was paid to race a motorcycle, and throughout all of that time I looked at life through the visor of my crash helmet. All I could see was the next corner, the finish line, the next race, the next championship. I have been selfish because the very essence of my being was to put myself first. During my recovery the visor wasn't just lifted for a bit, it was like they'd taken my helmet off and hidden the bloody thing! Now I'm looking around to see that there is another world that surrounds me 360 degrees, and I don't know which way to look first. It is all such a blur but I know I have to find a new direction to take my life forward – certainly for now, anyway – and a new way to provide for my kids.

I wasn't ready for this. I'm still not, but giving up on my lifelong dream? No chance.

*

The latest correspondence from the surgeons is that there's another type of scan they can do to my spinal cord in order to assess if or how likely it is that my ongoing health issues will ever be able to sort themselves out. The only problem is that the scan is really invasive and it carries the risk of paralysis, so their proposal is another interim MRI scan to see how the spinal cord is looking, give it some more time, then possibly consider this new scan. The letter went on to say that while this wasn't the news I was hoping for, these types of injuries are deeply complicated and require time to assess the risk versus reward. What do I even make of that? How much time do I actually have? Troy Bayliss came out of retirement at fifty and still won races at Australian Superbike Championship level, so that means I've got six years to get fixed then, right?

Some people have already started asking if in the future

I will race cars. I love cars, and I still dream about one day owning that Ferrari, but if I can't afford a bang on the head racing motorcycles at the minute, which is the one thing I am half sensible at doing, you have to imagine that sliding into a tyre wall in a car isn't going to be the best thing for me either. The television job is a much safer bet for now and something I really do enjoy, but I can guarantee you that whenever you see me on your screens talking about racing, I would rather still be out there on my bike.

One thing I would like to do is to share my experience with other young riders. I tried management once before, while still racing myself, but it didn't work out. I took a guy from paying for a ride in British Supersport to taking a wage in British Superbikes, but seemingly that wasn't enough for him. I am already making a move into rider management again, but this time I will get it right – it's not often I get caught out twice.

They say that as one door closes, another door opens, but for me to become something other than a motorcycle racer at the moment represents more than just a change of jobs. It's a change of life, a change of dreams. I would swap all six of my BSB titles for just one World Championship, but for now it is time to look forward, to spend lots more time with my beautiful wife, my children and my close friends, to draw inspiration from those around me and to try and buy some time.

In the meantime, I truly hope you've enjoyed my story so far. I hope it's taught you a few things you didn't know, and I hope it shows that nothing starts without a dream. If you have one, it is up to you to follow it. If you don't believe in it, how are you going to convince others to do the same?

We all have our own life's maze, I am sure of that. But it is up to you whether you make it to the other side. The route I took wasn't the most straightforward, but it has been true. True to me. I nearly lost my way on occasions, spent time doing shit I shouldn't have, but when the moment came, I made it happen. I aimed for the moon and, with the help of a lot of people, I guess I landed somewhere in the stars. I am truly thankful for that.

I am also truly thankful to the nurses, doctors and surgeons who have given me the best possible shot at a normal life again. It is an opportunity I intend to grab with the same vigour and determination that has defined my career and my recovery.

Finally, for every person who thinks I dodged a bullet, for every fan who came up to me in the paddock while I had a frame bolted into my head and told me I should retire, that I had nothing left to prove in the sport, I hope you finally understand. The whole point is that it never mattered to me what I had left to prove, because I wasn't trying to prove anything in the first place.

This is just me. I am a motorcycle racer. Who could ever tell me to be anything else?

Acknowledgements

Writing a book was something I always wanted to do, but it was something I expected to be able to do while still actively racing. I wanted a book that was going to come out while I was still at my most dominant in my sport, having celebrated perhaps another title or two, having maybe exceeded the hundred BSB wins. I wanted to be able to tell a story up until that point, but leave the potential to cover whatever successes may have followed after the book was released. Alas, here we are . . .

The theory started correctly. I'd spoken with a few people in the past who were keen to do something with me, but it was an off-the-cuff conversation with my good friend and Eurosport colleague, Matthew Roberts, who had written a few books already, that got the ball rolling. Matt and I started work on this book around February 2018 and spent an hour or two here, three or four there, going through a rake of questions Matt had in order to compile the basic layout. I truly believe he could be on to something with it too, because if you've enjoyed the book as much as I've enjoyed writing it with him, then you'll have been in for a treat!

Matt arranged a meeting in London with book agent David Luxton, a delightful guy who really knew the book industry inside and out, and having read just a few rough chapters and a synopsis, speaking with the two of us in the meeting – understanding our desire to make this not just a good book but a great one – he was convinced he could pitch and sell it.

Not long after came our first meeting with Robin Harvie, Matthew Cole and Kate Green from Pan Macmillan publishers, and immediately, to me at least, it was like, 'Wow, these guys and girls really believe in this.'

I have to say that, like with anything, it's very easy to underestimate just how much work goes into producing a book; for sure there are bits I've forgotten, people I've missed out, things removed for legal reasons, harsh words that have needed polishing. But, with the group of people I've been fortunate enough to have around me while writing this, it's been a pleasure. I never wanted this to be a dictation of my words turned into a script, and take the easy way out. I'm so keen for this book to win that I've personally given it the exact same levels of application and determination used throughout my race career.

I know for sure that if I tried to acknowledge everyone from throughout my life or career who's helped in one way or another I'd need to write another book, so for now I'm narrowing this right down. Petra, Zack and Lilly, I appreciate your love and patience; Mum, I guess I owe you!

Matt, thank you so much for helping me realize a dream and for structuring it so well. David, thank you for putting the whole deal together. Robin, thanks for your belief, your patience, efficiency and knowledge, and to the rest of the group at Pan Macmillan, thank you so much for all your support.